Internet Management

Internet Management

Nathan Dundee

Internet Management

ISBN 978-93-5111-442-0

Published in 2014 in India by

RANDOM PUBLICATIONS

4376-A/4B, Gali Murari Lal, Ansari Road
New Delhi-110 002
Phone : +91-11-43580356, +91-11-23289044
e-mail: randomexports@gmail.com, sales@randompublications.com, info@randompublications.com

Reprinted 2018

Type Setting by: Friends Media, Delhi-110089
Printed at : Sanat Printers

Preface

Internet Management or IT management is the discipline whereby all of the information technology resources of a firm are managed in accordance with its needs and priorities. These resources may include tangible investments like computer hardware, software, data, networks and data centre facilities, as well as the staff who are hired to maintain them. Managing this responsibility within a company entails many of the basic management functions, like budgeting, staffing, change management, and organizing and controlling, along with other aspects that are unique to technology, like software design, network planning, tech support etc. The central aim of IT management is to generate value through the use of technology. To achieve this, business strategies and technology must be aligned. IT Management is different from management information systems. The latter refers to management methods tied to the automation or support of human decision making. IT Management refers to IT related management activities in organizations. MIS is focused mainly on the business aspect, with strong input into the technology phase of the business/ organization. A primary focus of IT management is the value creation made possible by technology. This requires the alignment of technology and business strategies. While the value creation for an organization involves a network of relationships between internal and external environments, technology plays an important role in improving the overall value chain of an organization. However, this increase requires business and technology management to work as a creative, synergistic, and collaborative team instead of a purely mechanistic span of control.

Historically, one set of resources was dedicated to one particular computing technology, business application or line of business, and managed in a silo-like fashion. These resources supported a single set of requirements and processes, and couldn't easily be optimized or reconfigured to support actual demand. This led technology providers to build out and complement their product-centric infrastructure and management offerings with Converged Infrastructure environments that converge servers, storage, networking, security, management and facilities. The efficiencies of having this type of integrated and automated management environment allows enterprises to get their applications up and running faster, with simpler manageability and maintenance, and enables IT to adjust IT resources (such as servers, storage and networking) quicker to meet unpredictable business demand. The term *IT infrastructure* is defined in a standard called Information Technology Infrastructure Library (ITIL) v3 as a combined set of hardware, software, networks, facilities, etc. (including all of the information technology), in order to develop, test, deliver, monitor, control or support IT services. Associated people, processes and documentation are not part of IT Infrastructure. TIL documents define best practices and accepted techniques in the information technology community. This set of guidelines is widely used in both the public and private sector, essentially providing companies with a blueprint on how to organize and manage information technology operations at the company.

The book provides a clear, scientific and technical understanding of this subject. The information contained herein will equip the readers with latest and up-to-date knowledge.

I thank all members of my team who have helped in the preparation of the book. My special thanks go to "Random Publication" who have published the book.

—*Nathan Dundee*

Contents

1

Internet Technology

Internet

The arrival of the Internet made communication between machines much easier and a number of open protocols and applications were developed to make use of this. Of these, E-mail was the forerunner and there can be few academics and students that do not have access to this now. E-mail has its limitations and it was the World Wide Web that really brought the world of networked computers to the general public.

The open standards of many of the technologies and the ease with which anyone could publish information encouraged participation by all and we need to remember what is about these technologies that makes them attractive when we try to deploy them for education. However, initially, a relatively small number of University lecturers adopted it for a range of teaching purposes but even fewer did more than post information about their courses or actual lecture notes - usually not modified in any way to take advantage of the strengths of the media such as hypertext.

One of the strengths and principle attractions of the Web is that it can provide authoring access to anybody and this is quite different from the one-way nature of education through CAL or any other media that predated it. The fact that the technology facilitates this does not of course mean that it will take place but then this is true of any educational forum. While far from needing programming skills, it still takes a certain amount of technophilia to publish a Web page. Creating them is trivial but actually publishing them can be tedious if the institution has not provided a simple means to do so. This is all about information rather than teaching and learning and it soon becomes obvious to any treading this path that you cannot take the people out of the learning equation entirely. Learning is about interaction and interaction with information alone is not enough.

History

The original concept for the Internet was developed in 1962 by Paul Baran of the RAND Corporation. RAND in the 1960s was a Cold War military think tank. RAND was commissioned by the US military to find a way to maintain military communication in the event of a nuclear attack. The idea was to create a network that has no central control that could be targeted in an attack. Baran laid out a plan using packet switching technology to maintain communications through a network of multiple communications paths. The idea for multiple paths allowed communications to continue in the even that any one or more sections of the network were neutralized due to a nuclear blast.

In 1968, a contract was awarded by ARPA (Advanced Research Projects Agency) to a company called BNN to build the first network model, which was then called ARPANET. The original ARPANET used a Honeywell computer to handle the network switching. The original network linked four nodes: the University of California in Santa Barbara, the University of California in Los Angeles, the University of Utah and SRI in Stanford.

A major event in the history of the Internet occurred in 1972 when Ray Tomlinson of BNN developed the first e-mail programme. Also in 1972, ARPA changed its name to DARPA (Defence Advanced Research Projects Agency). DARPA and Stanford were collaborating on the development of TCP/IP, which became the main communications protocol for the Internet. TCP/IP was a huge breakthrough because it allowed different types of computers on different networks to communicate with one another. Prior to this breakthrough, computers could only communicate with other computers on the same type of network.

The name "Internet" was first used in the development of TCP. In 1976, Dr. Robert Metcalfe of Xerox's Palo Alto Research Facility developed Ethernet, which allowed data to be moved extremely fast. This breakthrough allowed local area networks (LANs) to become practical. Actually, in 1976, extremely fast meant a 56Kbps connection, which is the same speed that most narrowband dial-up connections still operate on due to the limitation of telephone wiring.

In 1983, every computer connected to ARPANET was required to use TCP/IP, which became the core Internet communications protocol. Also in 1983, the University of Wisconsin developed the Domain Name System (DNS), which allowed TCP/IP packs to be delivered to a server representing a domain name. Because the Internet actually operates on IP addresses, domain names must be translated into IP addresses by Domain Name Servers. This made it much easier to remember addresses for different nodes on the Internet.

1984 saw the Internet split into two entities. MIL NET became focused on the needs of the military and military development projects. ARPANET became focused on advanced research. The US Department of Defence continued to fund and support both networks. Also in 1994, the first high-speed Internet backbones were installed by MCI. The new network was called NSFNET (National Science Foundation Network) In 1985, the first.com domain name was registered by Symbolics, who still uses it today. In 1985, the Internet was strictly a text-based system. There were no images or web sites as we see today. Internet sites consisted of pages of text messages.

In 1990, the US Department of Defence replaced the old ARPANET infrastructure with the the new, high-speed NSFNET backbone. Also in 1990, Tim Berne's-Lee of CERN began working with a hypertext system that would eventually lead to the creation of the World Wide Web, for which he is best known. Tim Berners-Lee is frequently called the father of the world wide web due to his work in developing the concepts In 1992, the World Wide Web was introduced by CERN. The World Wide Web incorporated hypertext linking capabilities, a standardized HTML scripting language, standardized resource identifiers (URIs/URLs) and utilized a client-server model for requesting web pages and objects using a hypertext transport protocol (HTTP) model.

In 1993, the National Science Foundation created interNIC, which leads to the implementation of several Internet services, including formalized domain registration services by Network Solutions. Marc Andersen and the University of Illinois introduced Mosaic, the first graphical user interface for the World Wide Web. Andreessen would go on to start Netscape in order to further develop and commercialize the use of browsers. Compuserve and other subscription information services began offering businesses and home users access to the Internet through their information networks.

By 1995, large numbers of users were were joining the Internet community and business began thinking of ways to use the Internet to sell products and services. Since then, the evolution and growth of the Internet has been rapid.It is important to note that the Internet and the World Wide Web are not really one and the same. The Internet refers to the massive network of networks, which is basically the hardware infrastructure. The World Wide Web is a combination of methods and protocols for accessing the information over the Internet.

Size

No one knows for certain because it is growing so rapidly. Estimates range from 12 billion web documents to over 20 billion. It could actually be much larger than that.

Internet for Military

The original concept developed by RAND was for a military communications network. It evolved into more of an academic study involving better ways to communicate information. For many years the Internet was only available to universities and research facilities. There was military funding and research from DARPA, which kept the project alive, so there was a strong military interest as the project evolved through the 1960s, 1970s and early 1980s. There are people who played important roles in the history of the Internet project who say it was not a military project, but that is a bit of a denial regarding where the concept originated and where much of the funding came from. It is safe to say that by the time the concept of the World Wide Web started to emerge, the Internet was no longer a military project.

FireFTP is a FireFox-only add-on, which means that it will not work with Internet Explorer. Installation is simple. Just go to the FireFTP download page and click on the Download button. Make sure you are using FireFox when you visit the page. The browser add-on will automatically install in a few seconds.

After installation, you can find the FTP utility in the FireFox Tools menu. Click on it and it will open in a browser window. Just like FileZilla, FireFTP allows you to set up and save FTP connection accounts and allows quick connects for occasional FTP connections that you do not want to store. The only difference is that an Account is saved, while a QuickConnect is not. When you start up FireFTP, you will see multiple panes. The panes on the left side represent the local directories on your PC. The panes on the right display remote directories on your web site after you have connected to your server. To set up an account, click on the Create an account... selection from the drop-down menu in the top left-hand corner. The Account Manager dialog box will display. From there you can enter the FTP information for your web site.

The Account Name will be displayed on the drop-down menu. The account information can be obtained from your hosting company. The Category is optional and can be used if you have a lot of FTP accounts that you want to set up in logical group sonthe menu. The Host is typically your domain name, *i.e.*, tech-evangelist.com. If you are using a dedicated IP address, you can use the IP address.

Some hosting companies require the use of special Host addresses:

- The Login is your username for the FTP account.
- The Password is the password for the FTP account.

To set up an account, you only need to enter the Account Name. Any information that you enter will be stored when you same the account. If you are using a laptop that could be stolen, it is a good idea to leave the password blank. FireFTP will prompt you for missing information when you try to connect to your server.

The Account Manager also has a Connection tab where you can set up any special connection information, such as a non-standard port number. You can also designate default directories for both the Local (your PC) and the Remote (the server) sides of the connection. This feature saves a lot of time because you do not have to search for files on your PC if you store them in a special location.

Files

Use the Browse button to the right of the path displayed just above the Local pane. You can select any location that you have access to on your network. Make sure that the proper directories are selected in both the left-hand pane (Local) and the right-hand-pane (Remote). Highlight the files your wish to transfer in the left window and click the right arrow in the center bar. You can also transfer files from the server to your PC. It is important to make sure that you have the proper directories selected.

To disconnect from your server, use the Disconnect button to the right of the drop-down menu. Once a connection is made, the Connect button turns into the Disconnect button. This is easy to set up, although the location for the change is not very intuitive. On the top right-hand side of the FireFTP window there is a Tools selection. Select Tools > Options. Check the box named Show Hidden Files. This is found in the Connection tab in the Account Manager dialog box. The easiest way to set this up is to make the connection to your server, select the proper directories for both the left-hand and right-hand panes, then select the Edit button next to the drop-down menu. Select the Connection tab. You should see both the Local and Remote directory paths displayed. Click on the Use Current button next to each, and then click OK. The next time you connect to your server, the default directories will be used. If you need a real nice, lightweight and simple FTP utility, it is worthwhile to take a look at FireFTP. I was pleasantly surprised with this one.

Web Server

A web proxy server, sometimes called a web proxy, can serve a variety of purposes. Many of the purposes for using a proxy server are legitimate, but others are suspicious and sometimes malicious. Using a simple definition, a proxy is basically a server that sits between a user and the destination server that the user is accessing. It is an intermediary or go-between that requests resources from the destination server on the user's behalf. On of the most common uses of a proxy server is for anonymous web surfing. When a user is connected through a proxy server, the IP address of the web proxy is used to communicate with the destination server and thus the IP address of the user is hidden. This can be used to allow a user access to systems where their access might normally be blocked, or because an IP address identifies a user's geographic location, it can be used to disguise the country where a user is located.

There are thousands of free proxy servers set up in countries around the world, and lists of these servers can easily be found on the web. When a user visits one of these sites, they enter the web address of the site they wish to visit. From that point on, the true IP address of the user is protected and the destination server only sees the IP address of the proxy server.

Students use web proxies to allow them to access web sites whose IP addresses are blocked by their school's server. For example, if a school has blocked all the known IP addresses for porn sites, students might still be able to access these sites through a proxy. Because of uses intended to circumvent normal security, lists of the IP addresses of known proxy servers are available, which can also be blocked by a company or school network. If you are concerned about protecting your identity while on the web, a proxy server can help with anonymity. But be aware that these servers can have a malicious intent and can be used to cache information that passes through them, which means that you never want to use one of these intermediaries to log into your bank account or any web site where exposing user IDs and passwords can be detrimental. This can be a path to identity theft.

There are other malicious uses for these servers. Many e-commerce sites capture the IP addresses of customers who purchase products. They are used to identify the geographic location of a customer to help prevent fraud. If a customer's street address is in Boston, but their IP address identifies their geographic location as Nigeria or China, the chances are more than good that a stolen credit card is being used. Many sophisticated online thieves use domestic drop points or freight forwarding companies where products are shipped and later forwarded to the thief. They have also learned to use web proxy servers to hide their location, or make it appear that they are located in a country not known for credit card fraud.

There are many legitimate uses for proxy servers. AOL has traditionally cached commonly visited web pages and altered JPG images by compressing them to speed up web access for their users. They can also be used by schools and companies to filter content, and by ISPs that restrict access to family friendly content. If you are going to use a proxy server, try to identify those that are legitimate. Many are, but some are not. As a general rule, never access sensitive sites that require a user ID and password. This includes your e-mail accounts.

Using PHP

A shopping cart is an essential component of every e-commerce site. Although there are literally hundreds of shopping carts to choose from, only a few stand out. PHP is the preferred shopping cart language because it is the most popular web development language on the Internet. When combined with the MySQL database, PHP is unbeatable for cost effectiveness. The selection of the best shopping cart for your web site is an issue that should not be taken lightly. The user-friendliness built into your shopping cart can be a major factor when it comes to retaining visitors and converting them into customers. Numerous studies have shown that the checkout process associated with a poorly designed cart can be a major factor affecting shopping cart abandonment during the checkout process. The following is brief list of the most popular shopping carts that utilize both PHP and MySQL. Both PHP and MySQL are free (no licensing issues) and are offered with almost all non-Microsoft web site hosting. This gives this combination a low-cost advantage, both for the cost of obtaining, modifying and maintaining your shopping cart system. Indeed, many of the most popular shopping carts using PHP and MySQL are free and most have a wide range of support available through numerous forums. All of these shopping cart options are complete e-commerce storefronts, complete with category pages, product pages, checkout processes and much more. All have a wide range of mods available that add functionality to the e-commerce sites.

Os Commerce

First and foremost is os Commerce, the biggest player in open source shopping carts. osCommerce has been around for more than six years and includes a large community of users and supporters. osCommerce is a complete e-commerce storefront. The basic osCommerce download is very functional and there is a wide selection of plugin mods that add functionality and features. More than 100 templates are available that change the look and feel of a storefront. When considering shopping carts, CRE Loaded has been referred to as osCommerce on steroids. CRE Loaded is built on osCommerce. Different versions include large collections of already-installed mods so that you have a highly functional and heavily equipped version of of osCommerce as soon as it is installed. There are small one-time fees associated with purchasing a copy of CRE Loaded, but the costs are minimal.

Zen Cart is a derivative of osCommerce. The group that focuses on this cart started with a version of osCommerce a few years ago and used it as a basis for building their own open source shopping cart. it is therefore similar to osCommerce in some ways, but has its own user and developer community. Support is provided through a very active forum where members help each other to solve issues related to e-commerce and the use of Zen Cart. The best part is that it is a very stable cart with loads of built-in functionality and it is free. This is another contender when it comes to popular and very functional shopping carts. Cube Cart has both a free and low-cost version available. They are both the same, but it will cost you $89.95 if you wish to remove the Cube Cart copyright notice and link from the page footers. Sometimes this makes sense if you are in a competitive market and you do not want your competitors to know which shopping cart you are using.

Observations

Any of the choices listed above are good choices for an e-commerce web site. One thing to note is that most of the systems have all of the functionality turned on when you install the cart. This tends to degrade speed performance due to numerous unnecessary database lookups. After installing one of these shopping cart systems, you need to become familiar with the administration area and then should turn off every feature that you really do not need. Most of these systems have manuals available, either in hardcopy or downloadable format. Your learning curve will likely be shortened if obtain the manual and go through it in great detail. Which one did we like best? We decided to go with Zen Cart due to the very active user forum and the superior support we see from the development staff. You should, of course, make your own decision. You cannot go wrong with any of these PHP shopping cart choices.

Troubleshooting

Outbound e-mail uses a process called SMTP (simple mail transport protocol). SMTP is the standard for e-mail transmissions across the Internet. SMTP is generally used to send messages from a mail client (Thunderbird) to a mail server. The e-mail is stored on the server until retrieved by another e-mail client using a POP3 or IMAP retrieval protocol. Outbound e-mail problems can be frustrating to deal with because you rarely see an indicator as to what might be causing the problem. However, there are fewer factors involved when setting up the SMTP section in Thunderbird, so isolating the problem can be much simpler. Unlike setting up an e-mail retrieval for inbound e-mail, with SMTP, a single SMTP setup can be used to cover all of your e-mail addresses, regardless of how many different ISPs are involved.

Most SMTP mail servers are set up to allow e-mail accounts from other ISPs to be run through them. Thunderbird identifies the first SMTP account that you set up as being the default account. That is because in most cases it can be shared by all of your e-mail accounts.

Most of the configuration issues with sending e-mail can be resolved in the Server Settings section in Thunderbird.

- Select Account Settings from the Tools menu.
- Scroll down to the bottom of the list if e-mail accounts.
- Select Outgoing Server (SMTP).

When you are sure that this information is correct, click the OK button, shut down Thunderbird and then start it up again to make sure that any new settings are loaded. If you have multiple e-mail accounts and you know that inbound e-mail is working, try sending a test message to another of your e-mail addresses. If it still does not work or you see an error, make sure that you Internet access is active. If you can access the Internet using your browser, you should be able to send e-mail messages once the SMTP information is correct. If you are still having trouble connecting to the SMTP server, Thunderbird will usually display a message, but depending on the type of error, sometimes it does not. Most of the time the User Name is just the account name, but some configurations may require a complete e-mail address. If one way does not work, try the other.

If your SMTP server requires a secure connection, you may have to check the SSL box. I sometimes use the SMTP server at my AT&T account. AT&T connections usually require that you check the SSL box. If you are having connections problems, post your issues in the Comments below. Try to give us as much information as you can and we will see if we can help you to get connected.

Incoming E-Mails

Most e-mail addresses today use the POP3 (Post Office Protocol 3) Internet protocol for receiving e-mail. With POP3 your e-mail is held on a mail server. You can download your mail to an e-mail client. Typically, the e-mail is deleted from the server when it is downloaded, but it can be set up to retain the e-mail messages.

An alternative Internet mail protocol is IMAP (Internet Message Access Protocol). IMAP provides some enhanced capabilities and is useful for dealing with large volumes of mail that may need to be organized. Most hosing companies today use POP3. If you are not sure about your situation, ask the ISP or hosting company. The e-mail documentation they provide will usually tell you which protocol you are working with. Most of the configuration issues with receiving e-mail can be resolved in the Server Settings section for each e-mail address in Thunderbird.

Each e-mail address is configured separately:

- Select Account Settings from the Tools menu.
- Select Server Settings under the e-mail address you wish to troubleshoot.

The first thing to check is the Server Name. This identifies your mail server. You will need to get this information from your hosting company or ISP. Most mail servers are identified by using a subdomain preceding the domain name, such as mail.tech-evangelist.com. Some use other subdomain names, such as ipostoffice.tech-evangelist.com. Once again, the only way to know is to find out how your mail server is configured. Next, check the User Name. Sometimes this is the entire e-mail address and sometimes is is just the account name, which is the portion of the e-mail address to the left of the @ sign. The third item to test is the Security Settings. Most mail servers do not use a secure connection, so Never would be checked. I've seen a few that use TLS (Transport Layer Security), which is a type of secure connection. If Never didn't work, try TLS, if available.

There are also a few e-mail servers that use SSL (Secure Sockets Layer) for secure connections. Secure connections encypt the messages as they are downloaded, which prevents others from intercepting your messages. I have an AT&T e-mail account that requires SSL. When you click the SSL radio button, the port number will change. You can also try checking the Use Secure Authentication box, but thus far I have never had to do that when setting up an e-mail account.

There is a very small possibility that your ISP or hosting company is using a non-standard port. Thunderbird does allow you to change the port, but you should never do that unless instructed to do so by your ISP or hosting company. If the port is wrong, you will not make the proper server connection. If none of this works, make sure that you do indeed have an active Internet connection. If your browser can access the Internet, you should be able to retrieve your e-mail.

By now your problems receiving e-mail should have been resolved. Most of the time when I've run into issues setting up new e-mail accounts in Thunderbird, the issue was an incorrect User Name or Security Setting. Remember to save the settings each time you make a change by clicking the OK button. It is also best if you shut down and restart Thunderbird to make sure that your changes are reloaded. After that, test it again.

Creating E-Mail Signature

A signature in an e-mail is kind of like a footer on a web page. It is generally used to convey contact information, legal notices and other repetitive information. This is something that you may not want to re-type every time you send an e-mail message. Thunderbird allows you to create as many signatures as you wish. You can assign a different signature to each individual e-mail address.

The first thing you need to know is that you must create the signature file in a pure text editor, such as Microsoft's Notepad. Do not use Word or any type of text editor that may embed codes in the text. You can save these files anywhere on your PC, but it makes sense to store them somewhere where they will not get separated from the rest of your Thunderbird files. In a previous tutorial, I changed the file location for the Thunderbird files in order to make it easier to back up these files.

I simply created a new folder called "signatures" in the folder with the rest of the Thunderbird files. Like I said, you can store them anywhere, but when you do it this easy, the signatures stay with your Thunderbird files if you need to move them to another PC or if you have to restore a PC from your backup files.

Next, you will need to assign a signature to each e-mail address. From the Tools menu, select Account Settings... Highlight an e-mail address on the left-hand column. On the right, check the box that says "Attach this signature:" and then click the Choose button to navigate to your signatures folder. Select the file that you want to attach. Click the OK button to save your settings. You will need to repeat this process for each e-mail address where you wish to add a signature. If you add a URL to the signature file, most e-mail clients will turn it into a hyperlink. But if you need to spruce it up of if you wish to use HTML in a signature instead of plain text, here is what you need to do. Create a text file in the same manner as described above. When you save the file, save it with a.html extension, rather than a.txt extension. Thunderbird will then recognize it as an HTML file. You can then use coloured fonts, hyperlinks or just about any type of CSS, as long as you use inline CSS styles.

When you are using CSS in e-mail messages, make sure that you fully specify the URLs to images and store the images on your server. Don't try to embed images or send them with the message.

It won't work well with many browsers.One more thing that has to be mentioned about HTML in signatures is that the message must be sent in HTML mode for the HTML and CSS to work. When you send any message that contains HTML, Thunderbird will ask you if you want to send it in in Plain Text. You do have to click on the Send in HTML Only or Send in Plain Text and HTML for the HTML and CSS to render properly.

Spam and Junk Mail

No one want to receive spam, but today it is almost inevitable that most e-mail addresses will eventually end up on spam lists. I have always protected my e-mail addresses, but recently ended up receiving more than 100 spam messages per day on my most important e-mail address used only by my business clients.

It turns out that a client thought she was doing me a favour when she posted it on a forum, along with a recommendation. As part of my battle to eliminate spam, I found that Thunderbird contains some amazingly powerful spam and junk mail controls that are very effective at filtering unwanted e-mail. This tutorial shows you how to turn these filters on and configure them to meet your needs.

There are actually several methods for filtering out spam using Thunderbird's tools. I used all of them in conjunction and found that Thunderbird effectively filtered out almost every undesirable message. It is also amazingly accurate and only very rarely grabs a legitimate message and identifies it as spam.

Pre-Filtering Spam Messages

The first level for setting up spam filtering is to do it at the server level or on your personal computer. If you have a web site, your hosting company might already offer spam filtering software, such as Spam Assassin or Spam Pal. This step is not absolutely necessary, but it does make the process of identifying and filtering spam more effective. SpamAssassin is commonly found on Linux or Unix Apache servers. SpamAssassin checks messages coming through a hosting service's e-mail system. It does not actually filter the spam out, but rather uses heuristic algorithms that analyse a message. It then assigns a spam score. Thunderbird can use this score to determine if a message is likely to be spam. If your web site runs on Unix or Linux and uses a control panel such as Pleske or cPanel, check to see if SpamAssassin is included. You will find it under Mail, SpamAssassin. If the message near the top indicates that SpamAssassin is disabled, click the box labeled Enable SpamAssassin. Do not click the box labeled Enable Spam Box.

SpamPal is a different type of filtering system that installs on your PC. SpamPal uses spam block lists (lists of IP addresses used by spammers) to identify spam messages. I have not tried it, but if your hosting company does not use SpamAssassin, or if you do not have a web site (and therefore do not use a hosting company), you might want to try installing it. You will find it atspampal.org.

Configuring Junk Mail

The first step is to configure Junk Settings:

- Select Account Settings from the Tools menu. Thunderbird allows you to configure each e-mail address separately.
- Select Junk Settings under one of your e-mail addresses.

- Check all of the boxes in the Junk Settings display. If you don't use SpamAssassin or SpamPal, skip that checkbox. If you do use one of these tools, make sure the box is checked and the proper filter selected.
- Checking "Move new junk messages to Junk folder" will create a Junk folder under the selected e-mail address. You can set the nuber of days before spam is deleted from the junk folder. It is a good idea to move the messages to this folder so that you can periodically review it for messages that may not be spam.

Configuring Privacy Settings

- Select Tools, Options.
- Select the Privacy button.
- Select the Junk tab.
- Choose how you want spam to be handled when you manually select it when reviewing your e-mails. When you are viewing messages and you identify a spam message, you can click on the column to the left of the date to send the message to the Junk folder. This also helps the system identify spam messages.

Configuring Message Filters

When all else fails to identify spam, this is the way to do it. Message filters will search new messages for any keywords you designate. This section is pretty easy to figure out. Once again, you have to set up individual message filters for each e-mail address.

- Highlight an e-mail address in the main screen.
- Select Tools, Message Filters from the top menu.
- Click on the New button.
- Name your message filter at the top.
- Select the e-mail element that you wish to filter. Most spam keywords are going to be found in the Subject or Body.
- Select Contains.
- Enter the keyword or phrase you wish to use as a filter.
- Near the bottom of the displayed dialogue box, select the location to move any identified spam messages. The Junk folder for the current e-mail address is the most logical place for these messages so that you can review them.
- Click OK.

That's about all there is to configuring Thunderbird to filter out spam messages. Although the configuration sections are a bit scattered throughout Thunderbird, once you know where to find them they are easy to use.

View Source

If you are an avid Internet user and use Internet Explorer as your browser, you have probably noticed that there are times when the View Source function in Internet Explorer occasionally stops working. For a Web developer or designer who likes to view the HTML code for a Web site, this can be frustrating. Fortunately, both the explanation to the problem and the solution are usually simple.

The root of the problem is that the browser cache has filled because of all the Web page code and images stored by the browser. The solution is to clear these temporary files and start out with a fresh cache. To do this,

- Select Tools on the top menu in Internet Explorer
- Select Internet Options...
- Click Delete Files in the Temporary Internet Files section

It may take several minutes to delete all the files in the cache, so don't panic if it appears like your PC has locked up. As soon as the hour glass once again turns into a mouse pointer, you can shut down Internet Explorer and start it up again. The View Source feature should now work once again. If this does not fix the problem, you may have a more serious issue, such as a corrupted or deleted Notepad.exe programme file or problems related to the temporary files directory in Windows. Those problems are beyond the scope of this article. Other issues that have been reported that sometimes disable View Source include having a shortcut to Notepad on your desktop or having a shortcut named Notepad on your desktop. Renaming the shortcut should resolve those issues.

Most of the time, the problem tends to be related to the cache, so if you spend a lot of time on the Internet, it might be a good idea to clear the cache once a week.

Mozilla Thunderbird Tips and FAQs

Mozilla Thunderbird is, in my opinion, the absolute best free e-mail programme available. It doesn't have the vulnerabilities found with Outlook, primarily due to the fact that it is not an "attack target" like Microsoft products. Even when vulnerabilities are found, they are quickly patched by the community of developers that support Thunderbird. We've put together a list of tips to make your use of the Thunderbird e-mail application more enjoyable. If you have a specific question regarding how to do something with Thunderbird, post a comment below and if we have a solution we will include the answer on either this tips page or in a separate tutorial.

Where do I Find the Download for Thunderbird

You can find the most current version at the Mozilla Thunderbird download page. Installation is pretty simple. If you are using Outlook, Eudora or another e-mail client, you can easily import your address book and messages during the installation.

Including Previous Message Text

We found this to be one of the annoying default features with Thunderbird. Unless you change the settings, when you forward a message with Thunderbird it will include the forwarded message as an attachment. I personally prefer that the forwarded text be included in the body of the message that I send.

This is easy to change:

- Click on the Tools menu
- Select Options
- Select Composition
- Select the General tab
- *At the top change Forward messages*: "As Attachment" to "Inline"
- Click OK

Your forwarded messages should now include the text of the forwarded message in the body of the e-mail just below any message text that you add. If you selected the default settings during the installation, Thunderbird will automatically download updates and let you know when they are ready for installation. You will find the settings for this under Tools, Options, Advanced and then select the Update tab. Check out our tutorial about setting up Thunderbird mailing lists.

This is really simple to do, but like many things with open source software, the solution is not always intuitive. This is an area where Thunderbird excels. We did a separate post on that called Thunderbird spam and junk mail filters. We tried several different methods to eliminate spam and this was the only system that eliminated it almost completely and at zero cost. We were very impressed.

String E-mail messages

They are hidden, but you can find them using the tips we offer in Thunderbird file location. This is very useful information if you wish to move the location to a Windows folder that can be easily backed up.

Changing Passwords

Ah-h-h, grasshopper. Passwords used to access your e-mail accounts are easy to change if you follow the instructions we offer in Changing Thunderbird Passwords

Making Mozilla Thunderbird

When you set up Thunderbird as the default e-mail client, it will automatically open whenever you click on an e-mail address on a web page that uses the HTML mailto: protocol. To configure Thunderbird as the default e-mail client, simply Open the Tools menu, select Options and click on the General icon. Under system Defaults, check the box that says, "Always check to see if Thunderbird is the default e-mail client on startup." Click OK to save the setting. From now on, whenever the PC is booted it will check to see if Thunderbird is the default e-mail client. If one of the Windows programmes tries to change the setting to Outlook or if another programme changes it to something else, a message will be displayed that will allow you to change it back. Most people are not aware of this, but when you delete an e-mail message with most e-mail clients, you do not actually delete the message. The message is simple flagged so that it does not appear in the e-mail list. Thunderbird never actually deletes a message unless you take some extra steps. First, select File, Empty Trash. Second, select File, Compact Folders. This deletes all of the flagged messages in the data files. This issue keeps coming up. It looks like you can use Thunderbird with a Yahoo account if you subscribe to Yahoo Mail Plus. The standard freebie Yahoo account does not offer POP3 access. See the following articles. You will find all of the proper configuration information posted there.

- Can I use Thunderbird to read and send my Yahoo! Mail?
- Can I POP my mail into a different e-mail client (like Thunderbird)?
- Yahoo outgoing e-mail problems with Thunderbird.

Preventing Thunderbird

This was a feature that was turned on by default in older versions of Mozilla Thunderbird. I think the default is turned off in newer versions. It is something that is not only annoying, but also presents security issues. Turning the embedding feature off is easy. Just select the View menu. Make sure that Display Attachments Inline is unchecked. Changing Thunderbird's behaviour with outgoing e-mail attachments is easy to do, but is buried in the Config Editor. Make sure that you are using a current version of Thunderbird.

The location of the Config Editor has changed several times with different versions. Select the Tools menu, then Options, select the Advanced button, then the General tab and click on the Config Editor button. Scroll down until you find mail. content_disposition_type. If the value is not set to 1, double-click on that line and an Enter Integer Value dialog box will pop up. Change the value to 1 and click OK. Shut down Thunderbird and restart it for the change to take effect.

Programmer

When a non-technically inclined web site owner speaks with an experienced programmer, technical jargon frequently enters the conversation. Some programmers do that intentionally, just to show off their expertise. For others, it is just the way they talk because they are immersed in a technical working environment. If you get confused talking with IT people, you may find this jargon guide to be handy. The technical language of programmers can sometimes be very difficult to understand. It is loaded with shortcuts, euphemisms and analogies. Frequently, the full name or technical term for the many special symbols or characters used in programming is just too cumbersome or boring to use in everyday technical conversations. Unique names or monikers for programming symbols has evolved. Most are intended to be humorous and help to liven up the communications between programmers.

The following are a few of the most common jargon and techno-terms used by professional programmers in everyday conversations amongst themselves. Step outside of your box for a few moments and compare the special characters to the jargon terms and you can easily envision the evolution of the terms.

- . *(dot)*: A dot is just a period in a file name or domain name, as in google-dot-com.
- * *(star, splat or spider)*: An asterisk is a wild card symbol used with servers and computer programmes.
- # (hash, pound, crunch, sharp)–Most commonly referred to as a hash, this symbol is commonly used to designate comments in many programming languages.

- *! (bang, pling, shriek, not)*: The exclamation point serves different purposes in different programming languages, but it is most commonly used to reverse a Boolean evaluation. In other words, if a statement is true, it reverses it to false.
- *#! (hash-bang or sh-bang)*: When used as the first two characters on the first line of a programming script, a hash-bang causes Unix and Linux operating systems to execute that script using the interpreter specified by the rest of that line.
- *' (tick):* This is a single quote commonly used to surround a string of characters.
- *" (snakebite, rabbit ears)*: A standard double quote. This jargon goes way back to the 1980s, so if you hear this, you are talking to an old-timer.
- *$ (buck, bling, cash)*: Used to designate a string variable in many programming languages.
- *() (left paren, right paren, open, close)*: Commonly used to group portions of algorithms or comparison statements. Algorithms and evaluations of statements always start with the inner-most set of parens in all programming languages.
- */ (wack, slash, stroke)*: A common slash character, most commonly used in directory paths on servers or to define a mathematical division.
- *\ (backslash, backwack, hack)*: A common blackslash used in some networking paths and also as a common designation for a escape character, which means that the next character in line should be taken literally and not executed.
- *{} (left curly, right curly, hitchcocks*: Think Alfred Hitchcock silhouette, left banana, right banana)–Curly braces commonly used to group multiple programming statements.
- *~ (squiggle)*: A tilde character.
- *| (bar, pipe)*: A vertical bar character.
- *^ (hat)*: A caret character.
- *% (mod, grapes)*: Commonly used as a mathematical modulo character in programming languages.
- *& (amp, amper)*: An ampersand symbol.

W3C

You may find it interesting to learn how to eliminate every error message the W3C validator produces. It can be an educational process even if you are a very experienced developer. Although you may think you know a lot about HTML or XHTML, you will likely find that you do not know as much as you thought you knew about the W3C's coding standards. Before you use the validator, a page needs to have a Doctype declaration.

The Doctype declaration, or DTD, needs to be the very first line of code on a Web page. The DTD sets the standard to be used in the validation. It also serves another purpose. Many modern browsers contain multiple rendering engines. If you do not set a standard to be used for rendering, the page may not look consistent across different browsers.

Note that all valid DTDs from HTML 4.01 on contain a link to a standards document. If your web page editor already adds a DTD with every Web page, it may not be valid if it does not contain a URL to the actual standards document. Using the W3C validator is very easy. Just cut-and-paste or enter a complete URL to the Web page you wish to test. You may find some of the validation messages to be a bit cryptic, but the W3C provides links with most error messages that lead to additional information. There are some common page elements that always produce errors or warnings, even though they do not negatively affect either browsers or search engine spiders. Microsoft-specific entity codes, such as copyright and other symbols may not be code compliant. The validator handles these errors well and typically offers the code compliant equivalent.

Body tag attributes such as leftmargin, right margin (Internet Explorer), marginheight, marginwidth (Netscape) are browser extensions that are not part of the official coding standards. These types of issues will not typically produce negative effects with either browsers or spiders, but do show up as errors because they do not comply with the standard. One type of nuisance error is a missing alt attribute in image tags.

Current standards do require the use of the alt attribute in order to push designers and developers to use this attribute because it is beneficial for Internet users with vision impairments who utilize special browsers that describe images though the use of alt attributes. It may not make sense, however, to include text with every alt attribute. The code compliant workaround is to simply include an empty string value (alt="") for lines and other page elements that need no explanation. It can sometimes be very beneficial to eliminate every error message displayed, and to assure complete and 100% compliance with the DTD standard you chose. Once a page has been validated as compliant, the W3C offers a cut-and-paste snippet of code that can be added to your Web pages as both a "gold star" certification of compliance and as a link to re-validate the code when you make changes.

Avoiding Spam

Despite anti-spam laws, the amount of spam e-mail messages I receive has grown enormously. You probably feel the same way. The problem with spam laws is that someone has to enforce them, but the e-mail spam problem is so enormous that only the largest and most aggressive USA spammers get prosecuted. Foreign spammers are not subject to USA laws and are much harder to identify. There are, however, some fundamental things that you can do to lessen the amount of spam that you receive, particularly if you have a business.

First and foremost, the best way to prevent your e-mail address from finding its way to a spam list is to never, under any circumstances, publish the e-mail address on a web page. Why? Because most e-mail ends up on spam lists because one of the hundreds of spam bots–also called e-mail harvesters–found it on a web site and automatically added it to a spam list. If you need to publish an e-mail address, create an image file for the e-mail address and display that. Spambots cannot read text in images, so they will not find the e-mail address if you display it in an image.

Second, never, ever click on a spam message or any links in a spam message. This includes links that assure that the message will be removed from the spammer's database. While this may work for legitimate sources of e-mail, I am willing to bet that few spammers really care about the laws, especially if they are in a foreign country. When you click on any link, you are very likely just verifying that your e-mail address is valid, which pretty much guarantees that it will be added to hundreds of spam lists.

Third, much of the spam that we receive comes from spammer programmes that randomly generate e-mail account names using the domain names of popular ISPs and then send an e-mail to that address. If it bounces back, they know the e-mail address is not valid. If it does not bounce back, it may be a valid e-mail address.

Many spammers use a library of account names that are attached to other libraries of domain names. The account name if the portion of the e-mail address found to the left of the @ symbol. The domain is the part to the right. Due to the fact that we run several web-based businesses, we have noticed a pattern of account names that many spammers use to see if an e-mail address is valid. The account names are attached to lists of domain names that can easily be found on the web and are used to generate spam for commonly used e-mail addresses.

Internet Technology

The Internet has become critical to everyday life in domains as diverse as education, health, defence, commerce, travel and entertainment. The Internet was not designed for its current level of usage, and there is a need for simple constructs to allow the network to do better in terms of security, mobility and quality of service, among other things. A number of global and local programmes of research (in the US, EU and further afield, eg Asia) are looking at future network architectures and building testbeds to evaluate new protocols and systems based on these new ideas. The most notable, in the US are the NSF Find programme and the GENI project to build infrastructure. In Europe we find a number of projects, with some interesting high-level thinking (eg the Eiffel project) and a set of testbed initiatives under the FIRE Programme.

While some researchers think there is a need for a'clean slate' design of the network of the future, much successful work is evolutionary rather than revolutionary, and this can be seen in the articles in this issue. Future core networks will leverage IP over simple, super-fast optical core networks. A major trend is that of virtualization, featuring the construction of optimized virtual networks that answer the needs of a collection of users or applications. A wide variety of wired and wireless access networks are available or being developed: FTTH/FTTO in the wired domain, and 3G/CDMA, LTE, WiFi, WiMax and Satellite in the wireless setting.

Internet Modelling

It is quite important to comprehend how the complex systems that we build actually operate. This requires basic research on network modelling and simulation, eg, in order to derive the fundamental laws on network dynamics and control or to evaluate the ultimate capacity of self-organized wireless networks. It also requires advances in network measurements: traffic statistics, Internet probing and measurement, network inference and detection of anomalies and attacks.

Internet Algorithms

The future of the Internet will require a wide range of computer science tools: verification; distributed algorithms (eg for consensus, and election and epidemic diffusion); resource management algorithms: resource allocation and scheduling; database algorithms: content storage, update and retrieval, content replication and consistency; search engines and the semantic Web. A key cost in networking is the operations and management overheads. The scalability of the Internet is well known, but as distributed applications proliferate, a more autonomic approach is increasingly required. Spontaneous and self-organized networks emerge both in the wireless setting (eg with Wifi meshes or infrastructure-less wireless networks [MANETS]) and in the wired network setting (eg in peer to peer).

The Internet started by connecting computers and users to information, and then went on to connect users to each other with audio, video, games and social networking tools. Now the rapid evolution of pervasive, embedded networked devices means that we connect various types of devices to each other. There are far more computers in the world embedded in everyday objects (cars, domestic appliances etc) than there are on desktops. The interconnection of the Internet with the physical world through sensors and agents and the tagging of industrial production by RFIDs will lead to new traffic and architecture challenges, with possibly hundreds of billions of new devices that will collect information and will have to be upgraded and managed remotely and conveniently. This will require new paradigms for routing, search, naming, maintenance, data survival etc.

The Internet of things extends to cars and other vehicles. Here the key potential is in safety: ABS in cars could communicate road surface conditions to following vehicles, setting speed and braking reactions sooner rather than too late. Traffic management and pollution sensing on cars can also make use of networking between cars, and from cars to roadside infrastructure. Tracking goods in transit on the road would allow logistics companies to optimize their freight operations, saving time and energy and perishable goods.

There is an important diversification of the nature of the content transported across the Internet: initially it was files, then real-time games, video, telephony and whiteboards, and now TV, video on demand etc. There has also been diversification of the localization of contents: with each user potentially a content producer (peer-to-peer applications). New interactions with data are appearing, as in Web 2.0 or the semantic Web, and applications continue to evolve and require new systems, measurements and management tools. Since its beginnings in 1992, the World-Wide Web has offered remote transactions for goods and services. Recently we have seen a rapid growth in the number of attacks on identity, since acquiring such information allows miscreants to commit fraud that is hard to detect.

Estimates vary, but the Internet and all its services consume something on the order of 4% of the energy in the developed world. Only simple measures are required to improve this by a factor of two.

Furthermore, the Internet, as we have discussed above, can be used to monitor and control external devices (things, vehicles, services) and significantly reduce their unnecessary power consumption. Figures as high as 30% have been quoted for possible national savings of energy, if unused devices in all homes could be remotely turned off. The investment necessary to achieve this is relatively low, with what seems like a very big potential return.

The Internet Services

We are moving from a Web of documents to a Web of services and Web of knowledge. This has triggered an explosion of new applications such as SecondLife, FaceBook and LinkedIn. And there is more to come, with augmented reality, virtual worlds, real-time games and telepresence. New concepts such as service orchestrations are also emerging, and with them, new business models.

Setting The Context

- The invited article 'Starting the Debate: Agreeing on Disagreements' by Dirk Trossen, B.T., U.K., is a meta-discussion note, on how to trigger debate. As such, it is quite interesting as a methodology for encouraging architectural thinking in the long term.
- 'The Internet Engineering Task Force and The Future of Internet' by Emmanuel Baccelli, Thomas H. Clausen and Philippe Jacquet, INRIA Saclay, France, provides a useful reminder of the processes by which standards are created, and an analysis of how future research might be delivered in the short to medium term.

Architecture

- 'Network Virtualization, a Perspective' by Anja Feldman, Mario Kind, Olaf Maennel, Georg Shaffrath and Christoph Werle: Virtualization, briefly defined above, can be seen as a way to overcome the ossification of the Internet, namely the general idea that one should not change a system or architecture that works well. The technical challenges and the business models associated with overlay networks and more generally with virtualization are thoroughly discussed in this invited paper.

- '*Y-COMM*: A New Architecture for Mobile Heterogeneous Communications' by Glenford Mapp suggests that the symmetric architecture we are used to in the Internet is perhaps not well adapted to wireless, and proposes an alternative, useful for promoting discussion (cf the EU ANA Project).

Modelling, Measurement and Management

- 'Epidemic Information Dissemination' by Laurent Massoulie (Invited paper): Epidemic algorithms became popular at the turn of the century with Peer-to-Peer applications. They are now being investigated by major companies designing efficient distributed live streaming mechanisms over the Internet. This beautiful line of research combines the design of innovative algorithms and the modelling of their execution over a large network, which allows one to prove their quasi-optimality.
- Understanding traffic entails delivering information efficiently to humans so that they can decide on actions to take. The article 'iMyNetScope- a Platform for Network Traffic Visualization and Analysis' by Pavel Minarik discusses one approach to this, and presents one particularly interesting topic for today - the element of Cyber Defence.
- 'Unified Access to Internet Measurement Data' by Felix Strohmeier, Martin Nilsson and Demetres Antoniades: like the previous article, this touches on a timely topic - making sure we can all (as researchers or operations) access data easily (see also www.crawdad.org for an example of traffic archives in a standard form). Since the Internet is a federation of a vast number of networks (300 ISPs in the UK alone), we need clear and standard methods for exchanging data about operations. This applies equally to research networks such as those in FIRE.
- 'Privacy Aware Network Monitoring' by Peter Dorfinger, Carsten Schmoll and Felix Strohmeier describes a problem relevant to the research and operations community. Much work on the future Internet requires monitoring of research, but at the same time, real users require privacy. This article reminds us how important and difficult it is to reconcile these two aspects. Indeed, in gathering data about network use there are legal requirements relating to intercept laws and user privacy that must be met.

- 'Breaking the Weakest Link: Becoming a Trusted Authority on the Internet' by Marc Stevens is a reminder of the danger of security failures. The fact that even the basic technology of security is sometimes flawed is interesting. Systems are never perfect, and this is never more true than for security: we can never prove a system is secure, but only discover (eventually) when it no longer is!

Correctness and Robustness (and Self-Managed to Some Extent)

- '*ResiliNets*: Resilient and Survivable Networks' by David Hutchison and James P.G. Sterbenz: As discussed above, we need secure networks that are efficient and well managed. We also depend on these networks, and since individual components are never 100% immune from faults and failures, we need techniques to make the overall system more resilient than its components.
- 'Standardized Testware for Internet-Based Telecommunication Services' by Bostjan Pintar, Axel Rennoch, Peter Schmitting and Stephan Schulz: As Internet protocols grow in number and complexity each year, we need assurance that systems will behave correctly. This article outlines industrial solutions on the correct operation of the software systems (protocols) that make the Internet and its telecommunication infrastructure work.
- 'Network Description Tools and Standards' by Freek Dijkstra, Jeroen van der Ham and Ronald van der Pol: Setting up high-speed network connections - light paths - is still a manual effort taking two to three weeks. The network engineers need a clear picture of the network topology in order to plan and configure light paths. The Network Markup Language (NML) standardizes network topology and state information. The University of Amsterdam and SARA Computing and Networking Services in the Netherlands are contributing to this effort, with the ultimate goal being to automatically set up and manage light paths.

Novel Applications, Especially Multimedia

- 'Delay-Tolerant Bulk Internet Transfers' by Nikolaos Laoutaris and Pablo Rodriguez (invited paper): Using disruption-tolerant networking (DTN) techniques, but on the Internet rather than on challenged networks, produces very interesting results in terms of capacity. Throughput can be significantly increased for some applications, and there are some very well-motivated examples, such as backing up information between large data centres, using spare capacity in a smart and autonomic way.

- 'Resource Management for IPTV Distribution' by Henrik Abrahamsson and Per Kreuger: IPTV on AT&T and Telefonica's networks now has in excess of 12 million users, each with hundreds of channels of broadcast quality content. This makes for non-trivial deployments,– and the importance of resource management for the various different technologies is unquestionable.
- '*VISTO*: Visual Storyboard for Web Video Browsing, Searching, and Indexing' by Marco Pellegrini describes exciting work on future Internet killer applications.
- 'The New Role of Humans in the Future Internet' by Daniel Schall and Schahram Dustdar: Current service-oriented architectures typically orchestrate Web services. This article addresses architectures that combine Web and human services, where the latter are not limited to service consumption but may also undertake service production. The main emphasis is on the interfaces required in such architectures.

In The Home (Internet of Things, And Energy!)

- 'Orchestrating your Surroundings' by Pau Giner, Carlos Cetina, Joan Fons and Vicente Pelechano, UP Valencia, Spain, is an example of the 'Internet of Things' being at the centre of future Internet visions.
- 'An Autonomic Home Networking Infrastructure' by Thomas Luckenbach, Mario Schuster and Marc-Oliver Pahl: in line with the previous article but articulated with a vision of autonomic computing, this is on the important topic of home net automation. Home users are non-technical: they really do not want to become network managers, operators or system administrators. It is thus essential to make home networks 'plug and play'.
- 'Load-Balancing Energy-Usage of Household Appliances' by Lennart E. Fahlen: Energy is a highly relevant topic, as described above, and using the Internet to control consumer electronics in the household is a promising way to reduce unnecessary consumption.

On the Road, Vehicular

- 'The Internet of Vehicles or The Second Generation of Telematic Services' by Markus Miche and Thomas Michael Bohnert: Like the Internet of Things, vehicular networking is just taking off. There are car-to-car and car-to-infrastructure communications standards as well as integration of satellite navigation, traffic monitoring, tracking, and cellular map systems.
- 'Web-Enabled Tracking Operations in Distributed Supply-Chains' by Zsolt Kemény and Elisabeth Ilie-Zudor: Using the Web to track logistical information about goods in the real world is already a huge business. This is a very useful article on the topic, which also relates to the previous article.

Awareness, Identity And Society

- 'Knowledge-Based Collaboration Patterns in Future Internet Enterprise Systems' by Gregoris Mentzas and Keith Popplewell is supporting virtual community patterns, a bit like eScience community work.
- 'Experiences from the Public Safety Arena for the Future Internet' by Socrates Varakliotis, Peter Kirstein and Steve Hailes: Since the Boxing Day tsunami and Hurricane Katrina, it has become clear that the Internet might be better used in support of communications during disasters. This is a useful note on work in the area.
- 'With Joint Forces - Establishing Situation Awareness for the Future Internet' by Tanja Zseby and Thomas Hirsch: Like Mentzas' article, we can build systems to track patterns of use. This can be used to support collaboration or to detect misbehaviour. Increasingly, though, agencies are beginning to monitor social networks for this purpose.
- 'Social Networking for a Pervasive Future Internet: the SOCIALNETS Project' by Stuart M. Allen, Marco Conti, Andrea Passarella and Roger M. Whitaker: A timely article on an increasingly important topic. This outlines several new aspects of social networking that our readership should know about.
- 'Owner-Centric Networking: A New Architecture for a Pollution-Free Internet' by Claude Castelluccia and Mohamed Ali Kaafar proposes a new Owner-Centric Networking architecture that provides individuals control over their contents. This architecture would considerably improve privacy on the Internet by limiting data pollution.

- 'Semantic Web for e-Commerce' by Bernd Gruber: The Web is the basis for most new applications (Web mail, photo sharing, social nets, maps) and is the basis for commerce, which drives real economies.

Wireless, Embedded

- 'Management of Future Mesh-Based Radio Access Networks' by Vangelis Angelakis, Vasilios Siris and Apostolos Traganitis: Community mesh wireless nets are becoming pretty widespread in some areas as an alternative to expensive cellular data services. Automating management is important; related work at Intel and Microsoft in the last couple of years has covered some aspects (AP selection) but the topic continues to be relevant.
- 'Testing Mobile Data Applications on Smartphoes with SymPA' by Almudena Díaz and Pedro Merino discusses further the shortcomings of operating system platforms for data networking on cell phones and related devices. This is important, since the largest growth in Internet-capable devices is currently in this area.

2

Web Organization

Section

Markup Languages Section

Includes all markup languages including HTML, XML, and SGML. Documentation in this section currently includes an HTML Guide, XML Guide, and a Document Type Definition (DTD) reading reference.

CGI Section

Includes four documents describing implementation of the client to server web interface. It includes information about the common gateway interface (CGI), server side includes (SSI), JavaScript, and writing perl script programmes

HTTP Section

Thic section currently includes an HTTP Reference which is based on RFC 2616. It has brief descriptions of the HTTP request and response headers and also lists the possible response headers such as 404 (not found).

PHP - PHP is a scripting language that runs on the web server and the script code is embedded in the HTML document. It is easy to use with syntax similar to C which is why it is so popular.

PHP

JAVA

Documentation is being generated for this section. It currently contains some web links.

MIME Section

This section describes Multipurpose Internet Mail Extension along with its purpose and it also includes a few MIME related web links.

Graphics

Gif files used to add graphics to web pages.

World Wide Web

There are many types of technologies which are used to support the world wide web and more are being developed all the time. There are several groups involved in the development and coordination of these technologies.

IAB

Internet Architecture Board. Web site: IAB. The IAB websites states that"The IAB does not aim to produce polished technical proposals on such topics. Rather, the intention is to stimulate action by the IESG or within the IETF community that will lead to proposals that meet general consensus."

IANA

Internet Assigned Numbers Authority. Web site: IANA. They control the assignment of internet addresses and domain names.

IESG

The Internet Engineering Steering Group. Web site: IESG. According to RFC 2418, the IESG"has responsibility for developing and reviewing specifications intended as Internet Standards."

IETF

The Internet Engineering Task Force. Web site: IETF. Their web site says"The Internet Engineering Task Force (IETF) is a large open international community of network designers, operators, vendors, and researchers concerned with the evolution of the Internet architecture and the smooth operation of the Internet."

InterNIC

Internet Network Information Center, the authority for allocating internet addresses. Web site: InterNIC.

IRTF

Internet Research Task Force. Web site: IRTF. Their web site states their mission is"To promote research of importance to the evolution of the future Internet by creating focused, long-term and small Research Groups working on topics related to Internet protocols, applications, architecture and technology."

- *Isoc*: Internet Society, promotes internet policies. Web site:ISOC.
- *Istf*: Internet Societal Task Force. Web site: ISTF. Their mission is"To assure the open development, evolution and use of the Internet for the benefit of all people throughout the world".
- *W3c*: World Wide Web Consortium, sets standards for the web working with the IETF. W3C
- *Oasis*: Organization for the Advancement of Structured Information Standards. OASIS
- Internet2 Internet2 An Organization that supports internet related technologies including XML, DHTML, JAVA and more.
- *Irt*: Internet Related Technologies. Internet Related TechnologiesTheir website states"Internet2, led by over 180 U.S. universities working in partnership with industry and government, is developing and deploying advanced network applications and technologies, accelerating the creation of tomorrow's Internet."
- Graphic Communications Association A trade association that provides standards for the printing and publishing industries.

System Programming Language

System programming languages are higher level and they are strongly typed languages. The term "higher level" means that many details are handled automatically so that programmers can write less code to get the same job done.

System programming languages are well suited to building components where the complexity is in the data structures and algorithms.

System programming support following features:

- Register allocation is handled by the compiler so that programmers need not write code to move information between registers and memory.
- Programmers can use simple keywords such as while and if for control structures; the compiler generates all the detailed instructions to implement the control structures.

- Procedure calling sequences are generated automatically: programmers need not worry about moving arguments to and from the call stack.

Embedded System Programming

Embedded System Programming was first used in Apollo guidance computer to guide Apollo. Technological advancement brought the price of embedded system (ICs) lower making it possible to use them for commercial purpose. Today embedded systems are widely used in various devices performing specific functions with drastic improvement in processing power. Embedded system programming has been derived from the word embedded system. An embedded system is nothing but a special purpose system in which the computer is fully encapsulated by the device it controls. Embedded software designs have advanced enough to produce widely used devices performing specific function devices such as ATM, PDA, mobile phones etc. This widely used technological term in the field of Information Technology, is the combination of computer hardware and software which is either fixed in facility or programmable. In short it is purposely designed for a meticulous kind of application device. Systems that hosts this embedded systems are various industrial machines, automobiles, medical equipment, cameras, household appliances, and airplanes, vending machines, toys, cellular phone and PDA. Seeing its importance and worth embedded systems programming has gained lot popularity and people are looking for companies providing this service. If you are looking for a company providing embedded systems programming then your search is over as Softage is there for you.

Softage is Russia's leading IT service provider providing best and advanced embedded systems programming. Embedded systems programming is specially dedicated to unequivocal tasks so that design engineers can optimize it by reducing the magnitude and cost of the product. In fact nowadays, embedded systems are frequently mass-produced. This has resulted in the cost savings that may be multiplied by millions of items. Apart from the other devices embedded systems also range from portable devices such as MP3 players, to large stationary installations like traffic lights or factory controllers. According to the experts embedded systems are easily programmable and are provided with a programming interface. Embedded system programming is a tough and professional work which is efficiently handled by Softage. Backed by years of experience Softage hosts some of the best and professional programmers those are experts in embedded system software programming.

Windows System Programming

In old days, the operating system programme executes the program's instructions in sequence one instruction after another as they arranged by the programmer. When the programme calls a function or interacts with the Operating System (OS) by calling one of the OS's service functions, the function's instructions executed in similar way and the execution continue sequentially until the end of the last instruction of the main programme. In this traditional way of programming the programme only need one main function to start the execution. Nowadays, in event driven programming environment such as Windows, the interaction between the programme and the OS is a message-based interaction. In this interaction the programme start in a wait mode until the user create an event like for example, press a key or click a mouse button. The OS generates appropriate message and inserts it in application's message queue. The programme, when it ready, should dispatch the messages (read a message from the queue and send it back to the OS) one message after another for time scheduling purpose. After that, the OS then send the message again to the programme and the programme respond by taking appropriate actions. In this kind of interaction, a simple programme need at least two functions, the main function that start the message loop (WinMain ()) and the other called by the OS (Windows Function())and respond to the passed message.

Unix Systems Programming

The Unix systems programming API has been standardised by a large number of POSIX standards documents from the IEEE. For the majority of programmers the most important of these is POSIX 1003.1 which covers process primitives and environments, directories and files, I/O primitives and device specific functions. Later standards cover other issues, such as Shells and Utilities (POSIX 1003.2) and Administration (POSIX 1387.2). One of the unusual characteristics of POSIX 1003.1 is its use of the C language throughout. Whereas IEEE standards would normally be expected to be language independent, the history of Unix is so bound up with C that this was the only feasible route. The document claims that it will be the basis for definitions that are independent of particular programming languages. In fact, new language dependent versions have arisen, such as Ada (POSIX 1003.5) and Fortran.

Irrespective of the formal standards mechanisms, designers of libraries for other languages have used POSIX 1003.1 as the specification for their own libraries. For example, tcl [Ousterhout] and Perl [Wall] have well-developed Unix bindings that copy the syntax, and rely on the semantics, of POSIX 1003.1.

Java [Arnold] is the latest flavour in programming languages for all sorts of excellent reasons, despite some serious shortcomings. It is a full O/O language (although not as pure as SmallTalk or Eiffel); it is based on C/C++, but avoids the worst of both languages (not completely, though); by use of a virtual machine it is cross-platform (although some vendors have variant versions); it has a rich set set of libraries that deal with, for example, graphics and networking. These are combining to produce the "Web programming" environment where applications or applets are written once to run on any platform. Java extends the open authoring environment of HTML to an open programming environment.

How do Unix and Java co-exist? Very well in general terms. A Java application can do exactly the same things in a Unix environment that it can do in a Mac or Windows environment. With care, applications can even be written that transparently handle such issues as forward- versus back-slashes for directory separators.

Java currently lacks the depth of hooks into the POSIX API that tcl and Perl have. The standard must continue to have this lack or it will lose its universal applicability. However, *extensions* by *non-standard* libraries can supply this depth, as long as they are done in an appropriate manner. This paper reports on a project to make the POSIX API available to Java applications or applets using a non-standard library. It encapulates POSIX calls within Java methods for a new set of classes in the posix package.

This project must be contrasted in aims and methods to the Microsoft policy with J++: their attempt is to make J++ the best environment for doing Windows programming in Java J++, and this implicitly rejects the notion of a cross-platform environment. It may even turn out to be difficult for the programmer using J++ to be certain of how general their code is. The statements from Microsoft do not seem to dispel any uncertainty.

This project, on the other hand, makes it explicit about the introduction of non-standard features, by placing all the new classes in a package that is non-standard. No application using the posix package will ever pass the "Java Pure" tests. On the other hand, this package will develop by an open process method: the source code will be freely available to all, and can be freely modified. If interest is high enough, it can be divorced from individual control and given to a suitable co-ordinating authority.

Linkers

Definition

In computer science, a linker is a programme that takes one or more objects generated by a compiler and assembles them into a single executable programme.

In IBM mainframe environments such as OS/360 this programme is known as a “linkage editor”.

On Unix variants the term loader is often used as a synonym for linker. Because this usage blurs the distinction between the compile-time process and the run-time process, this article will use “linking” for the former and “loading” for the latter. However, in some operating systems the same programme handles both the jobs of linking and loading a programme; see “dynamic linking”.

Computer programmes are typically comprised of several parts or modules; these parts, if not all contained within a single object file, refer to each other by means of symbols.

Typically, an object file can contain three kinds of symbols:

- Defined symbols, which allow it to be called by other modules.
- Undefined symbols, which call the other modules where these symbols are defined.
- Local symbols, used internally within the object file to facilitate relocation.

When a programme comprises multiple object files, the linker combines these files into a unified executable programme, resolving the symbols as it goes along. Linkers can take objects from a collection called a “library”. Some linkers do not include the whole library in the output; they only include its symbols that are referenced from other object files or libraries. Libraries exist for diverse purposes, and one or more system libraries are usually linked in by default.

The linker also takes care of arranging the objects in a program’s address space. This may involve “relocating” code that assumes a specific base address to another base. Since a compiler seldom knows where an object will reside, it often assumes a fixed base location (for example, zero). Relocating machine code may involve re-targeting of absolute jumps, loads and stores.

The executable output by the linker may need another relocation pass when it is finally loaded into memory (just before execution). This pass is usually omitted on hardware offering virtual memory — every programme is put into its own address space, so there is no conflict even if all programmes load at the same base address. This pass may also be omitted if the executable is a position independent executable.

Concept

The basic job of any linker is simple: it binds more abstract names to more concrete names, which permits programmers to write code using the more abstract names. That is, it takes a name written by a programmer such as get line and binds it to "the location 612 bytes from the beginning of the executable code in module iosys." Or it may take a more abstract numeric address such as "the location 450 bytes beyond the beginning of the static data for this module" and bind it to a numeric address.

A linkers is used in the development of computer programming in systems. The earliest computers were programmed entirely in machine language. Programmers would write out the symbolic programmes on sheets of paper, hand assemble them into machine code and then toggle the machine code into the computer, or perhaps punch it on paper tape or cards. If the programmer used symbolic addresses at all, the symbols were bound to addresses as the programmer did his or her hand translation.

If it turned out that an instruction had to be added or deleted, the entire programme had to be hand-inspected and any addresses affected by the added or deleted instruction adjusted. The problem was that the names were bound to addresses too early. Assemblers solved that problem by letting programmers write programmes in terms of symbolic names, with the assembler binding the names to machine addresses. If the programme changed, the programmer had to reassemble it, but the work of assigning the addresses is pushed off from the programmer to the computer.

Libraries of code compound the address assignment problem. Since the basic operations that computers can perform are so simple, useful programmes are composed of subprograms that perform higher level and more complex operations. Computer installations keep a library of pre-written and debugged subprograms that programmers can draw upon to use in new programmes they write, rather than requiring programmers to write all their own subprograms. The programmer then loads the subprograms in with the main programme to form a complete working programme. Programmers were using libraries of subprograms even before they used assemblers.

By 1947, John Mauchly, who led the ENIAC project, wrote about loading programmes along with subprograms selected from a catalog of programmes stored on tapes, and of the need to relocate the subprograms' code to reflect the addresses at which they were loaded.

Perhaps surprisingly, these two basic linker functions, relocation and library search, appear to predate even assemblers, as Mauchly expected both the programme and subprograms to be written in machine language. The relocating loader allowed the authors and users of the subprograms to write each subprogram as though it would start at location zero, and to defer the actual address binding until the subprograms were linked with a particular main programme. With the advent of operating systems, relocating loaders separate from linkers and libraries became necessary. Before operating systems, each programme had the machine's entire memory at its disposal, so the programme could be assembled and linked for fixed memory addresses, knowing that all addresses in the computer would be available.

But with operating systems, the programme had to share the computer's memory with the operating system and perhaps even with other programmes, This means that the actual addresses at which the programme would be running weren't known until the operating system loaded the programme into memory, deferring final address binding past link time to load time. Linkers and loaders now divided up the work, with linkers doing part of the address binding, assigning relative addresses within each programme, and the loader doing a final relocation step to assign actual addresses. As systems became more complex, they called upon linkers to do more and more complex name management and address binding. Fortran programmes used multiple subprograms and common blocks, areas of data shared by multiple subprograms, and it was up to the linker to lay out storage and assign the addresses both for the subprograms and the common blocks. Linkers increasingly had to deal with object code libraries.

Including both application libraries written in Fortran and other languages, and compiler support libraries called implicitly from compiled code to handle I/O and other high-level operations.

Programmes quickly became larger than available memory, so linkers provided overlays, a technique that let programmers arrange for different parts of a programme to share the same memory, with each overlay loaded on demand when another part of the programme called into it. Overlays were widely used on mainframes from the advent of disks around 1960 until the spread of virtual memory in the mid-1970s, then reappeared on microcomputers in the early 1980s in exactly the same form, and faded as virtual memory appeared on PCs in the 1990s. They're still used in memory limited embedded environments, and may yet reappear in other places where precise programmer or compiler control of memory usage improves performance. With the advent of hardware relocation and virtual memory, linkers and loaders actually got less complex, since each programme could again have an entire address space. Programmes could be linked to be loaded at fixed addresses, with hardware rather than software relocation taking care of any load-time relocation.

But computers with hardware relocation invariably run more than one programme, frequently multiple copies of the same programme. When a computer runs multiple instances of one programme, some parts of the programme are the same among all running instance (the executable code, in particular), while other parts are unique to each instance. If the parts that don't change can be separated out from the parts that do change, the operating system can use a single copy of the unchanging part, saving considerable storage. Compilers and assemblers were modified to create object code in multiple sections, with one section for read only code and another section for writable data, the linker had to be able to combine all of sections of each type so that the linked programme would have all the code in one place and all of the data in another. This didn't delay address binding any more than it already was, since addresses were still assigned at link time, but more work was deferred to the linker to assign addresses for all the sections.

Linker Action

Programme Loading

Copy a programme from secondary storage (which since about 1968 invariably means a disk) into main memory so it's ready to run. In some cases loading just involves copying the data from disk to memory, in others it involves allocating storage, setting protection bits, or arranging for virtual memory to map virtual addresses to disk pages.

Relocation

Compilers and assemblers generally create each file of object code with the programme addresses starting at zero, but few computers let you load your programme at location zero. If a programme is created from multiple subprograms, all the subprograms have to be loaded at non-overlapping addresses. Relocation is the process of assigning load addresses to the various parts of the programme, adjusting the code and data in the programme to reflect the assigned addresses.

In many systems, relocation happens more than once. It's quite common for a linker to create a programme from multiple subprograms, and create one linked output programme that starts at zero, with the various subprograms relocated to locations within the big programme. Then when the programme is loaded, the system picks the actual load address and the linked programme is relocated as a whole to the load address.

Symbol Resolution

When a programme is built from multiple subprograms, the references from one subprogram to another are made using symbols; a main programme might use a square root routine called sqrt, and the math library defines sqrt. A linker resolves the symbol by noting the location assigned to sqrt in the library, and patching the caller's object code to so the call instruction refers to that location.

Although there's considerable overlap between linking and loading, it's reasonable to define a programme that does programme loading as a loader, and one that does symbol resolution as a linker. Either can do relocation, and there have been all-in-one linking loaders that do all three functions. The line between relocation and symbol resolution can be fuzzy. Since linkers already can resolve references to symbols, one way to handle code relocation is to assign a symbol to the base address of each part of the programme, and treat relocatable addresses as references to the base address symbols.

Two-pass linking Process

Now we turn to the general structure of linkers. Linking, like compiling or assembling, is fundamentally a two pass process. A linker takes as its input a set of input object files, libraries, and perhaps command files, and produces as its result an output object file, and perhaps ancillary information such as a load map or a file containing debugger symbols. Each input file contains a set of *segments*, contiguous chunks of code or data to be placed in the output file. Each input file also contains at least one *symbol table*. Some symbols are exported, defined within the file for use in other files, generally the names of routines within the file that can be called from elsewhere. Other symbols are imported, used in the file but not defined, generally the names of routines called from but not present in the file.

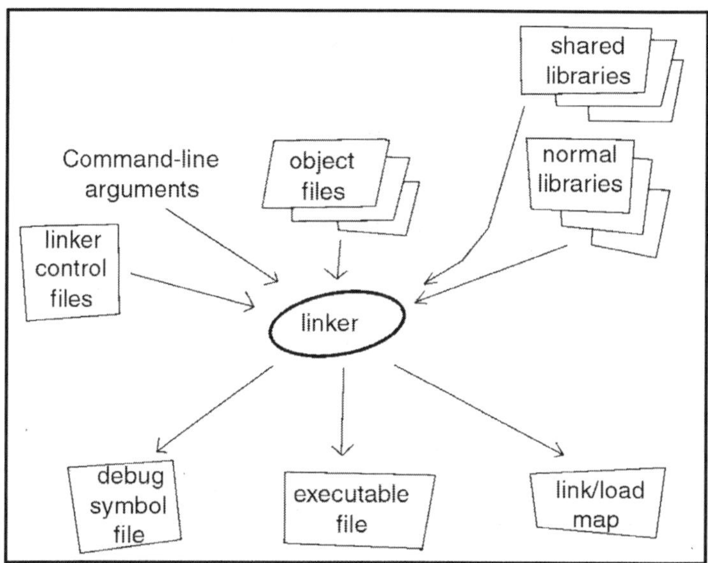

When a linker runs, it first has to scan the input files to find the sizes of the segments and to collect the definitions and references of all of the symbols It creates a segment table listing all of the segments defined in the input files, and a symbol table with all of the symbols imported or exported. Using the data from the first pass, the linker assigns numeric locations to symbols, determines the sizes and location of the segments in the output address space, and figures out where everything goes in the output file. The second pass uses the information collected in the first pass to control the actual linking process. It reads and relocates the object code, substituting numeric addresses for symbol references, and adjusting memory addresses in code and data to reflect relocated segment addresses, and writes the relocated code to the output file.

It then writes the output file, generally with header information, the relocated segments, and symbol table information. If the programme uses dynamic linking, the symbol table contains the info the runtime linker will need to resolve dynamic symbols. In many cases, the linker itself will generate small amounts of code or data in the output file, such as "glue code" used to call routines in overlays or dynamically linked libraries, or an array of pointers to initialization routines that need to be called at programme startup time.

Whether or not the programme uses dynamic linking, the file may also contain a symbol table for relinking or debugging that isn't used by the programme itself, but may be used by other programmes that deal with the output file. Some object formats are relinkable, that is, the output file from one linker run can be used as the input to a subsequent linker run. This requires that the output file contain a symbol table like one in an input file, as well as all of the other auxiliary information present in an input file. Nearly all object formats have provision for debugging symbols, so that when the programme is run under the control of a debugger, the debugger can use those symbols to let the programmer control the programme in terms of the line numbers and names used in the source programme. Depending on the details of the object format, the debugging symbols may be intermixed in a single symbol table with symbols needed by the linker, or there may be one table for the linker and a separate, somewhat redundant table for the debugger.

A few linkers appear to work in one pass. They do that by buffering some or all of the contents of the input file in memory or disk during the linking process, then reading the buffered material later. Since this is an implementation trick that doesn't fundamentally affect the two-pass nature of linking, we don't address it further here.

Relocation and Code Modification

The heart of a linker or loader's actions is relocation and code modification. When a compiler or assembler generates and object file, it generates the code using the unrelocated addresses of code and data defined within the file, and usually zeros for code and data defined elsewhere. As part of the linking process, the linker modifies the object code to reflect the actual addresses assigned. For example, consider this snippet of x86 code that moves the contents of variable a to variable b using the eax register.

```
mov  a,%eax
mov%eax,b
```

If a is defined in the same file at location 1234 hex and b is imported from somewhere else, the generated object code will be: A1 34 12 00 00 mov a,%eax A3 00 00 00 00 mov%eax,b Each instruction contains a one-byte operation code followed by a fourbyte address. The first instruction has a reference to 1234 (byte reversed, since the x86 uses a right to left byte order) and the second a reference to zero since the location of b is unknown. Now assume that the linker links this code so that the section in which a is located is relocated by hex 10000 bytes, and b turns out to be at hex 9A12.

The linker modifies the code to be:

```
A1 34 12 01 00 mov a,%eax
A3 12 9A 00 00 mov%eax,b
```

That is, it adds 10000 to the address in the first instruction so now it refers to a's relocated address which is 11234, and it patches in the address for b. These adjustments affect instructions, but any pointers in the data part of an object file have to be adjusted as well. On older computers with small address spaces and direct addressing, the modification process is fairly simple, since there are only only one or two address formats that a linker has to handle. Modern computers, including all RISCs, require considerably more complex code modification.

No single instruction contains enough bits to hold a direct address, so the compiler and linker have to use complicated addressing tricks to handle data at arbitrary addresses. In some cases, it's possible to concoct an address using two or three instructions, each of which contains part of the address, and use bit manipulation to combine the parts into a full address.

In this case, the linker has to be prepared to modify each of the instructions appropriately, inserting some of the bits of the address into each instruction. In other cases, all of the addresses used by a routine or group of routines are placed in an array used as an "address pool", initialization code sets one of the machine registers to point to that array, and code loads pointers out of the address pool as needed using that register as a base register. The linker may have to create the array from all of the addresses used in a programme, then modify instructions that so that they refer to the appropriate address pool entry.

Linker Command Languages

Every linker has some sort of command language to control the linking process. At the very least the linker needs the list of object files and libraries to link. Generally there is a long list of possible options: whether to keep debugging symbols, whether to use shared or unshared libraries, which of several possible output formats to use.

Most linkers permit some way to specify the address at which the linked code is to be bound, which comes in handy when using a linker to link a system kernel or other programme that doesn't run under control of an operating system. In linkers that support multiple code and data segments, a linker command language can specify the order in which segments are to be linked, special treatment for certain kinds of segments, and other application-specific options. There are four common techniques to pass commands to a linker:

- *Command line:* Most systems have a command line or the equivalent, via which one can pass a mixture of file names and switches. This is the usual approach for Unix and Windows linkers. On systems with limited length command lines, there's usually a way to direct the linker to read commands from a file and treat them as though they were on the command line.

Intermixed with Object Files

Some linkers, such as IBM mainframe linkers, accept alternating object files and linker commands in a single input file. This dates from the era of card decks, when one would pile up object decks and hand-punched command cards in a card reader.

Embedded in Object Files

Some object formats, notably Microsoft's, permit linker commands to be embedded inside object files. This permits a compiler to pass any options needed to link an object file in the file itself. For example, the C compiler passes commands to search the standard C library.

Separate Configuration Language

A few linkers have a full fledged configuration language to control linking. The GNU linker, which can handle an enormous range of object file formats, machine architectures, and address space conventions, has a complex control language that lets a programmer specify the order in which segments should be linked, rules for combining similar segments, segment addresses, and a wide range of other options. Other linkers have less complex languages to handle specific features such as programmer-defined overlays.

Loader

It is the Loader's function to fix absolute addresses for the relocated values in a relocatable module, thereby converting a relocatable module into an "executable" output file. The Loader is usually called automatically by the Linker but it may also be called separately by the user. As indicated below, several different Loaders are (optionally) available for use with Introl-C and, if the user has elected to obtain such optional Loaders, a variety of executable output file formats can be generated, depending on the Loader being used. Each resident Introl-C compiler package, and each Introl-C cross-compiler package, nominally includes a single, specific type of Introl Loader which is considered as being the "standard" Loader for that compiler's particular host system configuration. For resident Introl-C Compiler packages, the 'standard' Loader that is furnished is an "operating system dependent" type of Loader which generates an output file that is executable on that particular Compiler's host system.

For cross-compiler versions of Introl-C, the "standard" Loader furnished is typically a "hex" type Loader that generates a file of output load records, which can be either Motorola S-Records, intel Hex, Tektronix Hex, or Tektronix Extended Hex at user option. Besides the "standard" Loader that accompanies any given Compiler type, it is also possible for the user to optionally obtain and use other compatible "cross-Loaders" which generate output formats unrelated to the Compiler's host operating system. For example, "hex-type" Loaders are optionally available for use with resident versions of Introl-C; "operating system dependent" type Loaders are optionally available for use with cross-compiler versions; etc.

There are, therefore, several different species of Loaders, (as well as several different types of related Standard Libraries) that may potentially be used under Introl-C. The "standard" Loader supplied with your Introl-C package, as well as any other Loaders that may have been optionally ordered, are described in detail in the Loader Appendix of this Linker Reference Manual. This Loader section describes the general features that are common to all Loader types. Normally the input to the Loader is expected to be a relocatable file which has no unresolved external references; if unresolved references do exist in its input, loading will normally not be successful. A Loader option is provided, however, to force a file to be loaded even if it contains unresolved references.

Usually a relocatable file has to be linked before it can be used as input to the Loader. It is also possible, of course, to assemble a file which makes no external references and then use the relocatable output file produced by the Assembler directly as input to the Loader (ie without having actually linked it)

Functions of loader

- Allocate space in memory for the programme (allocation).
- Resolve symbolic references between object programmes (linking).

- Adjust all address dependent locations, such as address constraints, to correspond to the allocated space (relocation).
- Physically place the machine instruction and data into memory(loading) for execution.
- Loader: System programme that performs the loading function.
- Linker (or linkage editor): System programme that performs the linking operations (*i.e.* linking and relocation).

Kinds of Loader

Absolute loader

Performs Loading Only:

- Object programme contains:
  - H card (or record)
  - T cards (or record)
  - E card (or record)
- Check the starting address and memory size required (*i.e.* specified in H record), load Text records into memory sequentially, and then jump to the starting address specified by End record.

Absolute loader Algorithm

```
begin read Header record
verify programme
name and length read first
Text record while record type
'" 'E' do begin {if object code is in
character form, convert into internal
representation}
move object code to specified location in memory read next
object programme record
end
jump to address specified in End record
end
```

Relocatable loader

Perform allocation, relocation, and loading:

- Modification record: Used to describe the starting address and length of code to be modified.
- SIC computer: Most instructions use direct addressing. à Too many modification records are needed.

- Another approach: use relocation bit to indicate that the word should be modified or not.

Linkage editor

Performing linking only:

- Produce a linked version of the programme (called load module, executable image, or image programme).
- Solve external reference and library search, and perform relocation of all sections relative to the start of the linked programme.
- Although all linking has been performed, information concerning external reference is retained in the linked programme for further re-linking if necessary.

Linkage editor commands:

Example 1: new version of library routine

```
INCLUDE PLANNER (PROGLIB)
DELETE PROJECT
INCLUDE PROJECT (NEWLY)
REPLACE PLANNER (PROGLIB)
```

Example 2: combine subroutines into a package

```
INCLUDE READR(FINLIB)
INCLUDE WRITER(FIN LIB)
INCLUDE BLOCK(FINLIB)
SAVE FINIO(SUBLIB)
```

→The linked module name FINIO could be indexed in the directory of SUBLIB under the same name as the original subroutines.

- Linkage editor performs linking operation before the programme is loaded for execution. Linking loader perform linking operation at load time.
- Dynamic linking (or dynamic binding, load on call) perform linking operation until execution.
  - When a subroutine call is encountered and the subroutine is not resident in memory, load the subroutine into memory, perform linking, and finally jump to the subroutine.
  - Advantages: Load the routines when they are needed, the memory space will be saved.

Linking Loader

Perform allocation, linking, relocation, and loading:

- Modification record: Used to describe the starting address and length of code to be modified.
- SIC computer: Most instructions use direct addressing. à Too many modification records are needed.
- Another approach: use relocation bit to indicate that the word should be modified or not.

Loader Command Line

The "standard" Loader supplied with your Introl-C package is normally automatically called by the Linker when the Linker pass finishes. However, linker command line options exist that mav be used to alternatively force the Linker to automatically call other optional Loaders. Situations also arise when it is desirable to explicitly call the Loader alone, without first executing the Linker. When such situations arise, the Loader may be independently called by the user with a loader command line of the general form:

<c>ld <file> {<option>}

where <c>ld represents the Introl filename of the specific Loader being called, <file> is the name of the (linked) relocatable module which is to be loaded, and (<option>) represents zero or more Loader option specifiers.

Each of the potentially usable Introl Loaders is uniquely identified by a 3-letter Loader filename, the last two letters of which are always "ld". The <c> designator indicated in the "<c>ld" loader call on the command line therefore represents the first letter in the three-letter Loader name. For example, to call the Introl hex type of Loader, which has the filename "hld", the "<c>ld" entry on the command line would actually become "hld".

For further specifics on the names of the loaders which can be legally accessed. The relocatable file that is input to the Loader is expected to have a filenarne extension; if none is specified, the default filename extension ".RL" is assumed.

Normally the name of the executable output file will be identical to the name of the input file, but with a filename extension typically added by the Loader. The filename extensions each Loader appends are discussed in the Loader Appendices to this manual.

Loader Options

Each type of Loader available for use with the Introl-C has its own, generally unique set of options. When the Loader is being called separately, Loader options are specified directly on the loader command line when the Loader is being automatically called by the Linker, Loader options are specified on the link command line, together with the Linker options. If Loader options are specified on the link command line, any such options (ie those that do not apply to the Linker) will be automatically sent on to the Loader. For the most part Linker and Loader option specifiers tend to be distinct, so that there is little ambiguity when Loader options are specified on the link command line.

Library Files

A library file is a file which contains one or more linkable object modules of the type produced by the Introl Assembler. When a file is compiled and assembled, the result is exactly one linkable module which is placed into a file. This file is actually a library which happens to contain only a single module. When the user links a programme, one or more of these "libraries" are specified on the link command line.

Usually the "libraries" are those produced as a result of a compilation and contain only a single module, however, they may also contain several modules. The Library Manager, "libman", is a programme which allows the user to place several modules into a single library file. When the user has a large set of modules which are commonly used in programmes, it is usually convenient to place them all in one library and then simply specify the library once on the link command line.

The Linker will extract only those modules it requires in order to satisfy the external references of the programme. The Linker is designed to automatically search the "Standard Library", libc.R, if it still has external references to satisfy after it has exhausted all the alternatives provided by the modules specified an the link command line. For many C programmes, the Standard Library is usually where most of the external references are satisfied. Many users find it useful to add to, or modify routines in, the Standard Library. The Library Manager is the utility programme which allows the user to create new libraries and also to maintain existing ones.

Modes of Operation

The Library Manager has three modes of operation: Direct Mode, Interactive Mode, and Command File Mode. The most convenient to use for simple additions and deletions to the library is the Direct

Mode. For more extensive modifications the user may instead wish to use Interactive mode. The third mode is the Command File mode which causes the Library Manager to read its commands from a file rather than getting them from the user terminal.

Direct Mode: In Direct Mode the user is permitted to specify a single command on the library manager command line. When the Library Manager is called, it executes this single command function and then immediately exits from the Library Manager. When modifying libraries, however, a single command function is often all that is necessary to accomplish the change desired by the user. When Direct Mode is being used, the desired command is specified right on the command line, following the <lib> library specification. Any Library Manager command may be used in the Direct Mode. Interactive Mode: if no command is specified on the Library Manager call line, the Library Manager will enter its Interactive Mode of operation. In Interactive Mode the Library Manager will print a colon (".") as a promet and will accept a succession of commands directly from the user terminal.

Interactive Mode is useful when the user must make extensive changes to a library, or when the user wishes to step through the library checking and/or changing modules in an "interactive" manner. Once selected, the Interactive Mode will remain in effect until the user enters a "quit" or "omit" command. Command File Mode: One of the commands which the user can specify as an Interactive code or a Direct Mode command entry is the "Comfile" command. This command instructs the Library Manager to read subsequent instructions from a command file. When a "Comfile command is entered, the Library Manager will read from the file specified until it reads a "quit" or "omit" command or, alternatively, until it reaches the end of the file. when exiting the Command File Mode, the Library Manager will return to whatever mode it was in before the Command File Mode was entered. Command File Mode was entered as the result of a Direct Mode command, then the Library Manager will terminate when Command File Mode is exited. If entered from the Interactive Mode, it will return to the Interactive Mode.

Assembler

Definition

An assembler is a programme that converts simple commands into machine code. The simple commands, written in an assembly language, are used in groups to perform more complicated tasks.

Function

The function of the assembler is to translate programmes written in the assembler language into object modules. The code will then be in a suitable form for processing by the Linkage Editor. The assembler language is a symbolic representation of machine language. The correspondence between the two can be best understood by examining the listings produced by an assembler. The assembler, like the linkage editor, is supplied as part of VSE, CMS, and MVS, and executes under control of the appropriate control programme. It accepts, as input, a source programme written in the Assembler Language.

This consists of three types of instructions:

1. C Machine instructions.
2. C Assembler instructions.
3. C Macro instructions.

As expected with an IBM language, code can also be copied in from a source statement library (VSE) or a pds (MVS) or MACLIB (CMS).

Registers

- *AX*: This is split into half - into AL and AH (for low and high). They store the high part and the low part of the number in ax.
- *BX (BH/BL)*: same as AX
- *CX (CH/CL)*: Same as AX (used for loops)
- *DX (DH/DL)*: Same as AX (used for multiplication/division)
- *DI and SI*: are index registers and can be used as offset registers.
- *SP*: Stack Pointer. Does just that. Points to the current position in the stack. *Don't* alter unless you REALLY know what you are doing.

Interpreter

Definition

- An interpreter runs programme code by converting it to machine code on the fly. You save some time in the front by avoiding the compiling and linking steps, but interpreters generally run slower because they have to convert the same code (in a loop, say) again and again. An example of a common interpreter is the one that executes.bat files.

- An *interpreter* is also a programme that translates a high-level language into a low-level one, but it does it at the moment the programme is run. You write the programme using a text editor or something similar, and then instruct the interpreter to run the programme. It takes the programme, one line at a time, and translates each line before running it: It translates the first line and runs it, then translates the second line and runs it etc. The interpreter has no "memory" for the translated lines, so if it comes across lines of the programme within a loop, it must translate them afresh every time that particular line runs.

Consider this simple Basic programme:

- 10 FOR COUNT = 1 TO 1000
- 20 PRINT COUNT * COUNT
- 30 NEXT COUNT
- Line 20 of the programme displays the square of the value stored in COUNT and this line has to be carried out 1000 times. The interpreter must also translate that line 1000 times, which is clearly an inefficient process. However, interpreted languages do have their uses, as we will see in a later section.
- Examples of interpreted languages are Basic, JavaScript and LISP
- The Interpreter pattern discusses: defining a domain language (*i.e.* problem characterization) as a simple language grammar, representing domain rules as language sentences, and interpreting these sentences to solve the problem. The pattern uses a class to represent each grammar rule. And since grammars are usually hierarchical in structure, an inheritance hierarchy of rule classes maps nicely.
- An abstract base class specifies the method interpret(). Each concrete subclass implements interpret() by accepting (as an argument) the current state of the language stream, and adding its contribution to the problem solving process.

Structure

- Interpreter suggests modeling the domain with a recursive grammar. Each rule in the grammar is either a "composite" (a rule that references other rules) or a terminal (a leaf node in a tree structure). Interpreter relies on the recursive traversal of the Composite pattern to interpret the "sentences" it is asked to process.

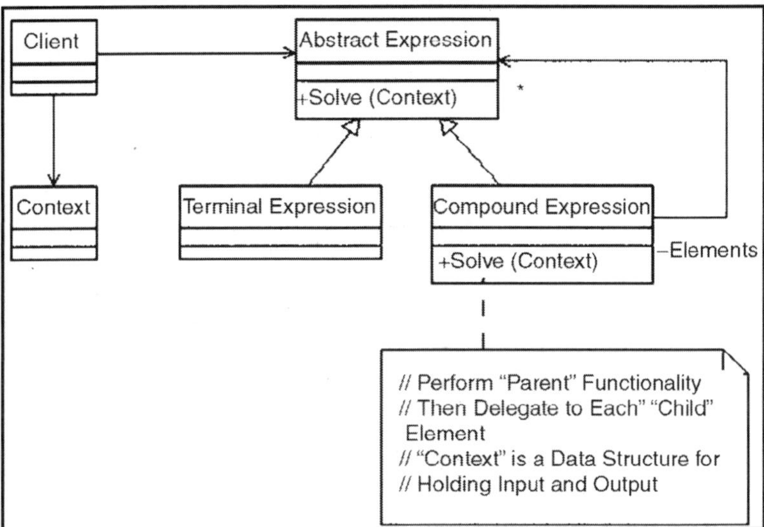

Compiler

Definition

A compiler completely converts programme code to machine code once. The computer user runs the machine code in the form of an executable command, ending in.exe say. Because the translation is complete before execution, compiled code is much faster.

The translation process should also report the presence of errors in the source programme.

Source Programme	→	Compiler ↓ Error Messages	→	Target Programme

There are two parts of compilation. The analysis part breaks up the source programme into constant piece and creates an intermediate representation of the source programme.

The synthesis part constructs the desired target programme from the intermediate representation. *Compilers* were the first sort of translator programme to be written. The idea is simple: You write the programme, then hand it to the compiler which translates it. Then run the result.

The compiler takes the file that you have written and produces another file from it. In the case of Pascal programmes, for instance, you might write a programme called my Prog.pas and the Pascal compiler would translate it into the file myProg.exe which you could then run. If you tried to examine the contents of myProg.exe using, say, a text editor, then it would just appear as gobbledy-gook. The compiler has another task apart from translating your programme. It also checks it to make sure that it is grammatically correct. Only when it is sure that there are no grammatical errors does it do the translation. Any errors that the compiler detects are called compile-time errors or syntax errors. If it finds so much as one syntax error, it stops compiling and reports the error to you. Here is an example of the C++ compiler reporting a whole list of errors:

Compiler Phases

The compiler has a number of phases plus symbol table manager and an error handler:

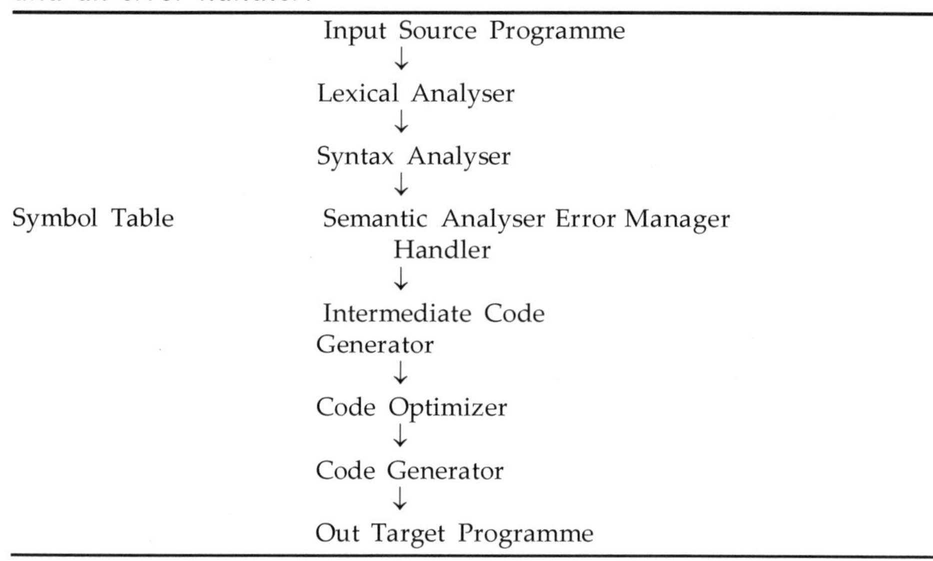

The cousins of the compiler are:

- Preprocessor.
- Assembler.
- Loader and Link-editor.

Front End vs Back End of a Compilers. The phases of a compiler are collected into front end and back end. The front end includes all analysis phases end the intermediate code generator. The back end includes the code optimization phase and final code generation phase. The front end analyses the source programme and produces intermediate code while the back end synthesizes the target programme from the intermediate code.

A naive approach (front force) to that front end might run the phases serially:

- Lexical analyser takes the source programme as an input and produces a long string of tokens.
- Syntax Analyser takes an out of lexical analyser and produces a large tree.
- Semantic analyser takes the output of syntax analyser and produces another tree.
- Similarly, intermediate code generator takes a tree as an input produced by semantic analyser and produces intermediate code.

Minus Points

- Requires enormous amount of space to store tokens and trees.
- Very slow since each phase would have to input and output to and from temporary disk

Remedy

- use syntax directed translation to inter leaves the actions of phases.
- Compiler construction tools.

Parser Generators

The specification of input based on regular expression. The organization is based on finite automation.

Scanner Generator

The specification of input based on regular expression. The organization is based on finite automation.

Syntax-Directed Translation

It walks the parse tee and as a result generate intermediate code.

Automatic Code Generators

Translates intermediate rampage into machine language.

Data-Flow Engines

It does code optimization using data-flow analysis.

Working of Compiler

Compiling a programme takes several stages of processing, which outlined as shown. The principles which are explained below also apply to interpreters, with the exception that the interpreters translate each programme one line at a time before running it, and then moving on to the next line.

Tokenising

This part of the process is also sometimes called *Lexical Analysis*. It involves turning the programme from a series of characters into a series of *tokens* that represent the building blocks of a programme. The tokens are keywords of the language *i.e.* important words such as *if, print* or *repeat*), variable names and mathematical operators (+, *, brackets etc.).

The tokeniser takes each of the characters in turn, and as soon as it recognises a legitimate token, it reports it to the next stage of the process. Each token has a label and a type, so a variable "count" in a programme would have the label corresponding to its name ("count") and the type "variable name". The tokeniser is also responsible for ignoring comments in the programme - these are words and phrases inserted purely for the benefit of any human reading the programme, and they have no function.

Syntax Analysis

Syntax means "grammar" and the syntax analyser in a compiler checks that the right tokens appear in the right order to make grammatically correct instructions. For instance, in C++, the instruction xyz++; is syntactically correct, but the instruction +;xyz+is not - the order of the tokens is wrong.

Semantic Analysis

The word "semantics" refers to *meaning*, and the semantic analyser checks the meaning of the programme. This refers to aspects such as whether the variables have been declared, *e.g.* xyz++; may be syntactically correct, but if the variable xyz has not been declared, then it is semantically incorrect! The semantic analyser checks not only variable declarations and scope, but whether the programme has entered or left loops, or subroutines, whether classes are accessed correctly etc.

Advantages

Choosing the right C compiler for your embedded-system projects may be a bigger challenge than you expect. The embedded-system-industry trend is moving from using assembly to using the higher level languages. Assembly language gives you more control over your code size and execution speeds. However, embedded C is easy to understand and portable from platform to platform. Another benefit is that developing code in C generally improves your product time to market. These features are advantageous if you expect your firmware to have longevity or if your staff changes periodically.

A variety of embedded-C compilers is available in the market today. Embedded-C compilers are available as shareware from controller- or processor-IC vendors; or from high-end, reputable software companies whose selling prices often reflect the sophistication of the software. Some compiler-software companies have great advertisements and competitive prices but inferior products. So, how do you choose your compiler software for now and for the future?

There are many issues to consider when choosing your compiler. The most important are ANSI compliance, size and speed optimizations, portability, and supporting tools.

Adherence to the ANSI standard for the C language is critical for about 80 to 85% of code. This feature facilitates portability from part to part, as well as from software platform to software platform. ANSI-compliant software also integrates easy-to-understand code into your library.

This type of code—if it is well-written—will have a shelf life like a good red wine. Even if portability is not an issue, it is important to understand how the compiler differs from ANSI and whether those differences will impact your development.

If the compiler of interest is ANSI-compliant, you should then examine the software's machine-code-generation capability. You might ask whether the compiler output code is optimized for small code (because memory is precious in controllers or processors) or whether the application executes in a timely or time-accurate manner. These features are somewhat mutually exclusive, but the compiler software should be able to optimize one or the other. Portability between platforms is critical in larger companies that have a diverse range of products. However, it can also be convenient in smaller companies that may want the flexibility to quickly change controllers during development. Portability allows you to change quickly from one controller to another during application development. It also makes your code libraries more valuable over time.

Some other characteristics that make up a good compiler are the availability of code libraries and library support. This concept does not fit into organizations with the NIH (not-invented-here) philosophy.

An NIH organization deserves everything it gets (or doesn't get). Libraries with code that implements useful functions help expedite your projects to completion. Many times, these libraries have gone through evaluations and debugging to ensure their value.

Some of the final details in your compiler evaluation have to do with customer service. You need to ask whether your compiler company supports your questions and helps with its software bugs. You will find this information in the company's application-notes library, discussion forums, and software-release history. Although frequent releases can be a sign of responsiveness, they can also be an indication of serious stability concerns. The ideal compiler vendor has more support than you'll ever need.

In the past, most firmware designers would write embedded-firmware programmes in assembly language. The embedded-C compiler transforms your source code into machine code. The C compiler you use determines the size as well as the execution time of your code. Many ways exist for determining these factors, so running your own test programmes is also important. Don't depend on the results from a compiler-software company that runs its own tests. Many times, these companies can consciously or unconsciously skew the results.

3

Network Communication

Communication

In a mobile communication terminal for starting and simultaneously using a plurality of applications, one desired application starts fast to improve the operability when the number of started applications reaches a present limiting number of applications. An application start determining unit searches a list of started applications in response to the instruction of the start of application to obtain the number of started applications, and determines that the application cannot start when the number of started applications reaches a preset limiting number of applications.

An ending-application selecting unit selects, as an ending application to be ended, the application with the low priority from the start applications based on the preset priority of application when the application start determining unit determines that the application cannot start. An application ending unit performs the ending processing of the ending application selected by the ending-application selecting unit and deletes the selected ending application from the list of started applications.

A mobile communication terminal for starting and simultaneously using a plurality of applications, comprising: application start determining means which compares the number of started applications with a preset numerical value that is a maximum number of simultaneously used applications, determines that the application can start when the number of started applications is less than the numerical value, and determines that the application cannot start when the number of started applications reaches the numerical value; ending-priority list creating means which calculates values indicating the using situation of the started applications in response to the determination of the application start determining means that the application cannot start and creates a list of ending priority indicating the order of applications with low influence.

Applications

In the case of ending the application; ending-application selecting means which selects the ending application based on the list of ending priority in response to the determination of the application start determining means that the application cannot start and clears the list of ending priority; application ending means which performs the ending processing of the ending application selected by the ending-application selecting means; application starting means which starts the application instructed by a user in response to the determination of the application start determining means that the application starts; and wherein the ending-priority list creating means collects data on evaluation items indicating the using situations including the total time displayed after starting the application, the number of switching times for display operation, and the last display time, obtains the order of started applications every evaluated item, multiplies the order by a weighting coefficient preset every evaluated item and every type of application, adds the multiplied result every application, calculates the values indicating the using situations, sorts the applications in order of the larger values, and creates the list of ending priority.

An application starting control method of a mobile communication terminal for starting and simultaneously using a plurality of applications, comprising the steps of: presetting a numerical value that is a maximum number of simultane-ously used applications; selecting, from started applications, an ending application to be ended based on a priority when the number of simultaneously used applications will exceed the numerical value; newly allowing to start an application after ending the selected ending application; and collecting data for the started applications, including a total time displayed after starting the application, the number of switching times for display operation, and the last display time, determining an order of the respective data for each of the started applications, multiplying each determined order by respective weighting coefficients for each of the started applications, adding the multiplied results for each of the started applications, and creating the priority by sorting the applications based on the added results.

Mobile Network

A mobile communication terminal for starting and simultaneously using a plurality of applications, comprising: application start determining means which compares the number of started applications with a preset numerical value that is a maximum number of simultaneously used applications, determines that the application can start when the number of started applications is less than the numerical value, and determines that the application cannot start when the number of started applications reaches the numerical value; selecting means which selects an ending application to be ended on the basis of low priority from the started applications, in response to the determination of the application start determining means that the application cannot start; application ending means which performs ending processing of the ending application selected by the ending application selecting means; application starting means which starts the application instructed by a user in response to the determination of the application start determining means that the application can start; and ending-priority list creating means for collecting data on evaluation items indicating the using situations including the total time displayed after starting the application, the number of switching times for display operation, and the last display time, obtaining the order of started applications every evaluated item, multiplying the order by a weighting coefficient preset every evaluated item and every type of application, adding the multiplied result every application, calculating the values indicating the using situations, sorting the applications in order of the larger values, and creating a priority list.

Memory

The present invention relates to a mobile communication terminal and an application starting control method thereof. More particularly, the present invention relates to a mobile communication terminal for starting and simultaneously using a plurality of applications and an application starting control method thereof. Recently, one type of mobile phones is sold to start a plurality of applications and simultaneously use a plurality of functions similarly to a personal computer or the like, under the improvement of CPU processing capacity. Such a mobile phone terminal enables a user to send an email while viewing a site screen on the Internet or to check the schedule by a scheduler while having a call.

However, the mobile phone terminal does not have a sufficient memory capacity or power capacity. Therefore, if many applications simultaneously start similarly to the personal computer, a malfunction is caused in the communication function or the started application operation becomes unstable. An unnecessary application must terminate without continuously staying resident in memory when the number of simultaneously-used applications reaches a predetermined limiting number.

Preferably, the unnecessary application automatically ends. As disclosed in the above-mentioned publication, the degree of importance is set to the application so as to use the application with the high degree of importance for a long time when the remaining amount of battery is reduced while a plurality of applications start, and the application with the low degree of importance ends when the remaining amount of battery reduces. However, when the number of applications to be started is over a predetermined number, the application to be ended does not automatically end.

Details

It is an object of the present invention to provide a mobile communication terminal and an application starting control method thereof, for fast starting a desired application and improving the operability by automatically selecting and ending the application to be ended when the number of started applications reaches a predetermined limiting number upon starting the application. According to the present invention, there is provided an application starting control method of a mobile communication terminal for starting and simultane-ously using a plurality of applications, comprising the steps of presetting a limiting number of simultaneously used applications; selecting, from started applications, an ending application to be ended based on the priority when applications over a limiting number are going to be started; and newly allowing to start an application after ending the selected ending application.

The priority may be preset or may be determined based on a using situation of the started application. The selected ending application may be displayed on a screen in response to the selection of the ending application. In this case, the selected ending application is ended in response to the approval operation of a user. According to the present invention, there is also provided a mobile communication terminal for starting and simultane-ously using a plurality of applications, comprising application start determining means which compares the number of started applications with a preset limiting number of simultaneously used applications, determines that the application can start when the number of started applications is less than the limiting number, and determines that the application cannot start when the number of started applications reaches the limiting number; selecting means which selects an ending application to be ended on the basis of low priority from the started applications in response to the determination of the application start determining means that the application cannot start; application ending means which performs ending processing of the ending application selected by the ending application selecting means; and application starting means which starts the application instructed by a user in response to the determination of the application start determining means that the application can start.

Network Applications

The application starting means may start the application instructed by the user in response to the ending processing of the application ending means. The application start determin-ing means may determine whether or not the application starts in response to the instruction to start the application from the user.

The mobile communication terminal may have a list of started applications indicating the started applications. In this case, the application start determining means searches the list of started application to obtain the number of started applications. The application ending means deletes the selected ending application from the list of started applications. The application starting means starts the application determined as the start by the application start determining means and registers the started application to the list of started applications. The mobile communication terminal may further comprises means for receiving the approval of the user before the ending processing of the ending application in response to the selection of the ending application by the ending application selecting means.

According to the present invention, there is also provided a mobile communication terminal for starting and simultaneously using a plurality of applications, comprising application start determining means which compares the number of started applications with a preset limiting number of simultaneously used applications, determines that the application can start when the number of started applications is less than the limiting number, and determines that the application cannot start when the number of started applications reaches the limiting number; ending-priority list creating means which calculates values indicating the using situation of the started applications in response to the determination of the application start determining means that the application cannot start and creates a list of ending priority indicating the order of applications with low influence in the case of ending the application; ending-application selecting means which selects the ending application based on the list of ending priority in response to the determination of the application start determining means that the application cannot start and clears the list of ending priority; application ending means which performs the ending processing of the ending application selected by the ending-application selecting means; and application starting means which starts the application instructed by a user in response to the determination of the application start determining means that the application starts.

The ending-priority list creating means may collect data on evaluation items indicating the using situations including the total time displayed after starting the application, the number of switching times for display operation, and the last display time, place a number to each of started applications in the order of their magnitude every evaluated item, multiply the number by a weighting coefficient preset every evaluated item and every type of application, add the multiplied results every application, calculate the values indicating the using situations, sort the applications in order of the larger values, and create the list of ending priority.

The mobile communication terminal may have a list of started applications indicating the started application. In this case, the application start determining means searches the list of started applications and obtains the number of started applications; the application ending means deletes the selected ending application from the list of started applications, and the application starting means starts the application determined as the start by the application start determining means and registers the started application to the list of started applications.

According to the present invention, the limiting number (maximum number) of applications for simultaneous use is set and when the start of a new application amounts to the number of applications over the limiting number, the application for ending is automatically determined and is ended in accordance with the priority from among the using applications.

Thus, in case that the number of applications reaches the limiting number, the new application is started quickly and the operability upon starting the application is improved.

Wireless communications

Wireless communications is a rapidly growing segment of the communications industry, with the potential to provide high-speed high-quality information exchange between portable devices located anywhere in the world. Potential applications enabled by this technology include multimedia Internet-enabled cell phones, smart homes and appliances, automated highway systems, video teleconferencing and distance learning, and autonomous sensor networks, to name just a few. However, supporting these applications using wireless techniques poses a significant technical challenge.

This course will cover advanced topics in wireless communications for voice, data, and multimedia. We begin with a brief overview of current wireless systems and standards. We then characterize the wireless channel, including path loss for different environments, random log-normal shadowing due to signal attenuation, and the flat and frequency-selective properties of multipath fading. Next we examine the fundamental capacity limits of wireless channels and the characteristics of the capacity-achieving transmission strategies. These strategies are typically not practical. Thus, our next focus will be on practical digital modulation techniques and their performance under wireless channel impairments, including flat and frequency selective fading. The next part of the course is spent investigating techniques to improve the speed and performance of wireless links.

We will investigate the design and performance of adaptive modulation and diversity techniques to compensate for flat-fading. Three techniques to combat frequency-selective fading are then examined: adaptive equalization, multicarrier modulation, and spread spectrum. We will also study the multiple access capabilities of spread spectrum with multiuser detection. The course concludes with a brief overview of wireless networks, including multiple and random access techniques, WLANs, cellular system design, and ad-hoc network design.

Applications for these systems, including the evolution of cell phones and PDAs, smart homes and appliances, sensor networks, and automated highways and skyways, will also be discussed. Presenting comprehensive coverage of this fast moving field, Wireless Communications and Mobile Computing provides the R&D communities working in academia and the telecommunications and networking industries with a forum for sharing research and ideas. The convergence of wireless communications and mobile computing is bringing together two areas of immense growth and innovation.

This is reflected throughout the journal by strongly focusing on new trends, developments, emerging technologies and new industrial standards. Under the guidance of an international editorial and advisory board drawn from academia and industry, this high quality, peer-reviewed journal, provides leading edge coverage of the opportunities and challenges driving the research and development of mobile communication systems.

All you need to stay ahead :

- High calibre survey papers

Written by leading experts in the wireless and networking communities.

- Rapid publication times

Due to electronic review and submission of original research papers

- Special Issues

Addressing key topics of interest and managed by high profile editors

- An international forum for the sharing of research and ideas

Key topics presented by leading individuals at the cutting edge of new technologies.

Computer Networks

In computer networks, bandwidth is often used as a synonym for data transfer rate - the amount of data that can be carried from one point to another in a given time period (usually a second). This kind of bandwidth is usually expressed in bits (of data) per second (bps). Occasionally, it's expressed as bytes per second (Bps). A modem that works at 57,600 bps hastwice the bandwidth of a modem that works at 28,800 bps. In general, a link with a high bandwidth is one that may be able to carry enough information to sustain the succession of images in a video presentation. It should be remembered that a real communications path usually consists of a succession of links, each with its own bandwidth. If one of these is much slower than the rest, it is said to be a bandwidth bottleneck.

In electronic communication, bandwidth is the width of the range (orband) of frequencies that an electronic signal uses on a given transmission medium. In this usage, bandwidth is expressed in terms of the difference between the highest-frequency signal component and the lowest-frequency signal component. Since the frequency of a signal is measured in hertz (the number of cycles of change per second), a given bandwidth is the difference in hertz between the highest frequency the signal uses and the lowest frequency it uses.

A typical voice signal has a bandwidth of approximately three kilohertz (3 kHz); an analog television (TV) broadcast video signal has a bandwidth of six megahertz (6 MHz) -- some 2,000 times as wide as the voice signal.

Bandwidth Monitor Pro

- Do you ever wonder how much bandwidth you are using?
- How fast you are downloading or uploading?
- Or if you're closing in on your monthly transfer limit?
- If so Bandwidth Monitor Pro is the utility for you!

Detailed Logging

Supports logging of all your network adapters at once with separate statistics for each adapter. You can go back and check your daily, weekly, monthly, yearly or total transfer.

Always Control

With the small transfer graph placed in the system tray you always have control of your bandwidth usage.

Highly Customizable

Bandwidth Monitor Pro can be customized to display the information you want. You can also change the graph type and colours.

Advanced Alert System

- You can set up rules with various actions and conditions.
- Lets say that you have a monthly transfer limit of 30GB.
- You can then set up Bandwidth Monitor Pro to alert you when your approaching that limit.

Mobile Internet WML

WML (Wireless Markup Language) is the new web language for making sites on mobile phones. Over the past few months new WAP (Wireless Applications Protocol) phones have become extremely popular and many large websites have created special 'mobile' versions of their site. Many people predict that, over the next few years, WAP sites will become even morepopular and e-commerce over mobile phones will be widely available.

Using WML

Although you might not have any plans immediately for creating a WAP version of your site, it is always a good idea to get involved in new technology. All you need to do is make a small site (even one page) which tells people a bit about your website. In the future you can develop the site further with things like e-mail and information for people to get directly off their phones. The main sites which will benefit from WAP are ones providing a service like e-mail, live sports scores or a calendar service etc.

But there are many other uses. For example, a site giving music reviews could put their reviews on a WAP site. People could then read the reviews on their mobile phone while browsing through the CDs in a shop.

Having WAP Phone

To create a WAP site you don't need a WAP enabled phone. You can get a WAP simulator for a PC. This is a piece of software which will give you a WAP phone on your desktop. You can then type in the URLs of WAP sites and can view them on your PC. You can get a very good free WAP simulator from YourWAP

Comparing Sites

WAP sites are not like standard web sites at all. As an example, you are looking at part of the Gowansnet web site. As you can see, sites written in WML are monochrome, very limited and there is very little screen space. Because of this you must be very careful when you are designing a WAP site as it is nothing like a web site.

Beginning WAP Site

After reading the introduction you should understand about WAP sites, WML and what you can do with them so I will go straight into how to create a site. Note that you should really either have a WAP phone or a WAP simulator so that you can view your site and a knowledge of HTML is useful.

Finding A WML Host

Unfortunately WML cannot be run on all web hosts. For WML content to be run, a web host must make some changes to the configuration of their web server. If your host cannot do this for you, you can try WAPHosts.net. They can provide you with a server which will support WML.

Declaring A WML Document

Cards

Instead of having pages, WAP sites have cards. These are what is displayed on the screen at one time, just like a page. More than one card can be inserted in each WML document. To declare a card, insert the following:

<card id="index" title="My WAP Site" newcontext="true">

This will make a card with the ID index (used for linking) and will display the text: My WAP Site at the top of the screen.

Closing Tags

Unlike with HTML, it is extremely important to close WML tags. If you do not, a page will certainly not work. You must close both the <card> and <wml> tags:

</card>

</wml>

Adding Text

In the last part I showed you how to create the basic file which will contain your WAP site. In this part I am going to show you how to insert text and how to format it.

The <p> Tag

Just like in HTML the <p> tag is used to show where a paragraph begins and ends. Unlike HTML, though, all text on a WML page must be inside these tags. You are not allowed to nest these tags either. One important thing to remember about WML is that, unlike HTML where a page will still display even if there is bad code, a WAP phone will just reject a page if there is and code it doesn't understand.

As with HTML you use the tags as follows:

<p>

information

</p>

Aligning Text

Aligning text in WML is nearly exactly the same as in HTML, except you can't use the centre tag. All aligning must be done using the following <p> tags:

Centre:

<p align="centre">

Right:

<p align="right">

The
 Tag

In WML (as mentioned earlier) all tags must be closed. This causes problems when using old HTML tags (like <Br>) which have no closing tag. To get around this, some tags have had a / put on the end e.g.

This, like in HTML will make a line break.

Text

In WML there is actually no font tag (as you can only display text in the phone's default font in black). To show text all you need to do is put it in between the <p> and </p> tags. Here is an example of a full WML document:

```
<?xml version="1.0"?>
<!DOCTYPE wml PUBLIC "-//WAPFORUM//DTD WML 1.1/
/EN" "http://www.wapforum.org/DTD/wml_1.1.xml">
<wml>
<card id="index" title="My WAP Site"
newcontext="true">
<p align="centre">
    Welcome to my new WAP site. You can view this on your mobile
phone anywhere in the world!<Br /> It is amazing!
</p>
</card>
</wml>
```

Hyperlinks & Images

In part 3 I showed you how to create a basic WAP site with one page and some text. This week I will show you how you can make this better by adding extra parts, linking to them (and other sites) and how to add images to your site.

More Cards

As I explained in the second part of this tutorial, WAP sites have cards instead of pages. They are really the same as pages except they can all be written in one file. To add another card, all you need to do is put in another <card> tag with a different ID to the others. For example:

<card title="About Me" id="about">

information

</card>

would be added below the first card but before the </wml> tag.

Linking

There are three ways to link to another WAP site, file or card. Just like in HTML these can either be the full path to a file or a relative link.

To link to a WAP site you use the following:

<a href="http://gowansnet.waphosts.net/">

Gowansnet</a>

in your text. To link to another file on your site you would use:

<a href="links.wml">My Links</a>

and to link to another card in the same page you use:

<a href="#about">About Me</a>

For suppliers, the thought of a uniform operating environment was disconcerting. Consumer lock-in was woven tightly into the fabric of the industry. Individual consumers, particularly those with UNIX system experience, envisioned standardized environments, but had no way to pull the market in their direction. However, for one category of consumer -governments- the standardization of the UNIX system was both desirable and within reach.

Governments have clout and are the largest consumers of information technology products and services in the world. Driven by the need to improve commonality, both US and European governments endorsed a shift to the UNIX system. The Institute of Electrical and Electronic Engineers POSIX family of standards, along with standards from ISO, ANSI and others, led the way. Consortia such as the X/Open Company (merged with the Open Software Foundation in 1995 to form The Open Group) hammered out draft standards to accelerate the process. In 1994, the definitive specification of what constitutes a UNIX system was finalized through X/Open Company's consensus process.

The Single UNIX Specification was born-not from a theoretical, ivory tower approach, but by analyzing the applications that were in use in businesses across the world. With the active support of government and commercial buyers alike, vendors began to converge on products that implement the Single UNIX Specification, and now all major vendors have products labeled UNIX 95, which indicates that the vendor guarantees that the product conforms to the Single UNIX Specification.

Vendors continue to add value to the UNIX system, particularly in areas of new technology, however that value will always be built upon a single, consensus standard. Meanwhile, the functionality of the UNIX system was established and the mid-life crisis was resolved. Suppliers today provide UNIX systems that are built upon a single, consensus standard. It is also important to remember that even when variance among UNIX systems was at its worst, IT professionals agreed that migration among UNIX system variants was far easier than migration among the proprietary alternatives.

TextProcessing and Word Processing

Almost every computer user needs a method of preparing documents. In the world of personal computers, word processing is the norm: editing and manipulating text in a ``What-You-See-Is-What-You-Get" (WYSIWYG) environment and producing printed copies of the text, complete with graphics, tables, and ornamentation. Commercial word processors from Corel, Applix, and Star Division are available in the UNIX world, but text processing, which is quite different conceptually, is more common. In text processing systems, text is entered in a page-description language, which describes how the text should be formatted. Rather than enter text within a special word processing environment, you can modify text with any editor, like vi or emacs. Once you finish entering the source text (in the typesetting language), a separate programme converts the source to a format suitable for printing. This is somewhat analogous to programming in a language like C, and ``compiling" the document into printable form.

Many text processing systems are available for Linux. One is groff, the GNU version of the classic troff text formatter originally developed by Bell Labs and still used on many UNIX systems worldwide. Another modern text processing system is TeX, developed by Donald Knuth of computer science fame. Dialects of TeX, like LaTeX, are also available. Text processors like TeX and groff differ mostly in the syntax of their formatting languages. The choice of one formatting system over another is based upon what utilities are available to satisfy your needs, as well as personal taste.

Many people consider groff's formatting language to be a bit obscure and use find TeX more readable. However, groff produces ASCII output which can be viewed on a terminal more easily, while TeX is intended primarily for output to a printing device. Various add-on programmes are required to produce ASCII output from TeX formatted documents, or convert TeX input to groff format.

Another programme is texinfo, an extension to TeX which is used for software documentation developed by the Free Software Foundation. texinfo can produce printed output, or an online-browsable hypertext ``Info'' document from a single source file. Info files are the main format of documentation used in GNU software like emacs. Text processors are used widely in the computing community for producing papers, theses, magazine articles, and books. (This book is produced using LaTeX.) The ability to process source language as a text file opens the door to many extensions of the text processor itself. Because a source document is not stored in an obscure format that only one word processor can read, programmers can write parsers and translators for the formatting language, and thus extend the system. What does a formatting language look like? In general, a formatted source file consists mostly of the text itself, with control codes to produce effects like font and margin changes, and list formatting.

Programming Languages and Utilities

Linux provides a complete UNIX programming environment which includes all of the standard libraries, programming tools, compilers, and debuggers which you would expect of other UNIX systems.

Standards like POSIX.1 are supported, which allows software written for Linux to be easily ported to other systems. Professional UNIX programmers and system administrators use Linux to develop software at home, then transfer the software to UNIX systems at work. This not only saves a great deal of time and money, but also lets you work in the comfort of your own home. (One of the authors uses his system to develop and test X Window System applications at home, which can be directly compiled on workstations elsewhere.) Computer Science students learn UNIX programming and explore other aspects of the system, like kernel architecture.

With Linux, you have access to the complete set of libraries and programming utilities and the complete kernel and library source code. Within the UNIX software world, systems and applications are often programmed in C or C++. The standard C and C++ compiler for Linux is GNU gcc, which is an advanced, modern compiler that supports C++, including AT&T 3.0 features, as well as Objective-C, another object-oriented dialect of C. Besides C and C++, other compiled and interpreted programming languages have been ported to Linux, like Smalltalk, FORTRAN, Java, Pascal, LISP, Scheme, and Ada (if you're masochistic enough to programme in Ada, we aren't going to stop you). In addition, various assemblers for writing protected-mode 80386 code are available, as are UNIX hacking favorites like Perl (the script language to end all script languages) and Tcl/Tk (a shell-like command processing system which has support for developing simple X Window System applications). The advanced gdb debugger can step through a programme one line of source code at a time, or examine a core dump to find the cause of a crash.

The gprof profiling utility provides performance statistics for your programme, telling you where your programme spends most of its execution time. As mentioned above, the emacs text editor provides interactive editing and compilation environments for various programming languages. Other tools include GNU make and imake, which manage compilation of large applications, and RCS, a system for source code locking and revision control.

Finally, Linux supports dynamically linked, shared libraries (DLLs), which result in much smaller binaries. The common subroutine code is linked at run-time. These DLLs let you override function definitions with your own code. For example, if you wish to write your own version of the malloc() library routine, the linker will use your new routine instead of the one in the libraries.

X Window System

The X Window System, or simply X, is a standard graphical user interface (GUI) for UNIX machines and is a powerful environment which supports many applications. Using the X Window System, you can have multiple terminal windows on the screen at once, each having a different login session. A pointing device like a mouse is often used with X, although it isn't required. Many X-specific applications have been written, including games, graphics and programming utilities, and documentation tools. Linux and X make your system a bona fide workstation. With TCP/IP networking, your Linux machine can display X applications running on other machines.

The X Window System was originally developed at the Massachusetts Institute of Technology and is freely distributable. Many commercial vendors have distributed proprietary enhancements to the original X Window System as well. The version of X for Linux is XFree86, a port of X11R6 which is freely distributable. XFree86 supports a wide range of video hardware, including VGA, Super VGA, and accelerated video adaptors. XFree86 is a complete distribution of the X Windows System software, and contains the X server itself, many applications and utilities, programming libraries, and documents.

Standard X applications include xterm, a terminal emulator used for most text-based applications within a window, xdm, which handles logins, xclock, a simple clock display, xman, a X-based manual page reader, and xmore. The many X applications available for Linux are too numerous to mention here, but their number includes spreadsheets, word processors, graphics programmes, and web browsers like the Netscape Navigator. Many other applications are available separately. Theoretically, any application written for X should compile cleanly under Linux.

The interface of the X Window System is controlled largely by the window manager. This user-friendly programme is in charge of the placement of windows, the user interface for resizing and moving them, changing windows to icons, and the appearance of window frames, among other tasks. XFree86 includes twm, the classic MIT window manager, and advanced window managers like the Open Look Virtual Window Manager (olvwm) are available. Popular among Linux users is fvwm--a small window manager that requires less than half the memory of twm.

It provides a 3-dimensional appearance for windows and a virtual desktop. The user moves the mouse to the edge of the screen, and the desktop shifts as though the display were much larger than it really is. fvwm is greatly customizable and allows access to functions from the keyboard as well as mouse. Many Linux distributions use fvwm as the standard window manager. A version of fvwm called fvwm95-2 offers Microsoft Windows 95-like look and feel.

The XFree86 distribution includes programming libraries for wily programmers who wish to develop X applications. Widget sets like Athena, Open Look, and Xaw3D are supported. All of the standard fonts, bitmaps, manual pages, and documentation are included. PEX (a programming interface for 3-dimensional graphics) is also supported.

Many X application programmers use the proprietary Motif widget set for development. Several vendors sell single and multiple user licenses for binary versions of Motif. Because Motif itself is relatively expensive, not many Linux users own it. However, binaries statically linked with Motif routines can be freely distributed. If you write a programme using Motif, you may provide a binary so users without the Motif libraries can use the programme.

A major caveat to using the X Window System is its hardware requirements. A 80386-based CPU with 4 megabytes of RAM is capable of running X, but 16 megabytes or more of physical RAM is needed for comfortable use. A faster processor is nice to have as well, but having enough physical RAM is much more important. In addition, to achieve really slick video performance, we recommend getting an accelerated video card, like a VESA Local Bus (VLB) S3 chipset card. Performance ratings in excess of 300,000 xstones have been achieved with Linux and XFree86. Using adequate hardware, you'll find that running X and Linux is as fast, or faster, than running X on other UNIX workstations.

Networking

Would you like to communicate with the world? Linux supports two primary UNIX networking protocols: TCP/IP and UUCP. TCP/IP (Transmission Control Protocol/Internet Protocol) is the networking paradigm which allows systems all over the world to communicate on a single network, the Internet. With Linux, TCP/IP, and a connection to the Internet, you can communicate with users and machines via electronic mail, Usenet news, and FTP file transfer.

Most TCP/IP networks use Ethernet as the physical network transport. Linux supports many popular Ethernet cards and interfaces for personal computers, including pocket and PCMCIA Ethernet adaptors. However, because not everyone has an Ethernet connection at home, Linux also supports SLIP (Serial Line Internet Protocol) and PPP (Point-to-Point Protocol), which provide Internet access via modem. Many businesses and universities provide SLIP and PPP servers. In fact, if your Linux system has an Ethernet connection to the Internet and a modem, your system can become a SLIP or PPP server for other hosts. NFS (Network File System) lets your system seamlessly share file systems with other machines on the network. FTP (File Transfer Protocol) lets you transfer files with other machines. sendmail sends and receives electronic mail via the SMTP protocol; C-News and INN are NNTP based new systems; and telnet,rlogin, and rsh let you log in and execute commands on other machines on the network. finger lets you get information about other Internet users.

The full range of mail and news readers is available for Linux, including elm, pine, rn, nn, and tin. Whatever your preference, you can configure a Linux system to send and receive electronic mail and news from all over the world. The system provides a standard UNIX socket programming interface.

Virtually any programme that uses TCP/IP can be ported to Linux. The Linux X server also supports TCP/IP, and applications running on other systems may use the display of your local system.

UUCP (UNIX-to-UNIX Copy) is an older mechanism to transfer files, electronic mail, and electronic news between UNIX machines. Historically, UUCP machines are connected over telephone lines via modem, but UUCP is able to transfer data over a TCP/IP network as well. If you do not have access to a TCP/IP network or a SLIP or PPP server, you can configure your system to send and receive files and electronic mail using UUCP.

Several conventions have sprung up around the development effort. Anyone who wishes to have their code included in the ``official'' kernel, mails it to Linus Torvalds. He will test and include the code in the kernel as long as it doesn't break things or go against the overall design of the system. The system itself is designed using an open-ended, feature-minded approach. The number of new features and critical changes to the system has recently diminished, and the general rule is that a new version of the kernel will be released every few weeks. Of course, this is a rough figure. New release criteria include the number of bugs to be fixed, feedback from users testing pre-release versions of the code, and the amount of sleep Linus Torvalds has had this week.

Suffice it to say that not every bug is fixed, nor is every problem ironed out between releases. As long as the revision appears to be free of critical or recurring bugs, it is considered to be stable, and the new version is released. The thrust behind Linux development is not to release perfect, bug-free code: it is to develop a free UNIX implementation. Linux is for the developers, more than anyone else.

Anyone who has a new feature or software application generally makes it available in an alpha version--that is, a test version, for those brave users who want to hash out problems in the initial code. Because the Linux community is largely based on the Internet, alpha software is usually uploaded to one or more Linux FTP sites and a message is posted to one of the Linux Usenet newsgroups about how to obtain and test the code. Users who download and test alpha software can then mail results, bug fixes, and questions to the author. After the initial bugs have been fixed, the code enters a beta test stage, in which it is usually considered stable but not complete. It works, but not all of the features may be present. The software may also go directly to a final stage, in which the software is considered complete and usable.

Keep in mind that these are only conventions--not rules. Some developers may feel so confident of their software that they decide it isn't necessary to release alpha or test versions. It is always up to the developer to make these decisions. You might be amazed at how such an unstructured system of volunteers who programme and debug a complete UNIX system gets anything done at all. As it turns out, this is one of the most efficient and motivated development efforts ever employed.

The entire Linux kernel is written from scratch, without code from proprietary sources. It takes a huge amount of work to port all the free software under the sun to Linux. Libraries are written and ported, file systems are developed, and hardware drivers are written for many popular devices--all due to the work of volunteers.

Linux software is generally released as a distribution, a set of prepackaged software which comprises an entire system. It would be difficult for most users to build a complete system from the ground up, starting with the kernel, adding utilities, and installing all of the necessary software by hand. Instead, many software distributions are available which include everything necessary to install and run a complete system. There is no single, standard distribution--there are many, and each has its own advantages and disadvantages. We describe installation of the various Linux distributions starting on. Of course, you may copy Linux from a friend who already has the software, or share the purchase cost with someone else. If you plan to install Linux on a large number of machines, you need only purchase a single copy of the software--Linux is not distributed with a ``single machine'' license.

The value of commercial UNIX implementations should not be demeaned. In addition to the price of the software itself, one often pays for documentation, support, and quality assurance. These are very important factors for large institutions, but personal computer users may not require these benefits. In any case, many businesses and universities have found that running Linux in a lab of inexpensive personal computers is preferable to running a commercial version of UNIX in a lab of workstations.

Linux can provide workstation functionality on a personal computer at a fraction of the cost. Linux systems have travelled the high seas of the North Pacific, and manage telecommuni-cations and data analysis for an oceanographic research vessel. Linux systems are used at research stations in Antarctica. Several hospitals maintain patient records on Linux systems. Other free or inexpensive implementations of UNIX are available for the 80386 and 80486.

One of the best known is 386BSD, an implementation of BSD UNIX for the 80386. The 386BSD package is comparable to Linux in many ways, but which one is better depends on your needs and expectations. The only strong distinction we can make is that Linux is developed openly, and any volunteer can aid in the development process, while 386BSD is developed by a closed team of programmers. Because of this, serious philosophical and design differences exist between the two projects. The goal of Linux is to develop a complete UNIX system from scratch (and have a lot of fun in the process), and the goal of 386BSD is in part to modify the existing BSD code for use on the 80386.

NetBSD is another port of the BSD NET/2 distribution to several machines, including the 80386. NetBSD has a slightly more open development structure, and is comparable to 386BSD in many respects.

Another project of note is HURD, an effort by the Free Software Foundation to develop and distribute a free version of UNIX for many platforms. Contact the Free Software Foundation (the address is given in Appendix C) for more information about this project. At the time of this writing, HURD is still under development.

Network Tools

VeriCenter remotely manages your network infrastructure, including routers, hubs, and switches, for the highest reliability and optimized performance. When a problem is detected and isolated, VeriCenter takes the steps necessary to coordinate with hardware vendors and carrier partners for problem resolution. At all times, you're able to access critical information about your network through our secure Web-based Customer Portal. Our services are designed to provide you with complete management of critical network devices within your environment, using the tools and expertise of our Network Operations Centre (NOC).

Every productive data network is made up of two intergral parts - infrastructure (communications environment) and active elements, which utilise the communications environment. The infrastructure can be made up of a structured cabling system based on melicke or optical lines, wireless transfer system etc. The quality and performance of the infrastructure directly affects the resulting attributes and output of the data network.

With the rapid development of Internet applications and technology, more and more emphasis is being put on securing access to data networks and on protection of the actual data with systems against misuse or attack. There is an evident trend of integrating various security functions into basic network elements, such as switches, routers etc.

The convergence trend for data and telephony into one communications infrastructure has brought the need to secure the necessary quality of service (QoS) for operations sensitive to the quality of the data network (IP telephony, video-conferencing). A modern data network is capable of working with several classes of operations and each of these classes is capable of securing the necessary quality of service. Since it was established, GiTy has been oriented to the most up-to-date technologies, which guarantee the maximum possible output for data networks and their long technological lifetime. Key components of data networks developed by us are products from the foremost technological manufacturers, such as Siemon, Cisco Systems, Enterasys Network, 3COM, Allied Telesyn and Crossbeam.

Data networks developed by us provide users with high performance, the maximum level of security and the tools needed for management of the quality of services for individual applications.

One way of conserving this network traffic is to slice the network up into smaller segments. These segments are connected to a bridge. Bridges are smarter than hubs and repeaters. They also use software to help get the job done. Bridges are able to read MAC addresses, which are also known as hardware addresses that are burned onto the NIC inside every computer on the network, of each data packet the is circulated on the network segments connected on the bridge. It is by learning which MAC addresses are live on the network that the bridge is able to control traffic that is local to a particular segment and keep it from spreading to other network segments that are being serviced by another bridge.

A bridge device filters data traffic at a network boundary. Bridges reduce the amount of traffic on a LAN by dividing it into two segments. Bridges operate at the data link layer (Layer 2) of the OSI model. Bridges inspect incoming traffic and decide whether to forward or discard it. An Ethernet bridge, for example, inspects each incoming Ethernet frame - including the source and destination MAC addresses, and sometimes the frame size - in making individual forwarding decisions.

Bridges serve a similar function as switches, that also operate at Layer. Traditional bridges, though, support one network boundary, whereas switches usually offer four or more hardware ports. Switches are sometimes called "multi-port bridges" for this reason. Computer networks serve the purpose of connecting many different computers or terminals to each other, host computers, printers, file servers etc. so that expensive computing assets, programmes, files and other data may be shared among many users. A large network may typically contain one or more gateways, routers and bridges operating in conjunction with one or more network segments.

A segment is section of a network connected to a group of machines which may communicate with each other via repeater operations without having to traverse a bridge or router. Bridges and routers are useful in that they allow connections of multiple segments such that more computers may communicate with each other than would otherwise be possible given the limited bandwidth of the media.

4

Basics of E-Commerce

Knowledge Economics in a Post-Capitalist Global Economy

"Knowledge remains an infuriatingly vague subject to write about-let alone sell. Telling a reasonably effective company that it should focus on "knowledge creation" is rather like telling an orchestra that it should concentrate on "music making"".

The Economist, 1997

On the macroeconomic scale, knowledge is also the focus of analysis of the "new" dynamics of the global economy. In an era of globalized, highly-mobile financial capital, multinational corporations can essentially "arbitrage" across national borders to find the best firms to integrate into their mode of production.

Reich (1991) writes that in the new "global web" of enterprise, "power and wealth flow to groups that have accumulated the most valuable skills in problem-solving, problem-identifying, and strategic brokering". Drucker (1991) claims that this globalization of enterprise and economic transactions is transforming the world economy from capitalism to a "post-capitalist society."

Capitalism and post-capitalism

"Our plan is to lead the public with new products rather than ask them what kind of products they want. The public does not know what is possible, but we do. So instead of doing a lot of market research, we refine our thinking on a product and its use an d try to create a market for it by educating and communicating with the public."

Akio Morita, Chairman, Sony Corporation

In a capitalist society, wealth flows to those who control the flow of financial capital. In the early days of manufacturing, the capital requirements of production facilities were modest, allowing the accumulation of physical capital to be financed internally by the increased production afforded by factory methods.

But as the technologies of production grew more sophisticated and their resource demands increased, economies of scale emerged. This placed greater emphasis on the ability of enterprises to access financial capital. Also, as noted by Chandler (1977), the rise of an entirely new class of industry, namely communications and transportation firms, required distributed facilities and closely-coordinated. Since financial capital is now widely available across them the development of these enterprises. The development of public capital markets increased the range of tools and the breadth of skills which managers could use to acquire financing.

This has led to the rise of financial markets of such tremendous sophistication that humans can navigate these environments only with the aid of computers. In turn, managers are concerned that their actions are now dictated by financial forces beyond their control; they are no longer able to channel financial capital, but instead are beholden to its demands.

In post-capitalist economics, wealth flows not to those who control financial capital, but to those who can acquire and direct intellectual capital. Since financial capital is now widely available across the world, effective money management is only one skill necessary to the success of firms. The increased velocity of commerce (especially electronic commerce) and competition demands multi-faceted expertise from a firm. In fact, the changes in the world economy are placing requirements of skills and resources that often exceed those of a single enterprise, necessitating the formation of multiple alliances to ensure that the members of each alliance can marshall the intellectual capabilities to deal with the complexities of their environment. Only through the judicious and experienced application of knowledge can firms hope to outperform their counterparts and achieve sustained competitive advantages.

The post-capitalist knowledge-based economy operates with dynamics which differ radically from those assumed by neo-classical economics. First, unlike other forms of capital, intellectual capital is not only unevenly distributed, but it tends to grow without physical limits. A firm which captures and exercises unique knowledge cap abilities will tend to attract more expert employees, thus exhibiting "increasing returns to scale." According to Arthur (1996), this dynamic leads to a new form of economics, namely knowledge economics, that is very different from traditional, process-o riented economics. He notes that "they call for different management techniques, strategies, and codes of government regulation".

Second, in traditional economics, free markets are the purest form of economic organization, and competition between diverse enterprises provides the "invisible hand" which Adam Smith (1776) claimed would guide market participants to mutual gains through trade. However, free market efficiency is predicated on numerous stylized assumptions, including perfect information symmetry provided by price signals. We now know that prices do not perfectly capture all information relevant to a transaction, leading in some cases to the use of bureaucratic organizations to conduct transactions (Williamson, 1985). Since information is often not distributed symmetrically, knowledge (which is based upon information) is also concentrated unevenly. Therefore, in knowledge-based markets, pure competition may not result in the most efficient solution. A direct corollary is that while a lack of competition is assumed to be a market failure in traditional economics, it may be an optimal solution in certain situations in knowledge-based economics.

Third, the forms of organization in knowledge-based economies differ from those in traditional markets. Chandler (1977) shows how mass production and mass distribution required a level of coordination best handled by bureaucratic mechanisms with in the firm. Transaction cost economics, as described in Williamson (1985), suggests that the "visible hand of management," in Chandler's terminology, will supercede the invisible hand of the market when the dimensions of the transactions, such as asset specificity, transaction duration or recurrence, complexity, and measurement problems, create a situation where internal coordination and control can govern those transactions more efficiently than market mechanisms.

A key assumption of transaction cost economics is that individual opportunism will require coercive control and monitoring to ensure economic efficiency in such transactions (Ghoshal and Moran, 1996). If opportunism is not assumed in all cases, or if opportunism is exercised along a continuum instead of assumed as an absolute, it is possible for other forms of organization to emerge, including internal markets (Halal, 1996) and hybrid organizations.

Andy Grove, Chairman, Intel Corporation

In its 1993 Agenda for Action and its 1995 Agenda for Cooperation, the Clinton Administration laid out its vision of the issues involved in promoting the spread and use of the National Information I nfrastructure (NII) and the Global Information Infrastructure (GII). In July 1997, the Administration plans to release another landmark report titled "A Framework for Global Electronic Commerce", that will outline the key domestic and international policies that will allow the Internet to develop and extend throughout the world at the core of NII and GII. The five key principles of the upcoming report are:

a. The private sector should lead in the development of NII and GII.
b. Governments should avoid undue restrictions on electronic commerce.
c. Where a governmental involvement is needed, its aim should be to support and enforce a predictable, minimalist, consitstent and simple legal environment for commerce.
d. Governments should recognize the unique qualities of the Internet.
e. Electronic commerce over the Internet should be facilitated on an international basis.

Furthermore, the report focuses on nine areas where international agreements and/or guidelines could facilitate the growth of electronic commerce by creating a predictable, market-oriented commercial framework:

a. financial issues :
   i. customs and taxation
   ii. electronic payment systems.
b. legal issues :
   iii. uniform commercial code for electronic commerce
   iv. intellectual property protection
   v. privacy
   vi. security.
c. market access issues :
   vii. telecommunications infrastructure and interoperability
   viii. content
   ix. technical standards.

Beyond the policy-making level, three key issues that will determine the long term viability of electronic commerce are:

a. technological feasibility: the extent to which technology—bandwidth availability and information reliability, tractability, and security— will be able to sustain exponentially increasing demands worldwide.

b. socio-cultural acceptability: the extent to which different cultures and ways of doing business worldwide will accomodate this new mode of transacting in terms of its nature (not face-to-face), speed, asynchroneity, and uni-dimensionality of transactions.

c. business profitability: the extent to which this new way of doing business will allow for profit margins to exist at all: no intermediaries, instant access to sellers, global reach of buyers. It is of course too early to pass judgment on any of these points: the technology is truly very young and also expanding so quickly that technology maturation is proceeding very slowly (Carayannis, 1996).

Moreover, the significance of privacy, security, and intellectual property rights protection as predicates for the successful diffusion, adoption, and commercial success of internet-related technologies both for the US and worldwide, especially i n places with less democratic political insitutions and free-market economies, is continually increasing.

The differentiation between the internet as a global network of computer networks and the intranets, corporate-based computer networks that are protected by "firewalls" and involve well-defined communities as potentially more promising technology platforms for fostering internet-related commerce (Intranet commerce has surpassed Internet commerce in terms of revenue and already more then half of the Web sites worldwide are commercial in nature). Strategic alliances such as the alliance of Cybercash with Netscape to post Cybercash's electronic wallet on the internet for using its electronic money or "cheets" to facilitate electronic commerce. More than 100 banks are supporting this technology and its users can have moneys in deducted from their accounts automatically while the security of the transactions is guaranteed.

Entry of new competitors such as the cyber market set up by Federal Express to allow commercial cyber-transactions: Fedex believes it is in the business of hauling information not just traditional mail packages. The industry has defined e-commerce too narrowly: many consumers reach a decision to buy on the Web and then buy using some other route (The Economist, 1997).

The online leaders are not the traditional commercial giants of the physical world, but outsiders who often had no prior experience about the markets they chose to enter (e.g.: Amazon.com).

Areas of business endeavor where electronic commerce matters (The Economist, 1997):

1. Financial services
2. Sex
3. Travel
4. Retailing
5. Music
6. Cars (Auto-by-tel)
7. Advertising & Marketing
8. Books (Amazon.com)
9. Business-to-Business commerce
10. Business-to-Government commerce.

General Electric is doing $1 billion annually with 1,400 of its suppliers through its Trading Process Network (TPN) Web site and has thus lowered the cost of business between 5 and 20% with 15% of the orders going abroad. With $30 billion annual purchases, GE "can use its purchasing power to pull entire industries into electronic commerce" (The Economist, 1997).

Issues of Security and Trust Affecting Electronic Commerce: Internet Thief Apprehended

A computer cracker who broke into a San Diego Internet service provider's computer and stole 100,000 credit card numbers has been nabbed.

The thief used a "packet sniffer" program to gather the information from a dozen companies selling products over th e Internet, and was arrested as he tried to peddle them to an undercover FBI agent for $260,000. "What is unique about this case is that this individual was able to hack into this third party, copy this information and encrypt it to be sold," says a Bure au spokesman. The cracker was using an account at the University of California at San Francisco, although authorities have not determined whether he is affiliated with the university. Concerns about security and privacy are significant factors affecting the spreading and growth of electronic commerce as all entities involved are treading technological virgin terrains. Recently, a small Danish start-up announced that all Netscape browsers had a "bug" that could allow a "hacker" to read the information on the hard drive of a computer "surfing" the WWW even if it were behind a protective "firewall" (CNN, 6/21/97).

At the same time, James Barksdale of Netscape contends that "I don't know of a dime that has been lost over the internet" (The Economist, 1997), while Visa and Mastercard are working together to on developing Secure Electronic Transaction (SET) technology that could make credit cards safer on the Internet than in the physical world. The uncertainty and risk involved highlight the strategic preponderance of well established brands (such as Visa) in gaining widespread consumer acceptance and trust (ibid).

Game Theory, Co-opetition, Strategic Inflexion Points and Strategic Capability Options

> *"You can not overtake the runner in front of you by following in his footsteps."*

Mao Tse-Tung

The essence of firm is the set of relationships among its stakeholders and between itself and other firms.... The most important objectives of commercial relationships are cooperation (the joint activity toward a shared goal), coordination (the need for mutually consistent responses), and differentiation (the avoidance of mutually incompatible activities). Game theory is a helpful way of describing these relationships. So although the discussion of cooperation begins from the familiar business problem of achieving success in a joint venture, we go on to explain how that issue can be described by the most famous of all games-the Prisoner's Dilemma. The objectives of coordination and differentiation are represented by the Battle of the Sexes and the Game of Chicken, respectively. I also describe the paradox of commitment-how it is possible to gain by limiting one's own options." (Kay, 1995).

By taking a game theory approach to strategy, Brandenburger and Nalebuff (1996) derive one alternative to pure competition as the basis for interfirm relations. They begin by noting that the concept of rationality, which underpins both traditional economics and the "bounded rationality" of transaction cost economics, is never absolute.

For example, "two people can both be rational and yet evalute the same outcome quite differently". They discuss the concept of allocentrism: evaluating a multi-player game from the points of view of all the players. Brandenburger and Nalebuff (1996) describe co-opetition as "a duality in every relationship — the simultaneous elements of cooperation and competition. War and peace. Co-opetition."

Instead of viewing all players as competitors, this approach can reveal that some opponents are in fact 'complementors,' who may add value to others. By focusing on turning apparent zero-sum situations into positive-sum games, Brandenburger and Nalebuff argue that firms should pursue a strategy of 'co-opetition,' combining cooperation and competition depending on the exact situation to achieve the greatest gainsharing among all players. Co-opetition is exercised through the formation of "value nets," where the firm interacts with suppliers, customers, competitors and complementors to maximize its own added value, in turn raising the returns to the other players in the net.

Co-opeting occurs when you collaborate with your rivals and compete with your partners in pursuit of "win-win" market players/ stakeholders configurations.

Cooperation vs. Coordination

There is a need for cooperation-to encourage individual persons to pursue a common goal against the contrary pressures of their own interests. There is also the problem of coordination. It often is important to that everyone do the same thing, eventhough precisely what it is that everyone does is not important at all. But there is also a need for differentiation. Although all different aspects of an activity need to be covered by an organization, if all firms in a market adopt similar strategies, the outcome is unlikely to be profitable for any of them. Strategic Inflection Points:

In an industry, a strategic inflection point is when the balance of forces shifts from the old structure, from the old ways of doing business and the old ways of competing to the new. Before the strategic inflection point, the industry simply was more like the old. After it, it is more like the new. It is a point where the curve has subtly but profoundly changed, never to change back again.

It is very difficult to tell when an strategic inflection point occurs even in retrospect. And it is even harder to tell while going through one. People who experience one develop a sense of it being an inflection point at different times. (Grove, 1995).

Strategic Technological Capability Options

The concept of creating strategic technological capability options implies that by investing in given technologies, firms create opportunities or 'options' for themselves, to make still additional investments in the future. The idea is more commonly understood in terms of "staying on the learning curve": machine tool companies that adopted numerically-controlled production technology in the early 1970's, found it easier to switch to integrated computer-based manufacturing a decade later... these firms developed capability options, which could be "exercised" to reduce the cost of adopting subsequent, more advanced technology vintages.

In this context, the capabilities developed in the first technology transition facilitated a subsequent transition to the more advanced technology. This implies that part of the benefit the original investment was the capability to work with automated processing equipment, a capability that translated more easily into the adoption of CIM technology in the 1980's.

Trust and Economic Transactions

Another focus of the recent economic analysis is the concept of trust. The rise of modern managerial capitalism from the old regime of family enterprise is viewed as a watershed in the move from craft production to mass production. These new companies were able to replace family ties with purely economic loyalties. Many economic historians argue that "how these loyalties were created...we cannot know for sure". One possibility is that these firms grew from military units who developed mutual loyalty in battle. But larger social forces seem to be at work to lead to the rise of entire economic systems based on economic loyalty. In particular, economists are now exploring the idea of "social capital," the ability of people to cooperate towards a common goal beyond purely financial motives. To form and lead the kinds of hybrid, cooperative organizatoinal forms described above, companies must command substantial social capital. Clearly, just as knowledge is the lever of intellectual capital, trust is the lever of social capital. Fukuyama (1995) defines trust as "the expectation that arises within a shared norms, on the part of other members of that community".

He attributes the development of shared norms to social activities such as religion. Thus, the economic development of various societies is the result of social development which determines whether a given society is "high-trust" (such as the United States) or "low-trust" (such as China), with high-trust societies more likely to adopt advanced forms of economic organization.

Knowledge Exchange as the Basis of Cooperation

Fukuyama ignores the development of global webs of enterprises, where entities from different societies coordinate and cooperate in individual action toward common goals. Such international alliances have increased in the past two decades. These groups themselves must be based on some kind of trust, although their members do not share common social backgrounds. We argue that building trust in such networks requires the sharing of intellectual capital to build social capital. In other words, knowledge exchange forms the foundation for trust in corporate alliances, linking intellectual capital with social capital.

Knowledge as a Medium of Exchange

Knowledge has certain characteristics which make it very distinct from other media of exchange, such as financial capital or physical capital (e.g. land).

Knowledge can be transferred between firms or individuals, like other forms of currency. But unlike money and land, knowledge, once transferred, is held by both the donor and the recipient. Hence, knowledge is not transferred in a formal sense; it is shared. The act of sharing knowledge allows both parties to utilize that knowledge independent of the other.

Knowledge sharing, then, is by nature a positive-sum game; neither party is deprived of knowledge by engaging in sharing. However, knowledge sharing may lead to a zero-sum game if one party is better able to use that knowledge in a market situation than the other.

For example, if a firm "reverse engineers" the products of a competitor, and then introduces an improved model onto the market, it can profit abnormally from the unintentional "sharing" of its competitor's knowledge. Intellectual property laws are intended to protect firms against the unintended appropriation of knowledge by outsiders. But since firms are notoriously "leaky" when it comes to knowledge, such legal protections are of limited value.

Knowledge Exchange, Co-operation and Competition

Given that firms are unable to protect their knowledge absolutely, they may be able to pre-empt the misappropriation of their knowledge by sharing it with their competitors. This, in turn, can create the expectation that the competitor will in turn share its knowledge with the donor firm. Thus, knowledge becomes an object of barter between firms towards the development of a new form of economic relationship. The equal exchange of knowledge constitutes a "quid pro quo" which, in turn, reinforces a growing trust between the parties to that transaction. As long as the knowledge exchanged between the firms is perceived by the recipients to be of equal value, trust can be built. In contrast, many alliances and joint ventures fail because the participants are either unwilling to share knowledge, on the faulty assumption that they are "parting with" that expertise, or because the parties are unable to attain a mutually-agreeable arrangement for the sharing of knowledge ex ante and the division ex post of the intellectual assets resulting from cooperation. Knowledge exchange does not rule out downstream competition between two firms.

Again, knowledge is simply the foundation of intellectual capital, not its equal. Possession of knowledge is one thing; its application and control is much more significant. Hence, firms may be willing to cooperate to share and develop jointly "generic knowledge," which they then apply in their unique ways in differentiated products on the market. The availability of that pool of generic knowledge adds value to the products of both firms, yet still allows them the freedom to compete with each other at the market level.

The Dynamics of Knowledge-Based Economics

The implications of knowledge sharing for the new knowledge-based economy are substantial. Knowledge-based competition is generally assumed to require that firms have different knowledge which they then use to create sustained competitive advantage. But knowledge sharing allows firms to access the same basic knowledge to cooperate and compete simultaneously for greater productivity. This, in turn, changes the way that firms must operate, and the mechanisms for governing transactions in the new economy.

Personal Trust Through Shared Knowledge

Within the firm, it is clear that individuals must share trust for the firm to survive and prosper. With the increasing mobility of human capital, it is no longer guaranteed that the employees of the firm have the same social and cultural background to provide a social basis for trust.

By encouraging knowledge sharing at the individual level, the firm gains in two ways. First, it can guarantee that knowledge will flow efficiently to those employees who are in the best position to utilize that knowledge at a given time. Second, however, it bonds individuals together in a collaborative mode to ensure that they work toward common goals, which in turn will drive firm innovation. As Foray (1991) observes, intra-firm cooperation is essential to innovation because the functions and resources of the firm are integrated together into a larger whole. He draws from the work of Aoki (1986) to show how Japanese firms are better organized through knowledge sharing to achieve higher-order innovation through the development of common, firm-specific knowledge using mechanisms of learning by doing.

Electronic commerce is tightly linked with the exchange of information and knowledge as these are the key mediums of exchange that underlie this new form of commerce. As such, the issues that are salient to the area of knowledge economics are also key in understanding the "co-opetitive" dynamics of electronic commerce. Primary among these are the issues of trust and non-linear change underscored by the concepts of strategic inflexion points and strategic capability options. These concepts are becoming increasingly important as business transactions are becoming more digital and the barriers to entry into markets and industries fuzzier promoting more openness in pursuit of win-win business configurations:

"Two major forces-fundamental technological change and a new ethos of openness-are driving through our era, forces that could bring about the long boom, a 25-year global expansion with all its consequences. Five waves of technology-computers, telecommunications, biotechnology, nanotechnology, and alternative energy-may bring about big productivity increases that lead to high rates of economic growth, in balance with nature. Meanwhile, we're seeing unprecented global integration....These two meta-developments lead to increasing integration and prosperity worldwide."

Economic Implications of E-commerce

The information revolution aided by the revolution in the telecommunications and institutional innovations had initially promised to change the nature of the market altogether. The market's primary role as merely a place where buyers and sellers meet (it had seemed) now has been revolutionized by the impact of the information revolution on its subsidiary role, i.e., as a transmission belt of information. Today market is a place where there is no intermediaries between a seller of a good and its final buyer to the mutual benefit of both parties (Sengupta, 2004). The Internet and its enabled technologies (especially electronic commerce) have caused the costs of many kinds of market mterachon to plummet (Saloner, 2001). Not only cost reduction, e-commerce has the potential to stimulate growth and employment in industrialized as well as developing countries. Further, e-commerce allows economics agents (both buyers and sellers) to interact more effectively by creating new market opportunities (Mukhopadhyay, 2002). Thus, e-commerce has strong economic implications at both micro and macro level.

E-commerce and Economic Growth

While e-commerce clearly has a positive impact on the business sector, doubts have been raised about its impact on the macroeconomic growth, and productive growth (2) in particular. Various studies show that e-commerce had an impressive performance particular in terms of productivity growth. The US, which leads the world in IT and e-commerce, has had a notable economic performance, particularly in terms of productive growth, since 1995. But, the same was not happened with the developing countries as they failed to catch up technologically with the industrialized world. To assess the broader economic impact of e-commerce and the ramifications of developing countries' catching up or not, UNCTAD has conducted a quantitative analysis based on two scenario: one in which the developing countries fall behind technologically and one in which they catch up with the developed countries. The analysis is centred on cost saving and assume that e-commerce can reduce costs of services, particularly in retail and wholesale trade, transport and financial and business services. Cost savings in services are stimulated through a productive growth scenario, which allow for the analysis of such macro-economic variables as GDP, welfare, wages and terms of trade. The analysis is a unique application of a computable general equilibrium model to e-commerce at the global level.

According to the report, under the first scenario developed countries would have welfare gains of $117 billion, while the developing world (excluding Asia) would lose welfare of $ 726 million. The Asian region, on the other hand, would gain $ 802 million, largely attributable to the transport services sector. Besides welfare and GDP losses, developing countries would also experience a reduction in wages and deteriorating terms of trade.

E-Commerce could therefore end up actually widening, and not narrowing, the gap between the developed and developing countries.Under the second scenario, however, if developing countries were to catch up with developed countries in productivity, they would increase output, wages and welfare.

A 1% productive growth m the service sector in Asia for example, would result in welfare gains of $12 billion, GDP growth of 0.4% and a 2 to 3% growth in the service exports. By reducing costs, increasing efficiency, reducing time and distance, e-commerce could thus become an important tool for development.

Impact of E-commerce on Economy

Business and the economy are inextricably linked with the development and implementation of new technology (Tassabehji, 2003). Growth and development of any modern economy has been recognized by many economic theorists, such as Kondratieff, Schumpeter, Mensch and Porter, to be based on innovation of new technology. In the early twentieth century, the economist Kondratieff introduced his 'Long Wave Theory (3)' of economic growth. He detailed the numbers of years that the economy expanded and contracted during each part of the half-century long cycle, which industries suffer the most during the 'downwave' and how technology plays a role in leading the way out of the contraction into the next 'upwave'. Building on this theory the economist Schumpeter (1961) assigned technological innovation an almost exclusive role, as engine of economic development: the fundamental impulse that sets and keeps the capitalist engine in motion comes from the new consumers' goods, the new methods of production or transportation, the new market, the new forces of industrial organization that capitalist enterprise creates. Mensch (1979) updates the Schumpeter theory, giving it an empirical base in history, where clusters of innovation take place and generate completely new sectors. He stressed that only technological innovations can overcome depression and that government must implement an aggressive innovation policy to stimulate the search for new and basic innovation. Further, Porter (1990), emphasizes that the prosperity and competitive advantage of a nation is no longer as a result of a nation's natural resources and its labour force, but rather the ability of its industry to innovate and upgrade. This can be seen as a disruptive technology on a macro environmental level. And today, whether economic community subscribes to these economic theories or not, the impact of new technology on the economy of a nation is indisputable. Continuous growth of e-commerce is expected to have deep impact on structure and functioning of economies at various levels and overall impact on macro-economy. Some key areas are discussed below:

Impact on Intermediation

Traditional production, transportation and distribution process is characterized by the liner-point-to-point path (4). In this process intermediaries play an important role. In physical world, because of large distance between production units and consumer units, it is not possible for consumers to approach producers directly and vice versa. The existence of intermediaries namely, distributors, wholesalers and retailers, this increase the transaction costs for both the producers and consumers.

But in the emerging economic scenario, liner-point-to-point information and knowledge flow no longer represent the reality. In the process of e-commerce transactions, it is possible for the consumer to conduct and place an order with the manufacturer instantly and directly (Singla, 2000). And same is possible within the various agents of this process (i.e., between producer and Retailers, Retailers and Distributors, Distributors and Retailers etc.). E-Commerce technology brings about the benefits of more accurate and timely information flow, administrative saving, lowering total distribution cost, closer trading relationship, improved cash flows, and moving closer to the end consumers.

No doubt that online ordering and delivery of product is reducing the role of intermediaries. Therefore, it is also feared that intermediaries would be completely eliminated in the e-commerce economy. However, this fear may be unfounded. In 'e-commerce economy, though it is possible to deliver a number of goods and services online, it may not be possible to eliminate the physical delivery of many goods because of their vary nature. Goods such vegetables and grocery, garments and shoes, toys etc. cannot be delivered online (they have physical existence). Though intermediaries like wholesalers and retailers can be eliminated in such transactions, it may not be possible to eliminate distributors and transporters. The demand for distributors and transporters is in fact expected to increase tremendously (Westland and Clark). Even with the advent of e-commerce technology, the functions of intermediaries will not change, because collecting information is a labour and time intensive task. However, this group can exploit new opportunities and challenges.

Impact on Agriculture

The open access architecture of the Internet, declining information technology costs, and high volume have resulted in progressive steps forward for the entire marketing system. Parallel changes in the structure of agriculture have also contributed to the popularity of the current generation of information technology. Chief among the changes is in the need for closer coordination of the supply chain-both upstream and downstream from the producer-and stretching' from seed, fertilizers, and machinery suppliers, to the food processors and retailers. Thus, technologies like electronic commerce have forced new relationships between and among the buyers of agribusiness to form a complex web interaction (Ehmake et al., 2001)

Various studies show that there is much about the potential success of e-commerce's in agriculture. Common agribusiness business-to-business transactions such as buying, selling, trading, delivering and contracting seem to be natural targets for conversion to e-commerce.

Many theoretical benefits of e-commerce in agriculture have been identified such as: (1) promotion of information flow, market transparency and price discovery (Poole, 2001); (2) facilitation of industry coordination (Nicolaisen, 2001); and reduction or elimination of transaction costs (Porter, 2001; Thompson, 1996). Internet based e-commerce also offer tremendous opportunities to create collaborative marketplaces in low-cost and effective way (Nicolaisen, 2001). E-commerce in agriculture could also potentially tighten the supply chain and cut marketing margins and transactions costs in way that benefit smaller, local producers as well as local agribusinesses. It also enables a vast array of products to be transacted, usually at a price that is competitive with local retailers. E-commerce can also change the situation of hard bargain caused by scattered farmers and lack of information. At the same time, the fast and convenient electronic bargain manner can accelerate the circulation of commodities, and lessen the risk, and increase the competitions of agricultural products in the international market (Cao and Chen, 2001). These theoretical benefits appear to be undisputed. However, these have yet to materialize into profitability. Study of Golman Sachs (2000) discussed the general barriers citied by business to Internet based e-commerce adoption and explained that these barriers also apply to agribusiness as well. These barriers include: (1) unclear return on investment (2) lack of budget (3) lack of stakeholders support and (4) complicated technology. Added to these, there may be some other factors (10) slowing down e-commerce adoption in agriculture. In fact, many of the issues faced by e-agribusinesses are the same as those faced by the firms in other sectors similar to changes brought by other new agricultural technologies (Hooker et al., 2001). However, characteristics of the agricultural sector and its participants present some inherent impediments to the implementation of e-commerce practices. Nonetheless, despite these challenges, there is room for creative solutions potentially leading to successful adoption. Those potential strategies touch on: structure of industry; market and product expertise; and organizational development. At this point of time it is not very clear-the impact of e-commerce on farms, agribusiness firms, markets, and rural communities. Are there only winners or are losers too? If so, who are they? What will government to do, with or against e-commerce in agriculture? Since e-commerce is still evolving, it is too early to definitive answer (Mueller, 2000). An inspection of current practices; however, suggest that success of e-commerce in agribusiness is undeniable. Factors specific to agriculture will create additional challenges, which must be overcome before success may be attained. The ability of each player to work though these challenges will determine the speed of implication of e-commerce in agriculture.

Impact on Labour Market

E-Commerce, consisting of marketing and other business processes conducted over the computer-mediated networks is changing the way organizations in many industries operate. It leads to the automation of some job functions and replaces others with self service operations, raising output per worker and dampening employment requirements in some occupations, as well as in the industries in which these occupations are concerned (Hecker, 2001). The introduction and implementation of new technologies has posed important challenges for the commercial workers and their trade unions worldwide. Among the issues that unions have to deal with are, both B2B and B2C, self-scanning, logistics system, multimedia and other in store sales support applications. In many ways, they are already deeply affecting labour market (Gottardi et al., 2004). In contrast, e-commerce has spurred employment in industries producing software, and systems used by e-commerce and other occupations associated with websites and networks.

Various studies showed that e-commerce has a positive impact on the labour productivity. At the theoretical level, since e-commerce reduces coordination costs between different work processes, they facilitate firms to fragment tasks to enable them to improve the labour productivity. At the same time when the routine tasks can be automated, e-commerce reduces unskilled work. In a recent study, Atrostic and Nguyen (2004) considered the impact of computer networks on the labour productivity in the US manufacturing sector, using micro data predominantly for 1999. They found a positive and significant impact of computer networks on plant level labour productivity, suggested that networks increase labour productivity by around 7.5 per cent. Motohashi (2001) provides evidence for the positive impact of different information networks on labour productivity in Japan. In the UK a recent study by Criscuolo and Waldron (2003), based on Annual Business Inquiry, shows that buying online positively affects the labour and total factors of productivity, while selling online has a negative impact on productivity.

But, perhaps the larger impact of e-commerce on labour market can be seen in the form of online job search. However, very little is known about the importance of online job applications or direct employer initiated contracts with potential candidates. Even then, online job posting has grown spectacularly (Autor, 2001). Estimates place the number of online job boards at over 3000, the number of active resumes online at over 7 million, and the number of job posting at 29 million. Kuhn and Skuterud (2000) reported that 7 per cent of employed workers regularly use the web to search for a new job in 1998. The leading job board, Monster.Com, offered 3.9 million resumes and 4, 30,000 jobs in August 2000. Further, the Internet is likely to change how some workers deliver labour services. For example, falling telecommunications traffic regardless of where it originates. Improvements in communication and control technology likely mean that people who monitor equipment or other workers can perform their task at the greater physical remove. Remote access to e-mail and company documents will enable many workers to perform some or all of their work from home to elsewhere.

On the flip side, it has also been feared that the reduction in number of intermediaries and sales persons due to reduction in number of supermarkets and showroom would reduce employment world over. The worst affected are expected to be the unskilled manpower. It is true that unskilled labour is getting displaced in a big way in the e-commerce economy. Internet and e-commerce by facilitating firms to employ home-workers on a contractual basis are seen to promote insecure employment opportunities. In India, as well as in the other low-income economies, the potential of e-commerce is seen to employment from the formal sector to small firms in the unorganized sector where employment is not protected by any legislation. Further, if this feature of e-commerce encourages the formation of small firms that are narrowly specialized, it also implies that there is less room for employee mobility within the firms, transforming the careers paths of employees (Francis, 1986).

Added to this, as with other tools, the internet is not without its limitations as a means of attracting qualified candidates. For example, companies listing opportunities on major job boards may receive applications from a much wider geographic region-and sometimes less qualified applicants-requiring additional sorting and review. Firms are also noting that some candidates who post their resumes online may be more passive job seekers; they want to "test the waters" and wait the results, versus proactively applying for open position.

Impact on Transportation

In a very short time span common sense has emerged within the world of transport, about the assumed huge impact of e-commerce and especially the Internet on relationships between companies (and consumers). Dholakia et al, (2000) concluded that in those regions of the world where there is old, established and often congested road infrastructure, any e-commerce-based methods that could lead to trip reduction and/or trip rationalization can contribute to an improvement in the quality of life. At least from a theoretical point of view, it seems quite clear that the online shopping could lead to reduction of transport demand. In some cases, online shopping eliminates any kind of physical transport (when goods can be dematerialized as software, books, music etc.).

In other cases, a goods transport is still necessary, but the journeys to shops are eliminated or reduced. Even if the purchase is finally made at the shop, the consumer can have used the Internet, looking for information, instead of visiting different shops. Thus, electronic commerce transactions have strong implications on transportation. In this context, numbers of studies have been conducted to measure the impact of e-commerce on the number of trips. Browne (2001) first quoted the study made by Farahmand and Young (1998). It modelled the effects of the number of trips by switch to home shopping of 10 per cent of the customers of a grocery store and a DIY store (of a typical size) in the UK. They assumed that delivery vans would carry the loads of nine customers on each round trip. In both the cases, the reduction in total trips is around 9 per cent. The vehicle kilometer made by the delivery vans for the 10 per cent of home shoppers suppose a reduction of 87 per cent in comparison with the vehicle kilometers previously made by car.

Further, the study (Coirm, 1999) also modelled a case of grocery home delivery in UK and their result shows that if 10-20 per cent of shoppers use home shopping, the reduction in the trips could arrive to 7-16 per cent. For the purchase made from home, the reduction in vehicle kilometers is 70-80 per cent even if each van only carries eight loads. Against this, study of Colin (2001) revealed that commerce has not had as great an impact on transport lows as some had expected, at least in terms of the volumes carried. However, some substitution effects are to be expected.

Not only on the retail transportation, e-commerce does have impact on the companies where heavy transportation is needed. E-transportation tool can enable seamless connectivity, provide dock-to-dock visibility of the supply chain, and deliver real time information that leads to better and faster decisions. E-transportation also enables shippers a choice of carriers to be used for shipments of merchandise varying in weights and service, and identifies all shipping packing, marking, labelling and communications requirements as well. (Vevaldi and Prasad, 2002). But many shippers still are not quite ready to put their faith in this relatively new e-commerce tool. Indeed, as with the introduction of new technology, e-commerce as it relates to the transportation industry, is going to take time to catch on.

For transportation companies it is expected that, with e-commerce, a whole new market will open up for transportation and logistics companies, or whatever they may be called in the future. At present e-commerce is pursued to a fairly high degree between companies, but is still not very developed between companies and private persons. The business-to-consumer (B2C) relation is expected to grow rapidly though, and when this happens it will result in several changes for actors in the logistics area. When delivering to private persons instead of companies, the demand for fast and accurate deliveries will increase. This is because one or more of the physical nodes will disappear when the goods can be transported directly from the producing company to the end customer. Direct home deliveries will request shorter lead times, and more complex distribution systems will be necessary to make this possible. Expected trends in traffic and distribution from a widely spread use of e-commerce are fewer passenger cars, an increased number of pickup trucks, and smaller consignments, especially on international transports. Further the study of Hultkrantz and Lumsden (2000) concluded that the logistics industry has to face the challenges and opportunities created by e-commerce, both from within the industry and from external players. The industry has always been pressed to cut costs and squeeze margins, and the future will be even more formidable as competition forces most companies to continue the streamlining of their business.

Impact on Taxation

When new technologies evolve, can taxation issues be far behind? If e-commerce is being billed as one of the greatest economic developments of the 21st century the taxation issues arising there from poses the single biggest challenge of the century to both-the businesses and the taxman's. (Girish, 20001) This is particularly true in the context of digitized products because transactions of such products are not backed up by any physical of goods. As e-commerce transcends the barriers of geographical boundaries the concept like the place of transactions and place of consumption become immaterial. International tax issues in the area of e-commerce are manifold and include nexus 0fthe vendor and tax enforcement agencies. Taxing authorities may have great difficulty collecting revenue form vendors conducting commerce through foreign Internet addresses. The foremost problem associated with Internet based commerce is fixing the place of transaction.

The place where a web-server is located, the place where the user initializes the transaction and the server where payment is collected may be different. Electronic transfer of funds heightens the risk of money being sent to tax havens. Further, many jurisdictions rely on the taxpayer to voluntarily identify himself, herself or itself as falling within its tax system. Tax authorities may not be able to effectively enforce their rights to collect tax in such an environment, especially if a business does not consider itself to be within a tax jurisdiction and simply choose not to disclose its activities to the relevant authority. It is trite, but true, that taxation of e-commerce is a major concern for the international agencies and the tax authorities worldwide.

In Europe, North America, and Australia and in many Asian Countries (particularly India and Singapore) substantial research have been conducted on the impact of the e-commerce on taxation. Among the plethora of books, reports, articles and papers produced on this topic however, the work of Organization for the Economic Co-Operation and Development (OECD) stands out as the most significant, given its commitment to consulting broadly with the governments worldwide as well as with the business community to develop an integrated and comprehensive approach to the taxation of e-commerce.The identification and analysis of the inter jurisdictional measures imposed by e-commerce is one thing. The formulation of domestic and treaty policies for dealing with e-commerce is another, even more controversial challenge. Perhaps, the most fundamental threat to the international tax system is the erosion of the worldwide tax base. It is increasingly possible for a company to try to divert income to a tax haven by locating its server there. This raises issues of allocation of business profits between the residence and source countries and leakage to tax haven (Cidambi, 2000).

The debate over how international tax principles ought to be revealed and may be reformed is still in its formulative stage. It would be necessary to equip the tax administration after reviewing the entire procedure in the light of the advent of e-commerce. First, the procedures have to be simplified. Second, it would be necessary top create an environment within the tax department to ensure that the tax laws are implemented appropriately, and that integrity of the tax base is maintained. (Mantravadi and Chowdary, 2002).For India, it is high time to learn from the experience of the work of OECD, Japan and the US to suggest a strategy to encourage e-commerce and integrate the tax system in such a way that it takes care of the twin problems of determining the sites of sales and also identifies the jurisdiction with regard to its authority to tax transactions. In doing so, we have to keep in mind the associated risk for the tax compliance.

Impact on Cost, Price and Competition

Logically, e-commerce reduces search and transaction cost (Mukhopadhya, 2002). Reducation in transaction costs are motivating businesses to incorporate e-commerce into their business strategy (Garcia, 1995 and Kambil, 1995) The net impact of e-commerce on UK Economy has been estimated to be between 2% to 3% of GDP. It has also been estimated that improved demand forecasting and stock management as a result of e-commerce will enable reduction in overall inventories by as much as 25% in the US. At the micro level, there is evidence that this will provides an one-off sustainable improvement in the profitability by an average of 5% or more for the enterprises currently working with low margin (Goldman Sachs, 1999). The e-commerce lowers costs because, the Internet lowers selling search costs as well as, by allowing seller to communicate product information cost effectively to potential buyers, and by offering sellers new ways to reach buyers through the targeted advertisement and one-on-one advertising. Thus it is helpful in reducing the search costs on both the sides. By reducing search costs on both sides of the market, it appears likely that buyers will be able to consider more product offering and will identify and purchase products that better match their needs, with a resulting increase in economic efficiency. But the reduction in the cost combined with new capabilities of technology can set off more complex market dynamics (Bakos, 2001).

The lower search and information cost should push markets towards a greater degree of price and competition, and this outcome is certainly possible, especially for the homogeneous goods. On the other hand the use of Internet technology to provide differentiate and customized products, and thus avoid competition purely on the price.

Lower search costs in the digitized markets will make it easier for the buyers to find low cost sellers and thus will promote price competition among the sellers. Thus e-commerce economy comes quite close to the features of the prefect competition, as larger numbers of buyers and sellers can instantly interact with each other. Many characteristics of e-commerce should increase competition because buyers will have access to a global marketplace and the ability to easily compare price and product features (Fletcher et al., 2000). E-Commerce technologies have the potential to significantly increase competition by increasing consumers' choice of products and traders (ACCC, 2001). However, some of the distinguishing characteristics of the e-commerce set up also have the potential for creating the monopoly power in the certain lines of products.

The e-commerce set up has negligible distribution cost for the intangibles and therefore marginal cost of the production and distribution is almost nil for these goods. Sales of these goods to a particular customer does not reduce its availability to the other potential customers. Economies of scale arising out of negligible marginal cost, along with network externalities and consumer preference for the already acquired skills, provide natural monopoly power to some of the products in the e-commerce set up. Early birds are thus expected to reap the benefits in these lines of production. Therefore, in the e-commerce environment, monopoly is expected to exist along with the prefect competition. Competition would be especially seen in those areas where goods and services cannot be digitized and economies of scale are not very prominent. Breaking the monopoly power to remain in the competition would require high speed of innovation and making the product visible all the time, whether there is a demand for the products or not. Competition would be basically in the forms of converting ideas, knowledge and brain power into innovation.

Impact on Money

With the new economic landscape now outline, let us return to the money. Not surprisingly, in the intangible (e-commerce based economy) economy, money is also becoming increasingly intangible. The relative weight on non-cash monetary transactions now exceeds the value of cash money by the factor often (Goldfinger, 2002). Money and payments are delivered via electronic networks as data bits and database entries. At the wholesale level, money representation and manipulation are fully automated. Beyond the alteration of the appearance and mechanics of money, there are deeper structural changes. The triumph of markets means that money is increasingly used to settle multilateral transactions rather that the bilateral commercial transactions.

The functional evolution in turn leads to profound modification in the design of the clearing system and networks, which need to handle large volume, work in real time, and offer more open access. Growth of e-commerce and development of various payment alternative channels (i.e.. Debit and Credit Cards, E-Cheque, Digital Purse, E-Cash etc.) assist payment channels. The delivery channels greatly impacted the retail banking and the wholesale markets of banks. And today, these new technologies have transformed the banking business almost beyond the belief in the last decade and the half.

Most of all the customers have benefited, as have the bank themselves. Added to this, digital currencies have many other advantages; some of the important are: cheaper, faster, safer, global, and more private than traditional credit cards and bank wires. In other words, digital currencies will prove to be as world-changing as the invention of the printing press and gunpowder. Digital currencies link together financial institutions and markets across the globe in a way that allows instantaneous value transfers with a mere fraction of the cost associated with traditional bank wires and credit cards. But, this new forms of money has also posed certain challenges before the banking sector, most of them are related to IT plans (Kamesan, 2003). Many schemes have been piloted or rolled out but the use of e-money is still tiny. This raises the question why e-money has not been more successful. One explanation may be that there is not sufficient demand. Another explanation is that we are merely observing the slow start that is typical for many inventions. Once critical mass has been reached, e-money will take off. Finally, the problems of e-money may stem from regulation.

No doubt, these changes make money more visible and pervasive but also less stable, more volatile in its value and more elusive. Therefore, in the new economy, monetary policy become more important as a lever of economic management at the same time that the classical monetary aggregates—lose their reliability as signals of the future economic growth and inflation' (Goodhar, 1984).

Nevertheless, one thing appears certain, electronic money will continue to emerge, rendering the overall money landscape more intricate and multifarious. To facilitate the emergence of electronic money, it is important to be open minded, to accept innovate vision of money and money transaction. At the same time it is also essential to recognize that many of these visions will either never be implemented or fail the critical test of customer acceptance.

Concluding Remarks

The emergence and rapid growth of Internet and E-Commerce has strong implications on economic and social actitivities. It is quite possible that these new technologies might transform the future of economic and societal landscape. At the economic front, there is a clear evidence that E-Commerce and Internet techonolgy have positive impact (UNDP, (2003), Pohjola (2000), Dewan and Kramer (2000), Kraemer and Dedrick (2000)}.

To study the economic implications of e-commerce, few areas of economy (transportation, Intermediation, Agriculture, Labour Market, Taxation, Cost, Price and Competition, and money) has been selected. On the basis of various studies it is revealed that e-commerce technology have strong economic implications. At the general level, there are two types of potential economic gains from the use of E-commerce and IT enabled technologies. First, are the gains in efficiency, both in static and dynamic.

Static gains are one-time, and come from more efficeint use of scarce resources, allowing higher consumption in the present. Dynamics gains come from higher growth, potentially raising the entire future stream of consumption and population. Efficiency gains of e-commerce also come about through the enabling of new digitized goods and services. The second type of potential benefits comes from cost reduction. Studies indicates that e-commerce is helpful in reduction of search cost, administration cost, distribution cost and even the labour costs. However, all these opportuities are yet to materlize in to profitability i.e. in agricultural sector, benefits of e-commerce exists, but, only theortically; not practically, as the implemetnation of e-commerce technolgy in agricultural sector has certin challenges. Addes to this, e-commerce based economic models has also posed number of challenges before the concerned people and community.

The area of e-taxation is one of the best example and most controversial issue all over the world. As e-commerce transaccends the barriers of geographical boundaries, the concept like the place of transactions and place of consumption become immaterial. With the emergence and growth of digital money in the economy, the chances of frauds have also incresased.

Another most difficult issue is the planning regarding the adoption and implemetation of e-commerce technology in the various economic activities. In nutshall, with the e-commerce based economic models, there is little to lose and more to gain.

5

Role of IT in Rural Marketing

Introduction

In recent years, rural markets have acquired significance, as the overall growth of the economy has resulted into substantial increase in the purchasing power of the rural communities.

Rural areas are evolving into strategic market for companies which include not only domestic but MNCs too. There is great potential that lies in rural market. More and more stress is therefore being given on marketing products. It is very interesting to notice that the rural markets are at par with the urban markets. The credit for this scenario goes to the marketing policies.

ITC e-Choupal is the greatest example of information technology in rural marketing. Launched in June 2000, 'e-Choupal', has already become the largest initiative in all internet-based interventions in rural India. ITC followed a different media/communication strategy which is more elaborate and extensive in rural marketing so far, which benefits both the farmers and the organization.

The strategy use the Information Technology and bridge the information and service gap in rural India which gives an edge to market its products like seeds, fertilizers and pesticides and other products like consumer goods etc.

They use the e-Choupal to order seed, fertilizer, and other products such as consumer good from ITC or its partners, at prices lower than those available from village traders. In this Paper we discuss about the role of IT in rural market, e-Chou pal, different strategy, vision and planning behind the e-Chou pal.

Significance

In recent years, rural markets have acquired significance in countries like China and India, as the overall growth of the economy has resulted into substantial increase in the purchasing power of the rural communities. On account of the green revolution in India, the rural areas are consuming a large quantity of industrial and urban manufactured products. In this context, a special marketing strategy, namely, *rural marketing* has taken shape.

Sometimes, *rural marketing* is confused with *agricultural marketing* – the later denotes marketing of produce of the rural areas to the urban consumers or industrial consumers, whereas rural marketing involves delivering manufactured or processed inputs or services to rural producers or consumers. Also, when we consider the scenario of India and China, there is a picture that comes out, huge market for the developed products as well as the labor support. This has led to the change in the mindset of the marketers to move to these parts of the world.

Also rural market is getting an importance because of the saturation of the urban market. As due to the competition in the urban market, the market is more or so saturated as most of the capacity of the purchasers have been targeted by the marketers. So the marketers are looking for extending their product categories to an unexplored market i.e. the rural market. This has also led to the CSR activities being done by the corporate to help the poor people attain some wealth to spend on their product categories. Here we can think of HLL (now, HUL) initiatives in the rural India.

One of such project is the Project Shakti, which is not only helping their company attain some revenue but also helping the poor women of the village to attain some money which is surely going to increase their purchasing power. Also this will increase their brand loyalty as well as recognition in that area. Similarly we can think of the ITC E-Chou pal, which is helping the poor farmers get all the information about the weather as well as the market price of the food grains they are producing. In other view these activities are also helping the companies increase their brand value. So as it is given above the significance of the rural market has increased due to the saturation of the urban market as well as in such conditions the company which will lead the way will be benefited as shown by the success of HUL and ITC initiatives.

Strategies

Dynamics of rural markets differ from other market types, and similarly rural marketing strategies are also significantly different from the marketing strategies aimed at an urban or industrial consumer. This, along with several other related issues, have been subject matter of intense discussions and debate in countries like India and China and focus of even international symposia organized in these countries.

Rural markets and rural marketing involve a number of strategies, which include:

- Client and location specific promotion
- Joint or cooperative promotion..
- Bundling of inputs
- Management of demand
- Developmental marketing
- Unique selling proposition (USP)
- Extension services
- Business ethics
- Partnership for sustainability.

Client and Location specific promotion-involves a strategy designed to be suitable to the location and the client.

Joint or co-operative promotion-strategy involves participation between the marketing agencies and the client.

'Bundling of inputs'-denote a marketing strategy, in which several related items are sold to the target client, including arrangements of credit, after-sale service, and so on.

Management of demand-Involves continuous market research of buyer's needs and problems at various levels so that continuous improvements and innovations can be undertaken for a sustainable market performance. Developmental marketing-refer to taking up marketing programmers keeping the development objective in mind and using various managerial and other inputs of marketing to achieve these objectives.

Media-both traditional as well as the modern media, is used as a marketing strategy. Unique Selling Propositions (USP)-involves presenting a theme with the product to attract the client to buy that particular product. For examples, some of famous Indian Farm equipment manufactures have coined catchy themes, which they display along with the products, to attract the target client that is the farmers. English version of some of such themes would read like:

- The heartbeats of rural India
- With new technique for a life time of company
- For the sake of progress and prosperity.

Extension Services-denote, in short, a system of attending to the missing links and providing the required know-how.

Ethics in Business-form, as usual, an important plank for rural markets and rural marketing.

Partnership for sustainability-involves laying and building a foundation for continuous and long lasting relationship.

> *"Building sustainable market linkages for rural products: Industry's role, scope, opportunities and challenges"*

E-Chou Pal Concept

ITC Limited is one of India's leading diversified conglomerates. Traditionally a tobacco and cigarette producer, it has grown into a conglomerate dealing in hotels, packaging, agribusiness, information technology, and fast moving consumer goods (FMCGs). ITC initiated its e-Chou pal project in 2000 to streamline its dealings with Indian farmers.

This is a project on a massive scale that ultimately aims to cover every sixth Indian village. Each Chou pal covers around six villages and 36,000 villages have been covered to date in Madhya Pradesh, Uttar Pradesh, Maharashtra, Rajasthan, Karnataka, and Andhra Pradesh.

Objectives and Goals

E-Chou pal aims to provide Indian farmers ready access to crop-specific real-time information and customized knowledge in their native language. By doing so, ITC wants to improves the farmers' decision-making ability, thereby helping them to better align their farm output to the projected demand in Indian and international markets.

Technologies

Typically, the Chou pals use Pentium computers along with a dot matrix printer and a UPS (500VA). ITC had initially upgraded telephone exchanges by using RNS (RAX Network Synchronization) kits, but eventually in most of the e-Chou pals, wireless VSAT links have been installed by bypassing the exchanges.

Even with these improvements, the bandwidth often remains limited. Hence, e-Chou pals have started compensating by caching static content locally. ITC also uses a specially designed template for managing data combined with new imaging techniques in order to speed up downloads and to optimize bandwidth use. To overcome the problem of sporadic electricity, several kiosk computers use back-up batteries recharged with solar panels.

E-Chou pals deliver relevant technology in the hands of the farmers, which can improve the economic condition of the entire village.

E-Chou pal is one of the very few ICT projects in India that has effectively utilized e-commerce transactions for poverty alleviation. One of the key lessons is that ICT can reduce the number of middlemen involved between agriculture commodity producers and final consumers.

Another key factor is that very simple technology solutions are available to create networks in rural areas, which can function as virtual agricultural commodity market places.

Marketing in Transition

Marketing is the management process that identifies, anticipates and satisfies customer requirements profitably. In pre-modern economies, the predominance of small enterprise and there was monopoly and there was no recognition of marketing as a separate field of expertise. Marketing emerged as a separate technical field only in the late 19th century. In the present scenario, the changing needs and wants or taste and preferences among the customers leads to paradigm shift in marketing. This is due to changing attitude and behaviour of the customers, globalization, increasing purchasing power and changing life style of the customers.

Causes for Marketing in Transition;

- Globalization – Globalization has brought changes in technology, quality, service, work culture and undoubtedly fierce competition.
- Emerging Middle-Class Consumers – the increasing Purchasing Power of the Middle-Class consumers creates the MNC's to seek opportunity in the emerging market.

- Changing Lifestyle and attitude of Consumers – since there is a change in the customers lifestyle due to western influence the customer's needs and expectations has increased.
- Increasing literacy rate
- Children influence in buying decision making
- Changing perspective of rural marketing in India
- Increasing penetration of mass media
- Consumer awareness
- Information revolution
- An Enormous growth in international business.

Formation of marketing concepts and practices;

- 1905-the University of Pennsylvania offered a course in "The Marketing of Products"
- 1908-Harvard Business School opens
- 1940s-electronic computers developed
- 1980s-emergence of relationship marketing
- 1984- introduction of guerilla marketing
- 1995-2001-the Dot-com bubble temporarily re-defines the future of marketing
- 1996- identification of viral marketing.

Emerging New Marketing Practices

Due to increased competition the companies had necessity to enhance additional features to their products to promote the sale of their products. Many companies followed different marketing practices to attract their customers.

Winning concepts and marketing practices are;

- Relationship marketing
- Co-branding
- Viral Marketing
- Sachet Marketing
- Green marketing
- Rural marketing
- Destination marketing
- Online marketing
- Cause related marketing.

A transition from a product oriented approach to a resource oriented approach;

	Transaction marketing	*Relationship marketing*
Focus on	Obtaining new customers	Customer retention
Orientation to	Service features	Customer benefits
Timescale	shorts	long
Customer service	Little emphasis	High emphasis
Customer commitment	Limited	High
Customer contact	Limited	High
Quality concern	Primarily an operations The concern to all	

Now a days many companies are practicing the new marketing concepts and practices. Some of the examples are as follows.

Relationship marketing: The domain of relationship marketing extends into many areas of marketing and strategic decision making. In the phenomenon of cooperation and collaboration with customers becomes the dominant paradigm of marketing practices. Relationship marketing has the potential to emerge as the predominance perspective in the paradigm of marketing. In the fierce competitive market customer relationship management is emerging as the core marketing activity in companies. For that to maintain companies practices customer retention strategies and having good relation with the customers.

Example: HSBC bank sent greeting cards to the customers on their birthdays to have good relationship

Whirlpool do very good post sale service to the customers.

Sachet Marketing

In India, Unilever successfully markets Sunsil and Lux shampoo sachets sold in units of 2-4 dollar cents; Clinic All Clear anti-dandruff shampoo sachets at 2.5 rupees each; and 16 cent Rexona deodorant sticks.

Idhayam gingili oil available for Rs. 4/-package.

Green Marketing

It refers to the process of selling products and/or services based on their environmental benefits. Such a product or service may be environmentally friendly in itself or produced and/or packaged in an environmentally friendly way. Green marketing can be a very powerful marketing strategy though when it's done right. Nowadays all companies are trying to produce eco-friendly products. And many companies have got ISO 14001 awards and strive to get.

Examples are; ITC products, in the note books it is environment friendly notebook.

Changing Perspective of Rural Marketing in India

The great Indian rural market is characterized by huge untapped potential and opportunities. It is estimated that almost 70% of Indian consumers live in rural areas, which generate almost half of the national income.

The number of middle income households in rural India is growing to above 111 million by 2007. There are almost twice as many lower middle income households in rural areas as in the urban areas. A large number of corporate are excited about tapping the potential of rural areas. The recent entry of some corporate like Bharti, ITC, DCM shriram consolidated, EID parry and Amul etc. proved their fascination towards this sector. These corporates tried to develop successful model of integrating information-technology in rural transformation in a profitable way.

The tamilnadu based EID parry has developed an agro-portal www.indiaagrline.com to cater the specific needs of the rural farming community. It is an endeavor to catalyze e-commerce in agricultural and non-farms products by offering a network of partnerships. The content is available in local Tamil language. The Anand, Gurajat based Amuls DISK dairy information system KIOSK project is yet another milestone of integrating corporate sector and information technology. These kiosk serve valuable information related to dairying, breeding and rearing cattle. ITC e-choupal has emerged as one of the most ambitious project integrating information technology and corporate sector for rural transformation. ITC e-choupal network has already covered approximately 3.1 million farmers through 5050 choupal in 29,500 villages.

The company has ambitious plan to reach 1,00,000 villages covering 10 million farmers by 2010 with whopping approximately 1,000 crore. It is opening 5-6 e-choupals everyday in six different states of India.

Pepsi Rural Marketing

Pepsi company India has entered into rural market by having joint programme with the Punjab agriculture university in ludiana and Punjab agro industries corporation in chandigarh. The programme focuses on evolving agricultural practices to help Punjab farmers produce crops that would make Indian products internationally competitive. To cultivate a range of sweet oranges for its Tropicana range. Apart from that, they have given advertisement to attract the rural people with the celebrity of Amitabh Bachchan and star cricketer Sachin Tendulkar.

Coca-cola Rural Marketing

With the help of Isha foundation coca-cola released the CD of the coca-cola Tamil CSR film "Nesa Karangal" and also acknowledged and appreciated coca-cola's efforts in promoting social cohesiveness and sportsmanship with an aim to transform rural lives.

Advertisements to attract the rural customers are maasa-actress Rani Mukherji acted in this advertisement and says "masti ka chataka", Satis shah's maaza ad is also based on village background. Aamir khan acted in the advertisement which showcases a beautiful village background with the punch line "thanda ka matlab cocacola" and also ad title "soni kudi" targeted the villagers.

Destination Marketing

Destination marketing is all about selling the experience. To sell the experience is far more difficult. In destination marketing media plays a major role. Word of mouth plays a vital role in destination marketing, people love to discuss their tour, infact they feel proud in telling their experiences,they bring gifts for their close ones they show their photographs and purchases to their relatives and neighbours e.g. Kerala has implemented the destination marketing very successfully and emerged as the most acclaimed tourist destination of the country in the recent past. Because of this destination marketing Kerala has achieved remarkable success in generating revenue and employment in state through tourism. It is estimated nearly $100 million which generate the employment opportunity in Kerala.

In the recent past all the successful stories of destination marketing that is Malaysia, Goa, Kerala, Singapore etc.

Emergence of theme parks such as ADHISAYAM, MGM, BLACK THUNDER – all are examples of destination marketing.

Transition from Kirana stores to modern organized retail outlets:

Modern retailing in India is growing rapidly. Although it commands just 3% of the overall retail market share, changing demographics and consumer taste are driving the growth of more than 30% of the modern retail formats.

It is expected to grow another 9% in the year of 2010. India is more attractive than ever to global retailers.

Major Players in India are;

Pantaloon retail India limited or future group, RPG group, Tata group, K.Raheja Corp. group of companies, RRL (Reliance retail limited), A.B.Birla group, Gati, Calvin Klein, Murjani group, Disney artist stores, Vishal group (Vishal Megamart)

Foreign players in India are;

Wal-mart stores, Carrefour, Tesco, Rosy blue group, LVMH Group, Metro.

Transition in Segmentation

Transition from demographic based segmentation to psychographic based segmentation, since 1950's market segmentation has been referred to as a process of identifying groups of individuals who are similar in attitudes etc. and the segmentation is of demographic segmentation after 1970s it is psychographic segmentation, know about the customer taste and preferences and collect at the real time point of purchase data. And now it is need based segmentation is using for different marketing functions like advertising and new product development.

Cause Related Marketing

Cause related marketing is practiced on the rationale that consumers are human beings are kind hearted. The customer pay the amount with some satisfaction that the specific amount is to for relevant social cause.

Example

A sanitary napkin brand "whisper" announced a contribution o Re.1 on every pack of sales for blind relief society. This helps in improving whisper's market share. HLL announced a contribution of Rs. 0.50 on the sale of each of its brand of lifebuoy brand soap to a diarrhea project.

Co-branding

Co-branding is when two companies form an alliance to work together, creating marketing synergy. This co-branding is innovative in the marketing practices.

Examples:

- Andhra bank and ICFAI university are using the strategy of co-branding.
- Andhra bank and Hindustan petroleum also launched their co-branded card
- SBI card and LG electronics India launched the LG-SBI card. This is the country's first co-branded credit card for the consumer appliances industry and can be used at more than 2 lakh outlets in India.
- Idea cellular and HDFC Bank launched two co-branded cards providing multiple benefits to customers of both.
- Pillsbury Brownies with Nestle Chocolate
- Dell Computers with Intel Processors

Online Marketing

Internet marketing, also referred to as online marketing, Internet advertising, or eMarketing, is the marketing of products or services over the Internet. Internet marketing also includes management of digital customer data and electronic customer relationship management (E-CRM) systems.

Samsung Marketing Practices

Viral Marketing, Interactive Marketing: Samsung created its "Fun Club" as a way to engage with Samsung mobile phone owners to help them get the most from their phones. Samsung provides content such as games, ringers, and wallpapers that are designed specifically for Samsung mobile phone models.

Hearing about new mobile content is one of the benefits of joining the "Fun Club." Samsung was looking for a new way to use rich multimedia to promote the game, Skipping Stone, to its customers. Samsung engaged Enpocket to create a mobile marketing campaign promoting Skipping Stone using the graphically rich MMS channel.

In the present competitive scenario, there should be transition in marketing practices in order to survive in the market. Since "change in the only thing which never change" in the world, companies have to adapt themselves according to the changing environment.

The best emerging practices in the corporate world is win-win concept to be the leader in the market.

The Imperative of Internal Marketing

People are the very essence of an organization. All the technological up gradation, state of the art facilities, et al, can come to a naught if all the employees in the company are not performing optimally. It is important for employees to be engaged as much to be developed, so that their productivity is aligned with the organizational requirements. Companies need to find out indigenous ways to challenge employees so as to keep them engaged.

The Internal Marketing concept was first proposed in the mid 1970's as a way of achieving service quality – a major problem in the services area. Its basic premise was 'to have satisfied customers, the firm must also have satisfied employs' and that this could be best achieved by treating employees as customers, i.e. by applying the principles of marketing to job design and employee motivation. Since then, the concept has seen a number of major developments and its application is no longer confined to the services area. It has been shown that any type of organization can use Internal Marketing to facilitate the implementation of it external marketing strategy or any other organizational strategies.

Despite the rapidly growing literature on Internal Marketing, relatively few organizations actually apply the concept in practice. One of the main problems contributing to this is that there does not exist, a single unified concept of what is meant by Internal Marketing. However, Internal Marketing can be holistically defined as "Internal marketing is a planned effort using a marketing-like approach directed at motivating employees, for implementing and integrating organizational strategies towards customer orientation".

Literature Review

Pete Naude opines that Internal Marketing orientation is an area within the broader market orientation that remains relatively under-researched. It shows how general managers, department managers and individuals can use internal marketing to increase employee involvement in reaching decisions, making commitments and taking action. David Ballantyne explores the structural relationships through which internal marketing can create value for an organisation, its customers and its employees. It is argued that internal marketing requires a relationship-mediated approach, where planned phases of learning activity in volunteer groups generate new internally valid knowledge critical to the improvement of external market performance.

Marelise Pitt, Johan Bruwer, Deon Nel and Paul Berthon state that internal marketing is a critical issue facing marketing professions, human resources and other executives. They argue that if poor service is provided between employees it is unlikely that good service will ultimately be provided to the external customer. Internal marketing (IM) focuses on acquiring and retaining customer-oriented employees. Critics of internal marketing claim that the term is simply a synonym for good human resources management. The concepts of internal marketing and human resource effectiveness (HRE), at both a strategic and technical level, are considered and suitable measures identified.

Gould states that when information is integrated with skills, understanding and experience, it becomes knowledge which the organization can use to its advantage. His research illustrates the importance of communication processes alongside business processes to achieve continuing improvement. He concludes that many businesses should give serious consideration to the idea that HR and marketing should be combined.

Nigel F. Piercy observes that while customer satisfaction measurement is currently one of the commonest prescriptions in both the marketing and management literatures, little attention has been paid to the effects of customer satisfaction measurement, particularly in terms of the impact on the internal market, i.e. the employees and managers inside the organization.

Gilbert D. Harrell & Matthew in their study, Marketing services to satisfy internal customers, conclude that staff unit managers in a range of disciplines who want to serve internal publics better can effectively market their services internally by understanding and responding to internal decision processes and expectations.

Walter E. Greene, Gary D. Walls& Larry J. Schrest in their article in Journal of Services Marketing, declare that the firms that do not or will not embrace the issues of internal marketing and incorporate those ingredients into their strategic marketing plan will see their market share and profit base erode. The article titled, Building brand values through Internal Marketing, shows that quality of service is central to building brand differentiation within industries that do not produce tangible products.

Internal marketing is an effective way of drawing attention to service, and encouraging staff in various ways to give the best of themselves. A paper titled, Internal brand building and structuration: the role of leadership, by Christine Vallaster & Leslie de Chernatony provides empirical insights about how change is brought about during internal brand building.

Carmel Herington, Lester W. Johnson& Don Scott have found that competitive advantage can be attained through development of a relationship-building culture which includes building relationships inside the organization as well as customer relationships. In fact, successful customer relationships rely on successful internal relationships.

Timothy W. Aurand, Linda Gorchels & Terrence R. Bishop in the, Journal of Product & Brand Management, have found that employees seem to have a more positive attitude toward the brand and are more likely to incorporate this image into their work activities when there is some degree of HR involvement in the internal branding process.

Robert E. Morgan in their study Business agility and internal marketing, have found that fundamentally, the same principles which are used to market solutions to the organisation's external customers can be employed to better segment, target and position the Information Service solutions to the internal customer base.

Need For Further Research

- Many enterprises are continually in some form of transformation-mergers, alliances, downsizing and rightsizing generating the need for constant communication.
- Some enterprises may rename themselves as a result and this rebranding requires communication to all stakeholders including employees.
- More companies are empowering staff to take on increased focus in the customer relationship. This needs full involvement, immersion and training in brand values.
- There is less reciprocal loyalty between employer and employee; the employee's time becomes transactional.The "internal" brand can be a way to bind the two parties together with shared goals and values.
- New ways of working require organizations and staff to constantly learn new skills and sometimes these are acquired through alliances. Building a learning company will be an important future consideration. Internal brand values can be an umbrella for this effort.

However, to date, there has been a considerable knowledge gap about the components of Internal Marketing. To reinforce this point, a study by Intercommunic reported in Marketing week showed that 85% of companies did not even have a human resources or marketing budget for internal promotions. It is commonly believed that sole role of marketing is to sell products and services outwardly to customers. In fact, the first and most urgent job of marketing is often to sell inwardly toward a company's people. For, it is only when the people of the company fully understand and are committed to the value proposition of the organization and its brands that external marketing can reach its full potential.

" Marketing is absolutely critical to being internally successful,"

Relationship Marketing-An Overview

Marketing is continually evolving in response to the changing environment. New strategies, techniques and tools for marketing managers are constantly being developed. Marketing has also moved away from the original idea of bringing about mutually satisfying benefits or exchanges. Consumers have responded to these changes and have become more sophisticated in their demand and expectations. Service marketing is a growing specialty, and concepts such as internal marketing have been developed with in the services sector, are now widely recognized to be highly relevant to all organizations.

Relationship marketing goes a step further. Organizations are urged to focus not only on their relationship with customers external and internal but with other elements within the industry and society. An emphasis to it is not on bringing about exchange processes but on building relationships.

The traditional perspective of marketing fails to bring the three critical areas such as marketing orientation, customer service and quality into closer alignment. Thus the relationship-marketing concept emerged as a new paradigm integrating customer service and quality with a market orientation.

Relationship Marketing-Definition

Relationship marketing is nothing but an effort directed at creating loyal customers. Philip Kotler defined relationship marketing as." The process of creating, maintaining and enhancing value-laden relationship with valued customers, distributors, dealers and suppliers by promising and consistently delivering high quality products, good services and fair prices". Marketing is shifting from trying to maximize the profit on individual transactions rather than to building mutually beneficial relationship with consumers and other parties.

Evolution

The concept of relationship marketing was first introduced by Franklin Berry (1983) in a service context to describe a long-term approach to marketing. Since then it has attracted considerable attention from both the practitioners and researchers.

In the 1950's marketing interest was primarily focused on consumer goods. In the 1960's increased attention was placed on industrial markets, while in 1970's considerable academic effort was placed on the area of non profit or societal marketing.

In the 1980's attention started to be directed at the services sector, an area of marketing that had received remarkably little attention in view of its importance in the overall economy. In the 1990's the marketing concept was shifted to relationship marketing.

Key Linkages in Relationship Marketing

Marketing orientation, quality and Customer service are the three basic elements in Relationship marketing. The linkage between these three factors will help to achieve a total customer satisfaction and long-term relationship.

As quality, customer service and market orientation are the three elements in relationship marketing, it is necessary to find the role of each factor in relationship marketing.

Role of Customer Service

Historically customer service has been seen from a narrow perspective where the primary role of the customer service is concerned with getting the right products at the right place at right time and the focus is much on distributors and logistics view points.

The new vision of customer service places it in a much broader context as a multi–dimensional issue with an impact on relationships with specific target groups across a broad range of company activities.

It is concerned with building of financial bonds (in which marketers offer pricing as an incentive to encourage customers to do more and more business with the firm), social bonds (which offer personalized service delivery) and structural bonds (which emphasize provision of quality services that are valuable the clients and not readily available with competitors which helps the customers to resist the temptation from the competitors) with customers and the other markets or groups to ensure long term relationships of mutual advantage.

Role of Quality

The role of quality is also undergoing review. The typical approach of the quality is changing from one of final inspection of outputs to one of assessing whether critical processes are in control and giving guidance to others in the techniques involved. Total Quality Management (TQM) programme is designed to constantly improve the quality of products, services and marketing processes. The idea of the total quality across all functions focuses the scope of quality on relationship between the firm and its customers, suppliers and other key elements on an ongoing basis.

Role of Marketing Orientation

Traditionally marketing has been seen as a process of perceiving, understanding, stimulating and satisfying the needs of specially selected target markets by channeling an organizations resources to meet those needs. It is concerned with the dynamic inter-relationship between a company's products and services, the customers need and want and the activities of the company. The marketing frame work mainly consists of marketing mix, market forces and the marketing process.

Relationship marketing places emphasis on building and maintaining a good workforce. Service quality depends to a very great extent on people, and developing long-term relationships with internal customers is just as important as building relationship with external ones.

Relationship Marketing-A Broader View

Traditionally marketing has been from the perspective of managing relationship with customer groups. However, a much broader viewpoint is appropriate in relationship marketing. Generally this can be done through two ways, viz:

1. By considering a wider range of markets; and
2. By expanding the marketing mix.

Widening the Markets

In traditional form of marketing, managing relationships with customer groups and new customers was given more importance than the existing ones. Later on companies realized the long-term advantage they would get by maintaining and enhancing the relationship with their existing customers. For providing quality products and best services, it is necessary to consider a wider range of markets. So in addition to formulating marketing activity directed at existing and potential customers companies are now considering other markets which includes:

a) *Supplier market:* The relationship between an organization and its suppliers is undergoing some fundamental changes mainly under the influence of Japanese. The old adversarial relationship where a company tried to squeeze its suppliers to its own advantage, is giving away to a relationship based much more on partnership and collaboration.

b) *Recruitment market:* The key resource for business (and other) organizations is no longer capital or raw materials but skilled people, a vital, perhaps the most vital element in customer service delivery. Companies maintain a good relationship with these markets, which assures a regular supply of skilled labour.

c) *Referral markets:* The best marketing is that which is carried out by your customer, that is why the customer loyalty ladder and the creation of advocates is important. But existing customers are not the only sources of referral. Referral markets go under many names intermediaries, connectors, multipliers, agencies and so on.

d) *Influence markets:* Influence markets tend to vary according to the type of industry or industry sector that an organization belongs to. Companies involved in selling infrastructure we items will place Government departments and regulatory bodies high on the list of markets they may address. Most companies also place the financial community, in its various forms-brokers, analysts, and financial journalists and so on in influence category.

e) *Internal markets:* Internal marketing involves two main concepts; the first is that every employee and every department in an organization is both an internal customer and an internal supplier. Specially formulated internal marketing programmes to communicate, train and motivate internal market members are very important if the relationship is to be a positive one. Service quality depends to a great extent on people, and developing long-term relationships with the internal customers is just as important as building relationships with external ones.

The optimal operation of the organization is ensured when every individual and department provide and receive excellent service.

Expanded Marketing Mix

While considering relationship marketing across different sectors, we need to identify more marketing mix elements, which are generic and have applicability to all areas of marketing.

The elements, which offer the customers same form of value satisfaction can be included in the marketing mix. So three more elements have been included in marketing mix, i.e.

People-The employee of the organization whom they consider as their greatest assets and can be categorized into contractors, modifiers, influences and isolated.

Processes-Which involves the procedures, task schedules, mechanisms, activities and routines by which a product or service is delivered ton the customer.

Provision of customer services-Which is considered as a crucial element in the marketing mix and seen in the content of the supply marketing channel, i.e., service is providing not only to its immediate customers and suppliers but also to its ultimate consumers and even the supplier's suppliers.

Integrating Relationship Marketing in a Firm

Relationship marketing implies a consideration of not just better relationships with customer markets, but also the development and enhancement of the relationship with other markets.

There is no need for a separate marketing plan for each market. But the companies must develop some strategies to address each of these markets.

The strategies must be deeply ingrained and understood by all staff within the organization. The following are the steps required for establishing relationship marketing in a company.

1. Identify key customers for the relationship marketing. The company can choose five to ten large customers and designate them for relationship marketing. Additional customers can be added who show exceptional growth.
2. Assign a skilled relationship manager to each key customer. The sales person servicing the customer should receive training in relationship marketing.
3. Develop a clear job description to relationship managers.
4. Appoint an overall manager.

Advantages of Relationship Marketing

Compared with other marketing concepts Relationship Marketing has got a lot of advantages. This marketing strategy ensures a better relationship with customers and other stakeholders of the organization. If relationship marketing is adopted in an organization, it will ensure a lower amortized cost for acquiring new customers.

Moreover, the customers will become less price sensitive. Later on they will become the word of mouth advertisers and referrals for the company. Relationship marketing ensures improved employee as well as customer satisfaction and thus retained them for a long–term. There will be a healthy relationship with suppliers if relationship marketing is practiced.

A good relation with government and other regulatory bodies is also visualized under relationship marketing.

6

Future of E-Marketing

Electronic market is relatively new concept and has crept into business vocabulary around 1970s. Electronic commerce denote the seamless application of information and communication technology from its point of origin to its end point along the entire value chain of business processes conducted electronically and designed to enable the accomplishment of a business goal. These processes may be partial or complete and may encompass B2B as well as B2C and C2B transaction (Wigand, 1997).

The E-commerce further leads to the emergence of the "market space"-a virtual world of information paralleling the real marketplace of goods and services-enables marketers to manage content, context, and infrastructure in new and different ways, thereby providing novel sources of competitive advantage. With electronic marketing one can think for business across the globe that was not possible earlier. Traditional way of market segmentation with an internet audience may not be fruitful. In electronic marketing, segmentation can be done effectively by considering two key dimensions i.e. potential value of the segment to the particular market sector and comparative attractiveness of the channel to the customer (Hymas, 2001).

The 4Ps frame work of traditional product marketing is not appropriate for electronic marketing due to unavailability of demographics and psychographics of electronic customers. Booms and Bitner (1981) considered 7Ps frame work for electronic Marketing. All most all the product can be made available for customer via electronic marketing but few product categories like Software, music, reports, games, videos etc., products can be delivered online at the same time, for other products it can be delivered later at the doorstep of the customers. It was initially believed that the Internet could benefit organizations because of the decreased costs involved with distribution, hence improving profit margins if they chose not to pass these benefits on to customers. But there are some electronic marketers like Amazon.com, have also contributed to price competition, effectively forcing the competitors to reduce the price. But same time Bromage (2001) argued that online customers buy online for convenience rather than for price advantages.

Regarding place, electronic marketing offers potential to shift from a non-virtual marketplace to a market-space instead, incorporating virtual transaction/distribution spaces. Websites have the potential to give information, to entertain and be interactive in their communication. Internet can take over some of the activities offered by the personal sales person (e.g. accepting purchase orders), but some of the activities undertaken by sales representatives cannot be replaced by technology.

The Internet allows organizations to make their service delivery system flexible. Because of the lack of physical proximity in electronic marketing, marketers make use of "virtual evidence" in the virtual environment. Lack of the personal interface may result in customer distrust of first-time interaction with electronic channels. It is also more difficult for marketers to build a relationship with customers whom they never see (Dobie et al., 2001); in such a situation trust (to reduce transaction cost) can be generated by other means, such as communication messages and brands.

Electronic marketing proved its effectiveness by reducing the time of shopping and made it easy for the people to shop. Most of the business houses adopted electronic marketing so far and many more are in pipe line.Although electronic marketing has proved its success in facilitating communication and exchange but still it has long way to travel.

E-Commerce and its Application in Indian Industries

Many international business researchers are of the opinion that increased globalization of markets and increasing international competition imply that firms in all nations will face similar, if not identical, competitive environments. In India due to liberalization of economy, the companies are facing acute competition in the international markets. In the new millennium, the internet-based way of doing business has certainly changed many industries and has influenced many customers and businesses. It has changed the shapes of whole set of industries and markets and has already had a great impact on consumers and is all set to have a very exciting future. It has improved services, reduce costs, open new channels and transform the competitive landscape. T

his paper is divided into two parts. First part deals with how E-Business is changing business environment. Second part of the paper is designed to examine the application of E-Commerce in selected Indian industries. For the purpose of the study, the e-business applications are divided into three categories:

- E – Commerce
- E – Procurement
- E – Collaboration.

E-commerce

E-Commerce, which primarily refers to buying, selling, marketing and servicing of products or services over internet. Business on the net is classified into B2B (Business to Business), B2C (Business to Consumer) and C2C (Consumer to Consumer).B2B transactions are largely between industrial manufacturers, partners, and retailers or between companies.B2C transactions take place directly between business establishments and consumers. B2B sites are essentially the net meeting points for buyers and sellers of the industrial world. They serve a limited number of customers.

The Turnover would be many times that of the most B2C sites and most importantly they make profits. B2C sites are offering low value items CDs, Cassettes, Food, Toys, Flowers, and Cards etc. because no complicated logistics are involved.

C2C sites don't form a very high portion of web-based commerce. Most visible examples are the auction sites. Basically, if some one has something to sell, then he gets it listed at an auction sites and others can bid for it.

E-procurement

The Internet offers a natural platform to facilitate efficient procurement as numerous buyers and sellers find each other and transact according to some pre-specified protocols. The following are the procurement strategies available for a manufacturer.

- Strategic Partnership
- Online Search Strategy
- Combined Strategy.

1. *Strategic Partnership:* Strategic partnership strategy is to develop a long-term supply relationship with a specific supplier.
2. *Online Search Strategy:* Online Search Strategy is to shop online for a better price.
3. *Combined Strategy:* The combined strategy is to combine both – sign a long-term purchase contract with a supplier up to a certain level, but if necessary additional quantity may be purchased online.

E-collaboration

We define e-collaboration as business-to-business interactions facilitated by the Internet. These include information sharing and integration, decision sharing, process sharing and resource sharing. There are many new cases that examine different elements of collaboration from information sharing and integration to process and resource sharing.

E-commerce Application in Banking Industry

New information technologies and emerging business forces have triggered a new wave of financial innovation – electronic banking (e-banking). The banking and financial industry is transforming itself in unpredictable ways (Crane and Bodie 1996), powered in an important way by advances in information technology (Holland and Westwood 2001).

Since the 1980s, commercial banking has continuously innovated through technology-enhanced products and services, such as multi-function ATM, tele-banking, electronic transfers and electronic cash cards. Over the past decade, the Internet has clearly played a critical role in providing online services and giving rise to a completely new channel. In the internet age, the extension of commercial banking to the cyberspace is an inevitable development (Liao and Cheung 2003).

E-banking creates unprecedented opportunities for the banks in the ways they organize financial product development, delivery and marketing via the internet. While it offers new opportunities to banks, it also poses many challenges such as the innovation of IT applications, the blurring of market boundaries, the breaching of industrial barriers, the entrance of new competitors and the emergence of new business models. Now the speed and scale of the challenge are rapidly increasing with the pervasiveness of the internet and the extension of information economy (Holland and Westwood 2001).

Products Offered: All of the major banks in India have an internet presence offering a range of products directly to consumers by way of proprietary internet sites.

While the initial focus of the banks has been in the retail-banking sector, there is a growing range of small to medium enterprise ("SME") and corporate banking products and services being offered. The products available include

Funds Transfer and Payment Systems: The major banks offer a range of online financial services including;

(i) Payment of bills;

(ii) Transfer of funds;

(iii) Remittances;

(iv) Applications for letters of credit; and

(v) Settlement through the MAS Electronic Payment System.

B2B E-Commerce: At least one of the major commercial banks offers an integrated B2B e-commerce product directly through its website, involving product selection, purchase order, invoice generation, and payment. However, integrated B2B products and services are not as yet generally available directly from the banks.

Securities Placement and Underwriting/Capital Markets Activities: Most commercial banks offer securities services such as online payment for shares and subscriptions for initial public offerings directly though their websites. However, more sophisticated online brokering services are generally only available through the banks' share-broker subsidiaries.

Securities Trading: A full range of online securities services are provided by the specialist securities subsidiaries of the major commercial banks including online trading.

Retail Banking: All of the major commercial banks have established websites for retail services. Typically such sites will offer the following services:

(i) a full range of personal account services, including foreign currency accounts;

(ii) funds transfers;

(iii) Bill payments;

(iv) Credit card services;

(v) Investment services; and

(vi) Online application for loan services including
  (*a*) Car loans;
  (*b*) Renovation loans;
  (*c*) Home loans; and
  (*d*) Personal credit lines.

E-Commerce has provided the platform that enables the implementation of core banking solutions (CBS). Today all the major banks have gone on to implement CBS. And with time being a premium among bank customers, banks have been ideating and developing newer modes of delivering banking services. Today there is a whole plethora of such platforms available ranging from the ATM to the mobile.

Banks like State Bank of India and its associates are recording over 100,000 transactions on a daily basis through their 5,000 plus network of ATMs. Incidentally the profile and usage pattern of ATMs in India matches that of ATMs abroad with an overwhelming (more than 80%) being used for cash withdrawal. Today with over 20,000 ATMs, India is recording one of the fastest growth in terms of ATM proliferation, though the per capita availability of ATMs doesn't compare anywhere to markets like Japan or the US.

With most banks now providing Internet banking facility, bankers say that customers are using the bank for a variety of purposes. One commonly used service being booking of rail tickets. Bankers also say that customers are using bank networks for online shopping. Most of the online banking channels are linked to major retailers. Estimates also indicate that today over 40% of the share transactions are being put through the internet.

E-commerce Application in Travel Industry

In India e-commerce is being driven by the growing online travel industry and online travel bookings have increased substantially after the entry of low cost carriers. Currently, online travel industry is contributing 50% to the revenue generated by e-commerce in India. To boot, online travel industry is growing at 125% (compounded annual growth rate) annually. Generating revenues of around $300-500 million (Rs.1,350-2,250 crore) currently, the size of the online travel industry is around 2% of the entire travel industry. Online travel industry is expected to become a $2 billion industry by 2008. In India, it is basically low cost carriers like Air Deccan and the Railways, which have significantly led to increased use of e-commerce. However airline industry is still exploring the advantages of e-commerce. Currently e-commerce is being used mostly for e-ticketing among the domestic airlines though e-ticketing penetration in India is as low as 17% against the world average of 49% and 42% in Asia Pacific. But according to the UN's International Telecommunication Union, about 400 million travellers worldwide are expected to book tickets on-line this fiscal.

Air Deccan launched its operations with a 100% web enabled ticketing service and in no time became India's largest e-commerce site, with Rs.30 million worth transactions per day. Electronic ticketing now accounts for 35%-40% of tickets sold by Air Deccan. E-ticketing not only make tickets more accessible for travellers 24/7 but also eliminates the need to invest in ticketing offices and other related infrastructure reducing operational costs. Also travellers could avoid the long queues and save the service charges payable to travel agents.

Being a 100% e-ticket enabled airline, Kingfisher not only offers e-ticketing but also electronic check-in, wherein after printing the boarding card on-line the customer can use web-enabled check-in on the airline's website and board the plane directly passing through only mandatory security check at the airport. One of the biggest advantage of e-ticketing is that one can neither lose an e-ticket nor destroy it by leaving it accidentally in the pocket. Also e-ticketing environment offers much better degree of connectivity and reachability.

E-commerce Application in Government

India is now getting used to e-tendering. The Andhra Pradesh government's initiative is now a model for other states. It began in the year 2002 in Andhra Pradesh State government projects had been stalled by delays in awarding tenders. Cartels regularly cornered the bulk of government contracts and bids were tampered with after closure. For N.Chandrababu Naidu, the tech-savy chief minister in a hurry, this was unacceptable. He needed a way around the mess and predictably by use of technology. Now, 90% of all the tenders in Andhra Pradesh are completed online. Last year, orders worth Rs.15,000 crore were placed. While it earlier took anywhere between 90 and 135 days to finalise a tender, today it takes only 35 days. Northern Railway is planning to implement E-Procurement (E-Works contracts) System from December 2006.

Globally, e-commerce growth has been led by the popularity of online shopping portals like amazon.com and ebay.com but in India that has not been the case. It is mainly driven by the online travel industry and banking sector. For instance, 29% of Indian Internet users book airline tickets online and the figure is expected to touch 46% next year. Online rail ticket booking stands at 39% of the total bookings. As far as banking is concerned, there are 4.6 million online banking users in India. This figure is expected to go up to over 16 million by 2007-08 that will include both internet and mobile banking users.

According to the Internet and Mobile Association of India (IAMAI), the e-commerce industry in India is expected to grow to a size of Rs.2,300 crore by 2007 against the Rs.1,200 crore. The total number of internet users which right now is 38.5 million is expected to reach 100 million by 2008.

E-Business and Supply Chain Management- A New Methodological Approach

Supply Chain Management has generated substantial interest in recent years for a number of reasons. Managers in many industries now realize that actions taken by one member of the chain can influence the profitability of all others in the chain. Many international business researchers are of the opinion that increased globalisation of markets and increasing international competition imply that firms in all nations will face similar, if not identical, competitive environments. In India due to liberalisation of economy, the companies are facing acute competition in the international markets. Many manufacturing companies are forced to improve the quality of their products and reduce their manufacturing costs.

Research in Supply Chain Management

Research in Supply chain management has identified twelve distinct management areas that are associated with the subject. Each area represents a supply chain issue facing the firm. For each area, we provide a brief description of the basin content and refer the reader to a few articles that apply. The twelve categories are,

- Location
- Transportation and logistics
- Outsourcing and logistics alliances
- Sourcing and supplier management
- Marketing and channel restructuring
- Inventory and forecasting
- Service and after sales support
- Reverse logistics and green issues

- Product design and new product introduction
- Information and electronic mediated environment
- Metrics and incentives
- Global issues.

1. *Location:* Of the twelve categories, decisions in this area have perhaps the longest time horizon. Decisions at this level set the physical structure of the supply chain and thus create constraints for more tactical decisions such as transportation, logistics and inventory planning. Engineering tools such, as mathematical models of facility location and geographic information systems are very useful in sorting the location choices.
2. *Transportation and logistics:* It includes all issues related to the physical flow of goods through the supply chain, including transportation, warehousing and material handling. This category addresses many of important choices related to transportation management including vehicle routing, dynamic fleet management with global positioning systems and merge-in-transit.
3. *Outsourcing and logistics alliances:* It examines the supply chain impact of outsourcing logistics services. With the rapid growth in third party logistics providers, there is a large and expanding group of technologies and services to be examined. These include fascinating initiatives such as supplier hubs managed by third parties.
4. *Sourcing and Supplier management:* This category addresses the issue of outsourcing components and the management of the suppliers who provide them. Make/buy decisions fall into this category. These decisions should involve top managers and strategic thinkers because they can literally define the future of the firm. For example, IBM to outsource its PC operating software to Microsoft and its central processing unit to Intel.
5. *Marketing and Channel restructuring:* It includes critical decisions related to getting the products from a firm's factories all the way into the customer's hands. As with facility location, these decisions impact the supply chain structure as well as define an interface with marketing.
6. *Inventory and forecasting:* It includes techniques for ongoing inventory management and demand forecasting. Industrial

engineers and operation managers have employed statistical models for forecasting and inventory planning. Stochastic inventory models can identify the potential cost savings from sharing information with supply chain partners, but more complex models are required to coordinate multiple locations.

7. *Service and after sales support:* This category covers the important issue of providing service and service parts. Some leading firms, such as Saturn and Caterpillar, build their reputations in this area, and this area and this capability generates significant sales.
8. *Reverse logistics and green issues:* This area examines both reverse logistics issues of product returns and environmental impact issues. Growing regulatory pressures in many countries are forcing managers to consider the most efficient and environment friendly way to deal with product recovery. Product recovery includes the handling of all used and discarded products, components and materials.
9. *Product design and new product introduction:* It deals with design issues for mass customisation, delayed differentiation, modularity and other issues for new product introduction. Traditionally, products destined for world markets would be customized at the factory to suit local market tastes. The customized product is desirable and managing worldwide. Thus if the French version selling well, but the German version is not, German products can be quickly shipped to France and customized for the French market.
10. *Information and electronic mediated environments:* This category addresses the impact of information technology to reduce inventory and the rapidly expanding area of electronic commerce. It focuses attention on integrative ERP software such as SAP and Oracle as well as supply chain offerings such as Manugistics, i2's Rhythm and Peoplesoft's Red pepper.
11. *Metrics and Incentives:* It refers to the measurement of both engineering and organisational processes and the related economic motivations. Several recent articles concentrate on the link between performance management and supply chain management.
12. *Global issues:* It considers the issues beyond local country specific operating environments to encompass issues related to cross-border distribution and sourcing. For example, currency

exchange rates, duties and taxes, freight forwarding, customs issues, government regulation and country comparisons are all included.

Supply chain management is indeed a large and growing field for both engineers and managers. Nearly all major manufacturing consulting firms have developed large practices in the supply chain field and the number of books and academic research papers in the field is growing rapidly. In fact, each of the twelve areas covered in our treatment of supply chains are important in themselves. Finally, the Internet continues to change many fundamental assumptions about business, pushing managers to continue to evolve their supply chain practices or find themselves driven out of the market.

Customer Relationship Management

We all know the meaning of customer, relationship & management, but by compiling these three words it is defined as C.R.M., which is a tool used by businesses in order to increase profitability, revenue & also customer satisfaction by segmenting the customers, then finding customer satisfying behaviour, and also implementing the process to satisfy the customers. C.R.M. technology should have the potential to seek the customer's satisfaction and which increases customer access and leads to deep and strong interactions. Take it like this: we all live in a society and we all are surrounded by some relationships. But, if these are having some grievances then our performance will be hindered.

Evolution of C.R.M.

With the very emergence of needs C.R.M. took birth and with the passage of time it has been coloured as per the market requirements.

1. *Traditional marketing:-*C.R.M. took birth, when people started exchanging goods to satisfy their needs and wants. This was the time of barter system.
2. *Mass marketing:-*At this time barter system became obsolete and industrial revolution took place and sellers were engaged in mass production, mass distribution. At this time production was given emphasis.
3. *Value-based marketing:-*At this time producers lay emphasis on offering better value to customers money by improving quality of products and services offered to customers.
4. *Relationship marketing:-*The scenario changed and producers started feeling the importance of customers and tried to build

long-term relations either by providing free gifts, or various services like guarantees etc. This was the time of customer-centred marketing.

5. *Marketing on web:-*This is also known as E-SHOPPING and is itself diversified in its nature. Doing just few clicks of mouse purchase variety and number of products. This is the most convenient and comfortable way of shopping. Many co. like Amazon, embay are the best-suited examples.
6. *Customized marketing:-*With the advancement in technologies this very advancement in marketing has become possible. Software database is used for this. Software databases help in providing & storing customers' information. Softwares like:- Sap, Siebel, Broadvison, Chordiant, Onyx, Selligent, Silknet, Lucent, Inference, IBM, Goldmine etc. are being used by the companies. Aircraft parts distributor Aviall, consumer product giant Kimberly-Clark, Lakme, Mattel's 'My Design Barbie', Dell computers, Nike shoes, electronic connector manufacturer Molex, and McDonald's are enhancing their sales, revenue and customer's loyalty with the implementation of this technology. Harvard business review depicts that by the end of 2010 almost 30% of U.S. commercial activity will involve customized marketing.

Types of C.R.M.

C.R.M. allows a company to address all types of customers at different points in its life and choose the market program that best fits a customer's attitude.

There are basically four types of C.R.M.:-

1. *Win back customers:-*This is the way of convincing the costumers to stay with the company at that point of time when they discontinue with the company. Coke, Pepsi and others soft drinks are the best-suited examples of this type.
2. *Prospecting:-*This is an effort to win new, first time customers. In this company needs to segment the market which helps organization to affectively target the offer.
3. *Loyalty:-*This is an effort in which company tries to prevent customers to leave the company. It is very difficult to gain it accurately. It uses two elements:-
   (a) *Value based segmentation:-*it helps in determining that how much company is willing to invest in retaining its customer's loyalty.

(b) *Need based segmentation:*-after determining its investment power, company can determine its customer loyalty program means either to use relationship marketing or marketing on the web or customized marketing.

4. *Cross sell/Up sell:*-In this company provides value addition in its product. In cross sell after getting customer data the value means offer to be provided is considered. And in up selling the product or service offered is an enhanced one means innovated.

Importance of Retaining Customers

Strong bonds provide that loyalty that turns out to be everlasting. Helps in recovering customer acquisition cost and also benefits by 'word of mouth' as it is more fruitful than television, direct mail and press put together. Harvard research also depicts that 5% increase in customer retention increases NPR by 20%-120%.

Why C.R.M.

Despite having best manufacturing capabilities, best marketing approach, best business strategy the organizations use C.R.M. WHY? Because each and every tool or strategy of a business can be copied by anyone but one's soft skills, one's way of handling relations can't ever be copied by anyone.

Because of all these advantages it is being use by many co. like Lakme employed 'Computer Touch Screen', Ponds Institute has a customer response center, HLL-Surf received 'Open Customer Feedback' and Surf-Excel is the result of that, Apollo Tyres offered 'Dia-a-Tyre, Asian paints is also providing home solutions. In short the CRM is a process enabled by technology to know your customers well and use the database to retain profitable relationship with high life time value customers. Retention of good customers and maximizing revenue through them is at core of CRM.

E-Commerce: Challenges and Opportunities

E-commerce as anything that involves an online transaction. This can range from ordering online, through online delivery of paid content, to financial transactions such as movement of money between bank accounts.

This paper has analysed some of the challenges and opportunities of e-commerce.

Elizabeth Goldsmith and others (2000) reported that the general category of e-commerce can be broken down into two parts:

1. E-merchandise: selling goods and services electronically and moving items through distribution channels, for example through Internet shopping for groceries, tickets, music, clothes, hardware, travel, books, flowers or gifts.
2. E-finance: banking, debit cards, smart cards, banking machines, telephone and Internet banking, insurance, financial services and mortgages on-line (Elizabeth Goldsmith and others, 2000).

Farooq Ahmed (2001) reported that the enormous flexibility of the internet has made possible what is popularly called e-commerce which has made inroads in the traditional methods of business management. All the facets the business tradition with which we are accustomed in physical environment can be now executed over the internet including online advertising, online ordering, publishing, banking, investment, auction and professional services. E commerce involves conducting business using modern communication instruments: telephone, fax, e-payment, money transfer systems, e-data interchange and the internet. The WTO has recognized that commercial transactions can be broken into 3 stages. 'The advertising and searching stage, the ordering, and payment stage, and the delivery stage.'

Growth of E-commerce

Electronic commerce or e-commerce encompasses all business conducted by means of computer networks. Advances in telecommunications and computer technologies in recent years have made computer networks an integral part of the economic infrastructure. More and more companies are facilitating transactions over web. E-commerce provides multiple benefits to the consumers in form of availability of goods at lower cost, wider choice and saves time. People can buy goods with a click of mouse button without moving out of their house or office. Similarly online services such as banking, ticketing including airlines, bus, railways, bill payments, hotel booking etc. have been of tremendous benefit for the customers. Most experts believe that overall e-commerce will increase exponentially in coming years. Business to business transactions will represent the largest revenue but online retailing will also enjoy a drastic growth. Online businesses like financial services, travel, entertainment, and groceries are all likely to grow.

Factors Influencing the Distribution and Forms of Global E-commerce

Nir B. Kshetri (2001) reported that the twin forces of globalization and the Internet have the potential to offer several benefits to individuals and organizations in developing as well as developed countries. Apart from economic benefits such as more choices and the convenience of shopping at home, the twin forces can make progress on educational and scientific development, mutual aid, and world peace; foster democracy; and offer exposure to other cultures. To fully exploit the potential of the Internet and e-commerce, policy makers in developing as well as industrialized countries are taking initiatives to develop the global information infrastructure (GII) and connect their national information infrastructures to the GII (Gore 1996).

All countries are not likely to benefit equally from the virtuous circle of Internet diffusion created by globalization and multiple revolutions in Communication technologies (ICTs). Forces influencing the distribution of global e-commerce and its forms include economic factors, political factors, cultural factors and supranational institutions. Economic factors mainly influence perceived relative advantage of Internet use whereas political and cultural factors influence the compatibility of the Internet with a society.

Supranational institutions' initiatives are influencing the price, quality and availability of ICT products and services, mainly in developing countries, thereby increasing relative advantage of Internet use. Moreover international institutions are influencing laws, regulations and policies in developing countries making them more compatible with Internet use.

Brief Review of Literature on E-commerce: Challenges and Opportunities

An attempt has been made to put forward a brief review of literature based on few of the related studies undertaken worldwide in the area of e-commerce as follows. Elizabeth Goldsmith and Sue L.T. McGregor (2000) analysed the impact of e-commerce on consumers, public policy, business and education. A discussion of public policy initiatives, research questions and ideas for future research are given.

Andrew D. Mitchell (2001) examined the key issues that electronic commerce poses for Global trade, using as a starting point the General Agreement on Trade in Services (GATS), the World Trade organization (WTO) agreement most relevant to e-commerce.

Nir B.Kshetri (2001) This paper attempts to identified and synthesized the available evidence on predictors of magnitude, global distribution and forms of e-commerce. The analysis indicated that the twin forces of globalization and major revolutions in ICT are fuelling the rapid growth of global e-commerce.

Jackie Gilbert Bette Ann Stead (2001) reviewed the incredible growth of electronic commerce (e-commerce) and presented ethical issues that have emerged. Security concerns, spamming, Web sites that do not carry an "advertising" label, cybersquatters, online marketing to children, conflicts of interest, manufacturers competing with intermediaries online, and "dinosaurs" were discussed.

Mauricio S. Featherman, Joseph S. Valacich & John D. Wells (2006) examined whether consumer perceptions of artificiality increase perceptions of e-service risk, which has been shown to hamper consumer acceptance in a variety of online settings.

Young Jun Choil, Chung Suk Suh (2005) examined the impact of the death of geographical distance brought about by e-marketplaces on market equilibrium and social welfare.

Prithviraj Dasgupta and Kasturi Sengupta (2002) examined the future and prospects of e-commerce in Indian Insurance Industry. (Arvind Panagariya, 2000) examined Economic issues raised by e-commerce for the WTO and developing countries. E-commerce offers unprecedented opportunities to both developing and developed countries.

Opportunities for E-commerce

Young Jun Choil, Chung Suk Suh (2005) reported that the development of the internet in the 20th century led to the birth of an electronic marketplace or it is called e-marketplace, which is now a kernel of electronic commerce (e-commerce). An e-marketplace provides a virtual space where sellers and buyers trade with each other as in the traditional marketplace. Various kinds of economic transactions and buying and selling of goods and services, as well as exchanges of information, take place in e-marketplaces. E-marketplaces have become an alternative place for trading. Finally, an e-marketplace can serve as an information agent that provides buyers and sellers with information on products and other participants in the market. These features have been reshaping the economy by affecting the behaviour of buyers and sellers.

E-business

E-business affects the whole business and the value chains in which it operates. It enables a much more integrated level of collaboration between the different components of a value chain than ever before. Adopting e-Business also allows companies to reduce costs and improve customer response time. Organizations that transform their business practices stand to benefit immensely from innumerable new possibilities brought about by technology.

E-commerce as anything that involves an online transaction. This can range from ordering online, through online delivery of paid content, to financial transactions such as movement of money between bank accounts. One area where there are some positive indications of e-commerce is financial services. Online stock trading saw sustained growth throughout the period of broadband diffusion. E-shopping is available to all these who use a computer. Over the past year Amazon.Com, ebay India, Indiatimes have seen a rapid growth in categories such as mobile handsets, jewellery, fashion apparel, books, gift items and other items.

Naukri.com – India's premier recruitment site has captured around 50% of the recruitment market.

Icicidirect.com-Stock trading simplified, Icicidirect.com is today the country's premier trading portal.

Baaze.com the country's premier shopping site started as an auction site and graduated to be the most popular platform-shopping site. Irctc.com-One of the best things about this site is that a credit card is not an essential requirement for buying tickets here. Instead the site offers a direct debit facility having tied with most of the popular banks.

It is being estimated that the online travel market in India was estimated at $300 million in 2005 and has crossed $750 million in 2006. By 2008, it is expected to exceed $2 billion.

Young Jun Choil, Chung Suk Suh (2005) reported that the economic consequences of the death of geographical distance due to the emergence of e-marketplaces. It has shown that overcoming spatial barriers by means of e-marketplaces lowers the price level. Since e-marketplaces achieve economies of scale by aggregating dispersed demands, they allow the economy to have more varieties that did not exist before their emergence.

E-commerce Integration

Zabihollah Rezaee, Kenneth R. Lambert and W. Ken Harmon (2006) reported that the rationale for infusion of e-commerce education into all business courses is that technological developments are significantly affecting all aspects of today's business.

An e-commerce dimension can be added to the business curriculum by integrating e-commerce topics into existing upper-level business courses. Students would be introduced to e-commerce education and topics covered in a variety of business courses in different disciplines e.g. accounting, economics, finance, marketing, management, management information systems. To help assure that all related business courses in all disciplines such as e.g., accounting, finance, economics, marketing, management, information systems pay proper attention to the critical aspects of e-commerce, certain e-commerce topics should be integrated into existing business courses.

Open and Distance Learning

Diana Oblinger (2001) reported that one is that education and continuous learning have become so vital in all societies that the demand for distance and open learning will increase. As the availability of the Internet expands, as computing devices become more affordable, and as energy requirements and form factors shrink, e-learning will become more popular.

In addition to the importance of lifelong learning, distance education and e-learning will grow in popularity because convenience and flexibility are more important decision criteria than ever before. E learning will become widely accepted because exposure to the Internet and e-learning often begins in the primary grades, thus making more students familiar and comfortable with online learning. In fact, for many countries, distance education has been the most viable solution for providing education to hundreds of thousands of students.

E-commerce and E-insurance

Prithviraj Dasgupta and Kasturi Sengupta (2002) reported that the recent growth of Internet infrastructure and introduction of economic reforms in the insurance sector have opened up the monopolistic Indian insurance market to competition from foreign alliances. Although the focus of e-commerce has been mainly on business to consumer (B2C) applications, the emphasis is now shifting towards business to business (B2B) applications. The insurance industry provides an appropriate model that combines both B2C and B2B applications.

Traditional insurance requires a certificate for every policy issued by the insurance company. However, paper certificates encumber problems including loss, duplication and forging of the certificate. The conventional certificate is now replaced with an electronic certificate that can be digitally signed by both the insurer and the insurance company and verified by a certifying authority.

Online policy purchase is faster, more user-friendly and definitely more secure than the traditional processes. Therefore it is more attractive to the insurer. At the same time it incurs less cost and requires fewer resources than traditional insurance and is therefore more profitable for the insurance company.

E-insurance also makes the insurance procedure more secure since the policy details are stored digitally and all transactions are made over secure channels. These channels provide additional market penetration that is absent in traditional channels and help in earning more revenue than traditional insurance processes.

Future media of E-commerce

Patric Barwise (2001) reported that Probability 99% of e-commerce today is done using PCs either desktops or laptops. For B2B e-commerce this is unlikely to change.For B2C e-commerce however, things will be more complex.

There will be wider range of relevant media, including interactive digital TV, and a range of mobile and wireless services. There will be huge difference between different consumers' ownership of equipment and access technology. Some will have broad band access and others have no digital communication at all.

Current and Future B2C Digital Media

Digital media able to support consumer e-commerce can be grouped under five main headings, with in the home PCS, IDTV and with in next five years a range of other online device such as games, computers, utility meters etc. In summary, the online PC is well established while the other B2C digital media are still emerging. Economic issues raised by e-commerce for the WTO and developing countries.

Arvind Panagariya, 2000) reported that access to e-commerce, which in the WTO parlance often means access to e-exports, has two components that must be distinguished sharply: access to internet services and access to services that can be traded electronically. The former deals with to access to Internet infrastructure while the latter relates to specific commitments in electronically tradable services.

E-commerce offers unprecedented opportunities to both developing and developed countries. In the short run, the gains are likely to be concentrated in developed countries have more to benefit. This is because, in the short run, developing countries lack the infrastructure necessary to take full advantage of Internet.

For many countries, especially developing ones, in these countries, most consumers do not have computers or Internet access. A likely scenario, therefore, is one in which a handful of independent entrepreneurs will receive the product by Internet, convert it into physical form such as CDs and sell the latter to consumers. But this activity may itself be costly, using up real resources. But in the long run, they can leapfrog, skipping some of the stages in the development of information technology through which developed countries have had to pass.

Some efficiencies issues must be addressed. The issue of tariffs, which are applicable to products imported in physical form but not when transmitted electronically. As long as the cost of electronic transmission is lower than that of physical delivery, the presence of tariffs on the latter poses no problem. Effectively, the electronic transmission offers the product to the country at a price lower than that available through physical delivery.

Challenges for E Commerce

Internet based e-commerce has besides, great advantages, posed many threats because of its being what is popularly called faceless and borderless. Some examples of ethical issues that have emerged as a result of electronic commerce. All of the following examples are both ethical issues and issues that are uniquely related to electronic commerce.

Ethical issues: Jackie Gilbert Bette Ann Stead (2001), reported the following ethical issues related to e-commerce.

1) *Privacy:* Privacy has been and continues to be a significant issue of concern for both current and prospective electronic commerce customers. With regard to web interactions and e-commerce the following dimensions are most salient:

(1) Privacy consists of not being interfered with, having the power to exclude; individual privacy is a moral right.

(2) Privacy is "a desirable condition with respect to possession of information by other persons about him/herself on the observation/perceiving of him/herself by other persons"

Security concerns: In addition to privacy concerns, other ethical issues are involved with electronic commerce. The Internet offers unprecedented ease of access to a vast array of goods and services. The rapidly expanding arena of "click and mortar" and the largely unregulated cyberspace medium have however prompted concerns about both privacy and data security.

Other ethical issues: Manufacturers Competing with Intermediaries Online.

"Disintermediation," a means eliminating the intermediary such as retailers, wholesalers, outside sales reps by setting up a Website to sell directly to customers.

Disintermediation include (1) music being downloaded directly from producers (2) authors distributing their work from their own Web sites or through writer co-operatives.

Dinosaurs – "Dinosaurs" is a term that refers to executives and college professors who refuse to recognize that technology has changed our lives. When an executive speaks in terms of the Internet being the "wave of the future," it is a sure sign of "dinosaur.

Perceptions of Risk in e-service Encounters

Mauricio S. Featherman, Joseph S. Valacich & John D. Wells (2006) reported that as companies race to digitize physical-based service processes repackaging them as online e-services, it becomes increasingly important to understand how consumers perceive the digitized e-service alternative. E-service replacements may seem unfamiliar, artificial and non-authentic in comparison to traditional service processing methods. Consumers may believe that new internet-based processing methods expose them to new potential risks the dangers of online fraud, identity theft and phishing swindles means schemes to steal confidential information using spoofed web sites, have become commonplace, and are likely to cause alarm and fear within consumers.

E-commerce Integration

Beside many an advantages offered by the education a no of challenges have been posed to the recent education system.

Zabihollah Rezaee, Kenneth R. Lambert and W. Ken Harmon (2006) reported that E-commerce Integration assures coverage of all critical aspects of e-commerce, but it also has several obstacles. First, adding e-commerce materials to existing business courses can overburden faculty and students alike trying to cope with additional subject matter in courses already saturated with required information. Second, many business faculty members may not wish to add e-commerce topics to their courses primarily because of their own lack of comfort with technology-related subjects. Third and finally, this approach requires a great deal of coordination among faculty and disciplines in business schools to ensure proper coverage of e-commerce education.

Online Advertising

A company needs to make marketing decisions not only in the areas of segmentation, product offerings, pricing and distribution but also in the areas of promotion. The successful promotion of a produce requires that, at a minimum, a positive message be received by potential customers. And advertising is the main and most commonly used source of communication to convey the message to the ultimate customers. Advertising is not a new concept. The principles of advertising have their root going back very deep into the history of man. About 3,000 years ago in Thebes, an advertisement was written on papyrus calling for information regarding a runaway slave.

This was not the first advertising, merely one of the first examples, which has survived. Pompeli is rich in advertisement scratched and painted upon its wall. But time changes; so do we. And the way people advertise their product or a service is no exception either. Online advertising is the latest addition in this genre. Online advertising is also known as Web advertising, Internet advertising and e-advertising. But whatever be the name, in essence, it is all advertising. In a very simple sense online advertising can be defined as the use of electronic communication resources (especially Internet and its enable technologies) to engage in the activities of advertising.

The realm of which is a relatively new, un-researched area with a huge untapped potential. What fascinates me about this topic is the fact that in the information age, the growing accessibility of the Internet among diverse sections of consumers, can become a powerful tool for endorsement and hence sale of products. What is unique and defining about this medium is that, the advertiser reaches only those who are interested (a focused audience), and more cost-effectively than with conventional advertising. With the new focused channels, the Advertiser can concentrate on timely and customized announcements, rather than the relatively static and mass appeal approach in conventional media. On an individual level, for example, the marketer may use the technology to make himself more accessible to the consumer thus adding to his service levels through interactive marketing. The introduction of interactive marketing and specifically interactive advertising heralds the beginning of an era where customers will choose the advertising they wish to see, when they want to see it. The Web can be transformed into a research tool, a brand builder and an advertising medium in one swoop, something not offered by other media.

Furthermore, unlike other media where the advertising agency is the only link between the client and the media-owner, the Web allows the client to become the media owner. The assortment of features of web advertisement notwithstanding, it provides a special challenge to marketers and planners due to its relative infancy, which brings previously un-encountered circumstances to the fore.

Why Online Advertising?

The Internet has produced a revolutionary new way for business to communicate and interact with customers. Everyone from small businesses to fortune 500 company's are racing to make their mark in cyberspace with their own "Home Pages" on the world wide web (www). The reason it presents great advertising opportunities for marketers because of its continuing growth.

The number of Internet users around the world is constantly growing. The computer industry almanac has reported that by the year 2005, 118 people per 1000 around the world will have Internet access.

As Internet users are growing day by day; so are Internet advertisers because they can easily, effectively and efficiently communicate their products or services to targeted mass audience. Add to this the fact that Internet users are well educated with high incomes, it is only logical to conclude that Internet surfers are a desired target for advertisers.

Other reasons why online advertising is growing rapidly are:

- Advertisement can reach very large number of potential buyers globally.
- Web superiority over other advertising medium.
- Web page (advertisement) can be updated any time and changes or corrections are painless.
- Online advertisement works 24 hours a day, 7 days a week, 365 days a year.
- In online advertisement specific interest groups or individuals can be targeted.
- Online advertisement can effectively use the convergence of text, audio, graphics, and Animation.
- Online advertisements are cheaper in comparison to traditional advertisement. There is no printing costs, no postage costs etc.

Forms of Online Advertising

The Internet is a great place to advertise. There are many forms of online advertising. Some of the main ones involved:

* E-mail sponsorship advertising
* Newsletter and E-zine advertising
* Rich media advertising (flash ads, Interstitials & Superstitials, streaming audio/video, etc.)
* Pop-up/pop-under advertising
* Online banner advertising
* Sponsorship (web sites, e-mails, sweep stakes)
* Advertorial (Paid-for editorial) placements.

Sector wise online advertising trends in world:

* Around 1/3 of net advertising is from FMCG Companies.
* Around 15% comes from finance companies.
* Around 11% from technology companies.
* Around 7% comes from communication a publication etc.
* And the rest from other sectors.

Online Advertising: Indian Scene

Online advertising is still in the embryonic stages in India, while in other parts of the world it has already taken deep roots. The share of India's online advertising in world pie is almost negligible. But developing countries like India; where Internet users are growing very rapidly, it has huge potential. India's leading advertisers are starting to advertise online, but at a very slow pace. Indian companies are also showing keen interest in promoting their products or services online.

Currently finance sector is most dominating sector in online advertising and accounted about 40% of total online advertising in India. Some of the leading companies from this sector are HDFC, Citibank, SBI, and UTI etc. FMCG goods have just started to come in led by companies like Hindustan Lever, Procter and Gamble etc. FMCG accounted about 20% of total online advertisement spending in India. Consumer durables companies are also coming and accounted 15% of total online advertisement. Share of media sector is about 10% and rest comes from other. In India, most popular form of online advertising is banner advertising. The reason, it is easy to create, place and use. E-mail advertising follows it. India has to cover a lot of grounds to come up to the level of online advertising as, say, a country like U.S.

There are many stumbling blocks in the growth of online advertising in India like, psychological fears of IT, high cost, low education and above all low awareness level. Still many Indian companies are hesitant, anxious and doubtful about the potential it offers. Unless these are dealt with online advertising can't really take off in India.

Benefits of Online Advertising

The Internet has great potential as media carrier compared to traditional media. It offers higher selectivity which is tailored to the user's profile. The customer can also customize the adverts as he/she is in charge of his own navigation.

Through the online advertising the advertiser can get quick, easy and inexpensive feedback in real time, which no other media offers, providing a higher feedback rate. Some other benefits of online advertising are as under:

- Online advertising facilitates the advertiser to reach an absolutely pinpointed and targeted audience.
- "Traditional advertising is usually a one-way mechanism there is no way for customers to act on the information in the advertisements. On the Internet, however, interested customers can click on a banner, learn more, and actually make purchase on the spot," states Arti Dwarkadas, business director, Ogilvy Interaction.
- The Internet as a medium knows no demographic boundaries and gives the advertiser a huge audience to tap and build brand image if not sell products.
- Internet's interactive nature allows for greater flexibility than traditional media in the type of information transmitted and the method of transmission.
- Online advertisement can facilitate purchase decision.
- Enhance customer company relationship.
- Protection of environment.
- Online advertisement expands the company's market to global market.
- It is easy to create, and place, it saves time, labor and money.
- No loss of quality even after a very long period of time.

Limitations of Online Advertising

Research, reveals that not many companies take advantage of online advertising opportunity. There are many reasons behind it. Some of the most common are as under:

- Online advertising is not simply a "Customer oriented" medium; it is a customer-dominated medium
- Online advertising is not emotional medium like T.V.; it is a cognitive medium
- Mindset shift in using online advertising
- Psychological fear of IT
- Infrastructure inadequacy
- High cost
- Limited space
- Limited information
- Users work on the net for a specific purpose; they are not interested in other things like advertising

Company can't target all the potential customers like those who are not Internet;

- Too many companies are trying to slice up a tiny online advertising pie, resulting in Commoditization of the business and leading to extreme competition pressure.
- Suggestions for online advertising
- Understanding the right way to advertise on the Internet is extremely important as the negative or downside potential is extremely great for a small startup or medium sized firm.

Ethics in Social Marketing

Problems faced by marketers in non-profit organizations are among the most important and interesting issues in marketing today.

For marketers in commercial organisations, ethical considerations are non-essential constraints. The ultimate aim is to make profits for shareholders, and ethical considerations may limit the methods employed to achieve this aim.

For social marketers the situation is different. By definition, their ultimate aim is ethical, and for them the question of whether the ends justify the means is real and challenging. For social marketers, therefore, ethical issues are fundamental.

Unfortunately, most social marketers, believe that it is important to define just what social marketing is, the different types of social marketing that exist, and how social marketing differs from commercial marketing.

Some of these points seem quite appealing at first as some social marketers typically believe that they have only limited resources for achieving such impressive objectives.

However, a moment's thought would show that this is not true. Some government agencies in India, for example, have comparatively large promotional budgets that would exceed those of many commercial marketers, particularly those who work in small companies. Thus, the overlap between commercial and social marketing is arguably much greater, and it would be helpful to explore common ground rather than create dubious distinctions.

Although it is worthwhile to argue that these concerns attached with the nature of social marketing are misplaced, it is still not clear whether these are the exclusive domains of social marketers. It is sometimes quoted that "Thoughtful social marketing practitioners are faced all too frequently with ethical dilemmas". This is clearly true, but the same is true of all marketers, who must make personal decisions regarding their activities and the implications these have for others. For example, commercial marketers have to decide whether it is appropriate to market products rich in highly processed carbohydrates while the social marketers have to decide whether it is appropriate to promote immunisation knowing that a very small proportion of children will suffer adverse effects to the vaccines. So, at times it becomes very difficult to demonstrate the ethical problems of social marketers from those faced by marketers in general.

Furthermore, it has been observed that both social marketers and commercial marketers have the same compelling interest; hence it is not surprising that social marketers borrow concepts first developed and applied in commercial marketing. However, it is surprising that there is little discussion of how social marketers can apply this commercial knowledge to the behavioural objectives they wish to tackle.

Ultimately, marketers interested in problems that involve social behaviours want to learn more about the options available for changing or reinforcing those behaviours, and the relative effectiveness of those options. These are difficult questions, as little has been empirically established. However, for social marketing to progress, these questions, as well as their ethical implications, need to be explicitly acknowledged and discussed, and actively researched.

The Emergence of Interdependent E-commerce Constructs

The innovation of e-commerce has affected not only the marketplace through the facilitation of the exchange of goods and services, but also human behaviour in response to the mechanisms of online services. Researchers have identified and hypothesized on relevant subject matters ranging from Web usability, marketing channels and other factors influencing online buying behaviour. Though researchers have focused on what appear different aspects of online buying behaviour, their studies may be shown to be interrelated and interdependent, even to the extent of revealing constructs upon which e-commerce, in terms of future design and research, could be built upon.

Constructs

A construct is defined as an abstract or general idea inferred or derived from specific instances (Hyperdictionary). This paper researched a number of studies on e-commerce with each providing examples in order to substantiate their respective hypotheses. Even with the varying number and nature of these studies, some constructs emerge which seem interdependent in contributing to the holistic view of e-commerce and associated consumer interactions. For example, Li, Kuo and Russel (2002) extrapolated from an online survey of 999 U.S. Internet users, that marketing channel knowledge is the strongest predictor of online buying behaviour. They draw this construct in the due course of presenting ten hypotheses. Three of their finding demonstrates that there is no difference in price, recreation orientation or age differences between those who make online purchases and those who don't. They did find that online buyers are better educated and male, with a higher income than those who don't purchase online. As would be expected, they further determined that online consumers are lower in experiential orientation than non-Web buyers and more convenience oriented. The remaining two hypotheses propose that online consumers view the Web as having higher utilities in communication, distribution as well as hold the self-perception that they are more knowledgeable about the Web as a marketing channel, than non-Web consumers. Ultimately however, these authors identify a weakness in their study in that their methodologies for measuring channel utilities may need to be modified to accommodate attributes such as information customization and degree of interactivity.

Web Usability Construct

Becker (2002) in a separate and unrelated study, which in contrast to the focus on individual users studied seventeen U.S. based e-businesses, theorizes on the construct of Web Usability. The weakness" with regard to information customization identified by Li et al above, appears addressable via Becker's mechanism of Web Usability. Becker represents Web Usability as the sum of eleven factors, which are navigation, design standards, personalization, design layout, performance, customer satisfaction, design consistency, reliability, security, information content and accessibility. The design standard speaks to the generalized "look and feel", which can be achieved by employing, for example, HTML style sheets. We could also include emerging World Wide Web Consortium technologies such as XHTML and CSS, used for data formatting. Personalization is the meeting, through customization (i.e., display of personal data, buying preferences etc.,) of individual needs.

Design layout is the presentation of the visual content as achieved through the positioning of Web-objects along with colours, fonts, styles etc. Navigation is the travellers mechanisms as well as the breadth and depth of search paths. Design consistency is the uniform placement of Web objects in all of the Web site's pages. Customer service is those added functionalities that enhance the online experience, such as, chat and e-mail. Reliability is the consistent availability of the customer's access to the Website as realized through the mitigation/elimination of any downtime. Security is the access limitation and privacy of personal information. Yeung, Shim and Lai for instance, state that, "Clearly, online payment security and data privacy are the major barriers for any business deploying e-commerce". Performance is the network related metrics of consumer wait and system response times. For example, Liu, Dixon and Murphy (2002) note that in China, "an underdeveloped infrastructure, expensive access, slow access speed...hamper Internet adoption". Information content is described as the accurate and complete translation of text into a native language. Finally, accessibility is how well its comprehension requirements are aligned with the visual, physical and cognitive limitations of the Web user.

Marketing Channel Construct

What seems to emerge here is that Web Usability is a construct upon which marketing's communication channel construct rests. In other words, when the Web site's intent transitions from conveying information to a true commercial venture, what appear super-imposable on the Web-usability infrastructure are the marketing channels; namely, communication channel, transaction channel and distribution channel. Li et al, argue that these three channels may or may not overlap through a commerce-oriented Website. The function of these marketing channels includes information, promotion, negotiation, ordering, financing, risk taking, physical possession, payment and the actual transfer of product ownership.

The purpose of the communication channel is to provide the customers' information needs for decision-making. Li et al argue that the communications channel can be judged on its characteristics of quality, quantity, and recency of information. It could be further argued that the communication channel, by holistically addressing the attributes of information, evolves the eleven Web Usability factors into the marketing activities of information and promotion. In short, this communication channel facilitates and perhaps even enhances, the flow of various types of information between sellers and buyers. If this line of reasoning is pursued, then the transaction channel seems responsible for the marketing functions of negotiations, ordering, financing, risk taking and payment. In essence, the transaction channel holds the range of activities between ordering and payment between buyers and sellers. The distribution channel could then be said to hold the remaining marketing functions of physical possession and the actual transfer of product ownership.

Design Construct

Nah and Davis (2002) take a different approach to Web Usability by simply distilling it to the ease of two distinct activities; namely, search and navigation. They present search, as an information seeking behaviour directed by goals. They give the example of a user seeking specific population growth data in her hometown over the last five years. In contrast, they make navigation synonymous with the common behaviour of browsing, defining it as an activity where the information space is explored without an explicit goal in mind. They also offer that, "searching tasks are best supported by a hierarchical information structure, such as those used by many online stores" in opposition to exploratory tasks, which are best supported by a network structure and a graphical browser. They suggest three design strategies or constructs, which are related in a top-down fashion:

(1) the task to be performed,

(2) how information is structured within the system, and

(3) navigational support.

Katz and Byrne (2003) use the same terms of searching and browsing to actually mean a subset of a goal-directed, information seeking behaviour. They define search as the "use of a site-specific search function accessed by typing a search query into a text field" and browsing as the "alternative methods of navigating a particular Web site, particularly the traversal of the site's menu of hierarchy". Furthermore, they hypothesize on information scent: "In the context of shopping online, information scent could refer to the amount of information a user could attain regarding the location of a product in a site based solely on the design of the site's home page...Presumably, information scent can play a large role in a user's decision to traverse the menus or use the site search function". Since all e-commerce transactions begin with either navigation/browsing or searching (as defined by Nah and Davis), these constructs along with the subset offered by Katz and Byrne, could act as strategic predecessors in building Becker's Web Usability segments.

Purchasing Decision Support Construct

Similarly, the decision support system presented by Nah and Davis could be said to precede Li et al's marketing channels. Nah and Davis (2002) define the decision support construct as one that supports the stages of the purchasing decision. The stages include product search, criteria management and comparison support. Product search contains the metaphor type of the site (search engine or browsable Web structure) and information structure (network or hierarchical). Criteria management is concerned with the product presentation type (graphics, colors, size, etc.,) and how the information on the product is provided (reviews from professionals, customers, etc.,). Of interest is Becker' note that, " many localized Web sites use national colors (e.g., yellow appears on many Germany Web sites) for navigation bars, images, and other Web objects to promote customer loyalty and national pride, as well as for 'branding' the customer experience". Lastly, comparison support involves the comparison scope (inter-site or intra-site) and comparison tools. In a Web site's transition from conveying information to a true commercial venture with marketing channels, Nah and Davis's three, decision support criteria could serve as the intermediary framework on which the e-commerce portion could be based.

Qualitative HCI Construct

The degree of interactivity, left opened by Li et al, is investigated in yet another separate study by Sun Lim of fourteen interviewees.

Lim argues that systematic analysis of human-computer interaction (HCI) must be predicated on the understanding of how and why users perform their activities (Lim 2002). He bypasses quantitative methods like the study of the progression of movement within Web pages, temporal differences in online actions, etc., in favor of a qualitative framework of study construct, which seeks to comprehend the cognitive processes fueling online behaviour. The tool that Lim uses is the Self-Confrontational Interview. In this technique, the subjects are asked to perform the behaviour being analysed, i.e., online activity, which is then recorded. Subsequently, the subjects view their recorded actions and are asked to recount both thoughts and emotions as best they can recall. The interviews are then transcribed to correlate the actor's actions with their thoughts and emotions.

Lim (2002) surmises that such qualitative understanding of human interaction will in turn contribute to improve Web usability. For example, he finds that online consumers favor sequential progression from larger activity units to smaller component units. This is illustrated in the narrowing process where online buyers begin with a search engine to identify pertinent stores and then funnel further to a range of stores within which to select a range of products until they get to the item they wish to purchase. Similarly, consumers expect hyperlinks to elaborate on parent hyperlink. This appears to further support the direction that Becker's Web usability factor of navigation should be divided to produce Nah and Davis's hierarchical model of search activity.

Lim also introduces the concept that Websites should mimic real life scripts. In other words, any online purchasing interface, should imitate a brick-and-mortar process. For example, if when one needs to purchase an airline ticket, all one has to do is state different destinations to the travel agent, then an online ticket system should mirror requiring the same, and not more information, in order to provide the service.

A study of an interviewee is given in this exact same scenario where the online interface requires more data input/additional traversal paths and the ensuing tension and confusion experienced by the consumer. This correlates with what Nah and Davis (2002) identify as cognitive overhead, "the challenge of maintaining several tasks or hyperlink trails simultaneously". They term the user's "experiences in planning, managing and executing digressions from a course of action", as the digression problem. In drawing a comparison between Becker's Web usability factor of accessibility and designing Web sites for real life scripts/cognitive overhead, it initially appears unrelated. For in fact, Becker discusses accessibility in terms of mitigating consumer's physical impairments and from an international perspective, the users' reading and language comprehension limitations. However, it could be argued that comprehension limitations exist not only due to physical or foreign language translations and understanding, but also as a byproduct of the consumer's specious expectation to use their real life shopping scripts to function in an Internet store and/or the consumer's inability to cope with the increasing cognitive demands. If this perception is considered, then Becker's view of accessibility is given an entirely new dimension.

Visual indicators as presented by Lim (2002), involve those clues which consumers have become accustomed to in a brick-and-mortar store. For example, one may look for box cover or a product design and logo rather than simply a product name when shopping. Becker's Web usability factor of information content might need to be deliberately stratified to accommodate emerging categories of information content such as these visual indicators. Nah and Davis (2002), take this further by calling for future studies in effective visual representations. For example, they query whether or not products should be presented on the Web using 3D imaging with interior and exterior views, for items such as automobiles. Li et al claim that such experience-oriented functionalities (e.g., 3D, virtual reality and surround video) will be dominant characteristics of the next generation of e-commerce stores. They state that simulating the real-life shopping experience, with which the consumer is familiar, will drive future, online consumer marketing.

Lim (2002) is careful to point out though, that functionality has to be dominant over aesthetics. He gives an example where a technically savvy user continued on a Website despite lack of functional clarity. A less technically competent user, he states, would simply have given up. There may be some correlation between this hypothesis and that of Li et al, which describes some online consumers belief that the Web has higher utilities in communication. It could be argued that the belief, the higher expectation of communication utility of the Web and the self-view of competency of experienced online consumers, allows them to persist in Web sites, which fail to meet the design layout, consistency and navigation as defined by Becker.

However, Lim (2002) makes the last point of guarding against Web site designs that encourage conditioning of automatic actions, as opposed to the thorough processing of information. For instance, a design layout that calls for pop-windows as a means of a communication channel, would fail in its intent if the shopper instinctively responds to remove these perceived obstructions to their line of vision, by summarily closing all pop-ups. Here again, Becker and Li's (2002) definition of design layout and communication channel respectively, achieve a greater level of granularity through the filter of Lim's hypothesis.

Trust Construct

Going beyond effective technical infrastructure, design and communication, a critical element influencing all e-commerce behaviour is the construct of trust. Wang and Vassileva distinguish between trust and reputation as; trust is "an agent's belief in an another agent's capabilities, honesty and reliability based on its own direct experiences", while reputation is the same belief, but based on other agents' recommendations. Smith and Brynjolfsson (2000) also offer that an Internet market, in response to lower search costs, yields a Perfect Bayesian Equilibrium in which buyers and sellers select actions based on their beliefs about each other.

Nah and Davis (2002) define trust as " the willingness of the consumer (trustor) to be vulnerable to the actions of an online party (trustee) by engaging in online relationship exchanges with the party". They outline thirteen principles of trust under three major categories of Content, Design and External Certifications and References.

Under Content as it pertains to trust, Nah and Davis (2002) state that it is necessary for e-commerce Web sites to provide the identity of the company (address, contact information, mission statement, etc.,) disclose performance history of the company and have a clear privacy and security policy. Becker notes that the "same security issues facing US users regarding the misuse and unauthorized distribution of credit card numbers, addresses, phone number, income and other personal data extend to all users in the international, online market".

Nah and Davis elaborate that these policies should have information outlining, "how and what types of consumers' personal and transaction information will be collected, how they will be used" and "how they will be protected from unauthorized access". They also indicate that the Web site must provide accurate and comprehensive product and pricing information along with a candid disclosure of all customer relationships aspects.

The latter includes specifications of each participant's obligations and responsibilities, guarantees and pertinent compensation along with support for mediation services and dispute resolution. Under Design, Nah and Davis suggest that the following traits will promote trust; timely and professional we site design, reliable and secure technology, informed consent and personalization. Nielsen states that, "a professional appearance brings confidence to consumers, clear navigation conveys respect for the customer and an implied promise of good service, and typos or difficult navigation communicate disregard for the users".

Nah and Davis suggest that informed consent can be achieved by providing consumers the technical functionality to opt-in/opt-out of those online interactions that can either potentially benefit or harm the users. They go on to say that with the customers' privacy protected, personalization (such as selective recommendations to customers) can provide the experience that will increase the levels of trust and loyalty. Becker defines personalization as meeting the needs of a user and Nah and Davis complements this by suggesting that customer's needs must be understood via mechanisms such as data mining and collaborative filtering.

Xu and Yadov, indicate "three sources of trust between trading parties in business relationship: familiarity, calculativeness, and values" with "the most practical trust source is calculativeness: trading parties estimate the trustworthiness of each other through calculation based on the other party's past performance, which is reflected by reputation".

Under External Certifications and References, Nah and Davis propose four guidelines for fostering trust indirectly. Credibility of online services can be cultivated by obtaining certifications either in the form of approvals from professional associations or from third party assurance services, which certify security and privacy practices. Online traders can be afforded protection from Internet fraud through escrow services. Reputation systems, which gather, disseminate and compile participant feedback, are also effective in aiding consumers' assessment of an online service's trustworthiness.

Finally, credibility can be enhanced by association, via hyperlinks to and from, with other credible third parties. It could be argued that trust, (in the accuracy of information, competency of the vendor to deliver expected service, privacy of client information, reliability of performance and security of all data transfers and transactions), permeates the entire cycle of e-commerce constructs.

Consumer shopping behaviour is being fundamentally changed by electronic commerce. Recent, independent and seemingly unrelated studies, show general patterns of dependencies or constructs, in how the virtual marketplace, as presented by e-commerce Web sites, need to be approached in terms of construction in order to accommodate consumers' needs. Nah and Davis's design paradigm of the task to be performed, structure of the information within the system (with Katz and Byrnes subsets of information seeking) and navigational support, all appear to be a unifying design construct in building Becker's eleven segments of Web Usability. In turn, Web Usability itself seems to be a construct upon which Li et al's marketing-communication channel rests. Another of Nah and Davis's constructs, the three, purchasing decision support criteria of product search, criteria management and comparison support, could then serve as the intermediary framework on which the e-commerce portion, including Li et al's remaining marketing channels of transaction and distribution, could rest. The maturing marketing channels are then likely to complete the construct circle as constructs themselves in evolving and effectively leveraging not only the current quantitative mechanisms of data mining, collaborative filtering, real-life scripts (mimicking shopping and support), but also in contributing to the genesis and use of new constructs of qualitative techniques, such as Lim's Self-Confrontational Interview, cognitive overhead research and social constructs of trust.

Understanding the Quality and Customer Service

Customer Service

Customer service is the provision of service to customers before, during and after a purchase. According to Jamier L. Scott. (2002), "Customer service is a series of activities designed to enhance the level of customer satisfaction – that is, the feeling that a product or service has met the customer expectation."

Its importance varies by product, industry and customer; defective or broken merchandise can be exchanged, often only with a receipt and within a specified time frame. Retail stores will often have a desk or counter devoted to dealing with returns, exchanges and complaints, or will perform related functions at the point of sale.

Customer service may be provided by a person (e.g., sales and service representative), or by automated means called self-service. Examples of self service are Internet sites. However, In the Internet era, a challenge has been to maintain and/or enhance the personal experience while making use of the efficiencies of online commerce. Writing in Fast Company, entrepreneur and customer systems innovator Micah Solomon has made the point that "Online customers are literally invisible to you (and you to them), so it's easy to short-change them emotionally. But this lack of visual and tactile presence makes it even more crucial to create a sense of personal, human-to-human connection in the online arena."

Customer service is normally an integral part of a company's customer value proposition. In their book *Rules to Break and Laws to Follow*, Don Peppers and Martha Rogers, Ph.D. write that "customers have memories. They will remember you, whether you remember them or not." Further, "customer trust can be destroyed at once by a major service problem, or it can be undermined one day at a time, with a thousand small demonstrations of incompetence." From the point of view of an overall sales process engineering effort, customer service plays an important role in an organization's ability to generate income and revenue. From that perspective, customer service should be included as part of an overall approach to systematic improvement.

Some have argued that the quality and level of customer service has decreased in recent years, and that this can be attributed to a lack of support or understanding at the executive and middle management levels of a corporation and/or a customer service policy.

Instant Feedback

Recently, many organizations have implemented feedback loops that allow them to capture feedback at the point of experience. For example, National Express, one of the UK's leading travel companies invites passengers to send text messages whilst riding the bus. This has been shown to be useful as it allows companies to improve their customer service before the customer defects, thus making it far more likely that the customer will return next time.

Setting the Right KPIs

A challenge working with Customer Service is to ensure that you have focused your attention on the right key areas, measured by the right Key Performance Indicator. There is no challenge to come up with a lot of meaningful KPIs, but the challenge is to select a few which reflects your overall strategy. In addition to reflecting your strategy it should also enable staff to limit their focus to the areas that really matter. The focus must be of those KPIs, which will deliver the most value to the overall objective, e.g. cost saving, service improving etc. It must also be done in such a way that staff sincerly believe that they can make a difference with the effort. One of the most important aspects of a customer service KPI is that of what is often referred to as the "Feel Good Factor". Basically the goal is to not only help the customer have a good experience, but to offer them an experience that exceeds their expectations. Several key points are listed as follows:

1. Know your product-Know what products/service you are offering back to front. In other words be an information expert. It is okay to say "I don't know", but it should always be followed up by... "but let me find out" or possibly " but my friend knows!" Whatever the situation may be, make sure that you don't leave your customer with an unanswered question.
2. Body Language/Communication-Most of the communication that we relay to others is done through body language. If we have a negative body language when we interact with others it can show our lack of care. Two of the most important parts of positive body language are smiling, and eye contact. Make sure to look your customers in the eye. It shows that we are listening to them, not at them. And then of course smiling is just more inviting than someone who has a blank look on their face.
3. Anticipate Guest Needs-Nothing surprises your customer more than an employee going the extra mile to help them. Always look for ways to serve your customer more than they expect. In doing so it helps them to know that you care and it will leave them with the "Feel Good Factor" that we are searching for.

Standardization

There are few standards on this topic. ISO and The International Customer Service Institute (TICSI) have published the following ones:

- ISO 9004:2000, on performance improvement
- ISO 10001:2007, on customer service conduct
- ISO 10002:2004, on quality management in handling customer complaints
- ISO 10003:2007, on dispute resolution
- The International Customer Service Standard (TICSS).

There is also an Information Technology service management standard: ISO/IEC 20000:2005. Its first part concerns specifications and its second part the code of practice.

Understanding and Managing Customer Perception

In today's globalising economy competition is getting more and more fierce. That means it becomes more difficult for products and services to differentiate themselves from other offerings than ever before. Not only is the number of competitive offerings rising due to globalisation ofproduction, sourcing, logistics and access to information. Many products and services face new competition from substitutes and from completely new offerings or bundles from industry outsiders. Since product differences are closed at an increasing speed and many companies try to win the battle for customers by price reductions, products and services tend to become commodities.

On the other hand, customer behaviour becomes more hybrid. On one hand, customers are increasingly price sensitive – searching for bargains at marketplaces like ebay or buying their groceries at discount markets. On the other hand they enjoy branded and luxury goods. One and the same person may plan a weekend trip with a no-frills airline and a stay at a five-star-hotel.

In the result, customers have a wider choice of often less distinguishable products and they are much better informed. For many offerings the balance of power shifts towards the customer. Customers are widely aware of their greater power, which raises their expectations on how companies should care for them. Bringing it all together, it becomes ever more difficult to differentiate a product or service by traditional categories like price, quality, functionality etc.

In this situation the development of a strong relationship between customers and a company could likely prove to be a significant opportunity for competitive advantage. This relationship is not longer based on features like price and quality alone. Today it is more the perceived experience a customer makes in his various interactions with a company (e.g. how fast, easy, efficient and reliable the process is) that can make or break the relationship. Problems during a single transaction can damage a so far favourable customer attitude. The consequence for companies is that they have to adapt their ways of competing for customers. Traditionally, companies have focused their efforts of customer relationship management on issues like customer satisfaction and targeted marketing activities like event marketing, direct marketing or advertising. Although doubtless necessary and beneficial, these activities are not longer enough. They narrow the relationship between company and customer down to a particular set of contacts in which the company invests its efforts. Most likely this will produce not more than a satisfied customer who is well aware of the companies offerings and has a positive attitude towards them. However, a satisfied customer is not necessarily a loyal one.

If a customer is satisfied that means that a product of service has met his expectations and that he was not dissatisfied by it. Customer satisfaction is doubtlessly very important. It is the precondition for repeat purchases and it prevents the customer from telling others about his disappointing experiences. A loyal customer, however, is more than a customer who frequently purchases from a company.

The difference is the emotional bond which links the customer so closely to the company that he develops a clear preference for these products or brands and is even willing to recommend them to others. Loyal customers truly prefer a product, brand or company over competitive offerings. Thus loyalty goes beyond a rational decision for known quality or superior price-performance-ratio. It is about the customers' feelings and perceptions about the brand or product.

When the customer makes his buying decision, he evaluates the benefits he perceives from a particular product and compares them with the costs. The value a customer perceives when buying and using a product or service go beyond usability. There is a set of emotional values as well, such as social status, exclusivity, friendliness and responsiveness or the degree to which personal expectations and preferences are met. Similarly, the costs perceived by the customer, normally comprise more than the actual price. They also include costs of usage, the lost opportunity to use an other offering, potential switching costs etc. Hence, the customer establishes an equation between perceived benefits and perceived costs of one product and compares this to similar equations of other products.

Based on this, customer loyalty can be understood as to how customers feel about a product, service or brand and whether their perceived total investments with a it live up to their expectations. The important point here is the involvement of feelings, emotions and perceptions. In today's competitive marketplace, these perceptions are becoming much more important for gaining sustainable competitive advantage. Customer perceptions are influenced by a variety of factors. Besides the actual outcome – i.e. did the product or service deliver the expected function and did it fulfil the customers need – the whole process of consumption and all interactions involved are of crucial importance. In today's globalised information driven economy this can also comprise issues like

- How other customers or influencing groups perceive the product or brand.
- The degree to which the customer feels the actual marketing campaign addresses the most important issues.
- Responsiveness and service quality of any affiliates, e.g. distribution partners.

Customer perceptions are dynamic. First of all, with the developing relationship between customer and company, his perceptions of the company and its products or services will change. The more experience the customer accumulates, the more his perceptions will shift from fact-based judgements to a more general meaning the whole relationship gains for him. Over time, he puts a stronger focus on the consequence of the product or service consumption.

Moreover, if the customers' circumstances change, their needs and preferences often change too. In the external environment, the offerings of competitors, with which a customer compares a product or service will change, thus altering his perception of the best offer around. Another point is that the public opinion towards certain issues can change. This effect can reach from fashion trends to the public expectation of good corporate citizenship. Shells intention to dump its Brent Spar platform into the ocean significantly altered many customers perception of which company was worth buying fuel from. Research has been don on the impact of market share on the perceived quality of a product. Depending on the nature of the product and the customers' preferences, increasing market share can have positive or negative effects on how the customer perceives the product.

Positive Effects of Increasing Market share on Customer Perception

Increasing market share can send out positive signals by acting as an indicator of superior quality that is recognised by more and more other customers. This effect is particularly strong for premium priced products. Customers normally assume that a product must be of exceptional quality if it can gain such an unexpected market success despite its high price.

Many brands offer positive emotional benefits of using a product that is popular in the markets.

The value of a product or service can rise through increasing number of users of the same product, e.g. number of members of an online community, better availability of software for popular computer systems.

Negative Effects of Increasing Market share on Customer Perception

For premium and luxury products, customers may translate an increasing market share into a loss of exclusivity and thus perceive it as less valuable.

The quality of services may suffer if they are consumed by increasing numbers of users. Dis-economies of scales and congestions can be observed with busy airports and many other services so that customers may look out for other providers that promise more timely service and convenience.

The concept of customer perception does not only relate to individual customers in consumer markets. It is also valid in business to business situations. For example, a competitor Benchmarking survey of a large industrial supplier revealed that the market leader, although recognised for excellent quality and service and known to be highly innovative, was perceived as arrogant in some regions. If we take into consideration that there are about four other large players with a similar level of quality and innovative ideas, this perceived arrogance could develop into a serious problem. Customers here are well aware the main characteristics of all the offerings available at the market are largely comparable. So they might use the development of a new product generation of their own to switch to a supplier that can serve them not better or worse, but with more responsiveness and understanding.

Companies have done a lot to improve customer satisfaction and customer relationships in the past. As discussed above, this will not be enough any more.

Any serious effort to manage customer perceptions starts with a good measurement system. Companies must be truly willing to look at the whole process of interaction through the customers eyes. For many companies, this requires a more or less extensive shift in mindset, since most departments from development to sales will be involved.

7

New Age Media

New media is a term meant to encompass the emergence of digital, computerized, or networked information and communication technologies in the later part of the 20th century. Most technologies described as "new media" are digital, often having characteristics of being manipulatable, networkable, dense, compressible, interactive and impartial. Some examples may be the Internet, websites, computer multimedia, computer games, CD-ROMS, and DVDs. New media is not television programs, feature films, magazines, books, or paper-based publications.

History

In the 1960's, connections between computing and radical art began to grow stronger. It was not until the 1980's that Alan Kay and his co-workers at Xerox PARC began to give the power of a personal computer to the individual, rather than have a big organization be in charge of this. "In the late 1980s and early 1990s, however, we seem to witness a different kind of parallel between social changes and computer design. Although casually unrealated, conceptually it makes sense that the Cold War and the design of the Web took place at exactly the same time." Until the 1980s media relied primarily upon print and art analog broadcast models, such as those of television and radio. The last twenty-five years have seen the rapid transformation into media which are predicated upon the use of digital computers, such as the Internet and computer games. However, these examples are only a small representation of new media. The use of digital computers has transformed the remaining 'old' media, as suggested by the advent of digital television and online publications. Even traditional media forms such as the printing press have been transformed through the application of technologies such as image manipulation software like Adobe Photoshop and desktop publishing tools. Andrew L. Shapiro (1999) argues that the "emergence of new, digital technologies signals "a potentially radical shift of who is in control of information, experience and resources" (Shapiro cited in Croteau and Hoynes 2003: 322).

W. Russell Neuman (1991) suggests that whilst the "new media" have technical capabilities to pull in one direction, economic and social forces pull back in the opposite direction. According to Neuman, "We are witnessing the evolution of a universal interconnected network of audio, video, and electronic text communications that will blur the distinction between interpersonal and mass communication and between public and private communication" (Neuman cited in Croteau and Hoynes 2003: 322). Neuman argues that New Media:

- Will alter the meaning of geographic distance.
- Allow for a huge increase in the volume of communication.
- Provide the possibility of increasing the speed of communication.
- Provide opportunities for interactive communication.
- Allow forms of communication that were previously separate to overlap and interconnect.

Consequently it has been the contention of scholars such as Douglas Kellner, Callum Rymer and James Bohman that new media, and particularly the Internet, provide the potential for a democratic postmodern public sphere, in which citizens can participate in well informed, non-hierarchical debate pertaining to their social structures. Contradicting these positive appraisals of the potential social impacts of new media are scholars such as Ed Herman and Robert McChesney who have suggested that the transition to new media has seen a handful of powerful transnational telecommunications corporations who achieve a level of global influence which was hitherto unimaginable.

Recent contributions to the field such as Callum Rymer (2009) and his recent presentation on wikipedia, as well as Lister et al. (2003) and Friedman (2005) have highlighted both the positive and negative potential and actual implications of new media technologies, suggesting that some of the early work into new media studies was guilty of technological determinism – whereby the effects of media were determined by the technology themselves, rather than through tracing the complex social networks which governed the development, funding, implementation and future development of any technology.

Brave New Media World

Possibly the greatest testament to the media's power over mass consciousness is its ability to rewrite and even erase history. As the world plunges headlong into what's been labeled the Information Age, for example, Western-dominated mass media-with the sometimes unwitting assistance of new Internet-based enterprises-have so far convinced most of their avid consumers that we're dealing with unique issues and a revolutionary new environment that makes old debates about mass communication irrelevant. In reality, it's just a case of media-induced amnesia.

Concern about press responsibility and information policy actually dates back to the 1890s, particularly after the impact of media propaganda was dramatically demonstrated during the Spanish-American War. In 1922, the president of General Electric warned Europe about the downside of radio, urging nations to stop hurling insults at each other "in furious language." Five years later, the League of Nations passed a resolution opposing "obviously inaccurate, highly exaggerated, or deliberately distorted" news, urging the press not to undermine international peace. By the early 30s, an International Federation of Journalists had established a tribunal to deal with information that promoted hate and violence. From the start, however, the US opposed or remained aloof from proposals designed to impose sanctions or promote balance, even though its leaders recognized the danger of a European news cartel and, later, the power of fascist and Nazi propaganda. The US stand, then as now, was that only private-sector ownership could ensure the so-called "free marketplace of ideas."

The fact that commercially-based media are subject to abuses and distortions was ruled irrelevant, while arguments for a "new international information and communication order," one that would be democratic, support economic development, enhance the exchange of ideas, share knowledge among all the world's people, and improve the quality of life, was called demagoguery, the leading edge of a plan to impose a global socialist state. In the early 80s, this battle came to a head in the US effort to discredit the UN Educational, Scientific, and Cultural Organization (UNESCO), established in 1945 to promote the worldwide exchange of thought and ideas in hopes of promoting peace and prosperity. Although never completely comfortable with this agenda, the US went along until the late 70s, when calls for a New International Information Order (NIIO) directly challenged the West s "cultural imperialism."

Information flows shouldn't be one-directional, all nations should have equal access to information and international transmission channels, the power of existing transnational media monopolies should be reduced, and additional media voices should be heard-these were some of the NIIO's lofty goals. Not surprisingly, the response from the US government and corporate media was negative and savage, using all the power at their disposal to derail this challenge to the "free marketplace" gospel.

Once Ronald Reagan became president, the Heritage Foundation, a conservative think tank that developed many of Reagan's policies, led the charge. Now, the goal was not only to squelch any talk about media reform, but also to discredit UNESCO and the entire UN system. Mainstream media pitched in, casting the issue as a power play by Third World dictators to destroy the "free press"-a widely accepted euphemism for media in private hands, largely financed by advertising, and not subject to government controls or demands for social responsibility. At the same time, they played the technology card. In response to complaints about information flow imbalances, cultural dependence, unequal facilities, and distorted coverage, government and business leaders asserted that high tech would eliminate age-old gaps and even enable under-developed countries to "leapfrog" into a post-industrial future. The argument was persuasive, but the record since then shows that the main beneficiaries have been corporations and the US military-intelligence-industrial complex. The communications revolution has dramatically enhanced the mobility of capital, while helping the military to impose a global surveillance regime that would shock George Orwell.

The attack on UNESCO climaxed with the US withdrawal in 1985. After that, hopes for a "new world information and communication order" evaporated. Some critics suggest that the approach was doomed anyway, since it was promoted by political and intellectual elites, and focused on the role of states rather than individuals and civil society. In short, they argue that such a campaign for "democratization from above" would empower only governments, and likely produce new forms of censorship and control. Today, the information superhighway, like other media, is mainly driven by the market, which defines what services consumers get and how much they'll pay. Those lacking sufficient bucks-a group that includes the vast majority of the world's population are simply shut out.

The companies investing in this highway want control of access to consumers to recoup their investments. The Internet-at this point still largely a public meeting place where people exchange information, search databases, play games, and chat-has clearly attracted the attention of the international business community. Once its effectiveness as a vehicle for advertising and sales is further refined, this public, relatively un-regulated, un-censored, pluralistic network may become essentially a global electronic shopping mall.

A century after the power of global communications was first acknowledged, we're still being fed the same old line: The market best protects the free exchange of information, and is certainly preferable to any form of state or global intervention. There is another point of view, though not one our corporate gatekeepers have deigned to mention. It's embodied in the People's Communication Charter (PCC), a global initiative developed by Third World Network in Malaysia, the Centre for Communication & Human Rights in Amsterdam, the US-based Cultural Environment Movement, and the World Association of Community Radio Broadcasters.

The PCC articulates essential rights and responsibilities that ordinary people should have in relation to their cultural environment. "All people are entitled to participate in communication, and in making decisions about communication within and between societies," it asserts. "The majority of the world's peoples lack minimal technological resources for survival and communication. Over half of them have not yet made a single telephone call.

Commercialization of media and concentration of media ownership erode the public sphere and fail to provide for cultural and information needs, including the plurality of opinions and the diversity of cultural expressions and languages necessary for democracy. Massive and pervasive media violence polarizes societies, exacerbates conflict, and cultivates fear and mistrust, making people vulnerable and dependent."

In 18 articles, the charter outlines a set of principles that provide the basis for a campaign to transform global communications. Building on existing treaties and the Universal Declaration of Human Rights, it calls for broad rights to access and literacy, international protection of journalists, and the right of all people to "reply and to demand penalties for damage from media misinformation." It addresses the issues of cultural identity, language diversity, and protecting children from harmful media products. In addition, it focuses on privacy rights, equitable use of cyberspace, protection of consumers from promotion disguised as news or entertainment, and accountability through self-regulatory bodies, based on the standards outlined in the charter.

Finally, reflecting its focus on "democracy from below," the PCC also deals with the vital question of independence. The right to participate in and benefit from self-reliant communication structures, it explains, "requires international assistance to the development of independent media; training programs for professional media workers; the establishment of independent, representative associations, syndicates or trade unions of journalists and associations of editors and publishers; and the adoption of international standards."

At this point, corporate media's response has been to ignore that there's anything to discuss, aside from some self-indulgent hand wringing about whether the press focuses too much on polls and conflicts and not enough on content. Of course, we know what they're really focused on-ratings-which, in the end, means money. Still, the charter's agenda does go straight to the heart of what worries most people about our brave new media world. The questions are whether, this time, enough people will see through the "free marketplace" spin-and whether civil society will seize the initiative before it's too late.

BBC News Online

BBC News Online is the website of BBC News, the division of the BBC responsible for newsgathering and production. The website is the most popular news website in the United Kingdom and forms a major part of BBC Online. The site records around 14 million unique users a week (around 60 to 70% of visitors are from the UK). The website contains international news coverage, as well as British, entertainment, science, and political news. Many reports are accompanied by audio and video from the BBC's television and radio news services, while the latest TV and radio bulletins are also available to view or listen to on the site together with other current affairs programmes.

BBC News Online is closely linked to its sister department website, that of BBC Sport. Both sites follow the same layout and content options and respective journalists work alongside each other.

The site was named best news website at the BAFTA Interactive Entertainment Awards every year from 1998 until 2001 when the category was withdrawn.

History

The site launched in November 1997 headed by founding editor Mike Smartt. There had already been a special site marking the 1995 Budget, as well as the death of Princess Diana in 1997, but nothing on the scale of the launch of the main site itself. The original design was created by a team, including Matt Jones, based on designs commissioned from consultancy Lamby-Nairn, and has been redesigned several times mainly to match the visual style of BBC News television bulletins. A major overhaul in 2003, primarily by Paul Sissons and Maire Flynn, coincided with a relaunch of the BBC News Channel (then BBC News 24) and featured a wider page design. New features were gradually introduced, including the publicising of video content more prominently, and the introduction of live streaming of the BBC News channel.

The site saw its largest redesign on 31 March 2008, with wider centred page designs, clearer links and more of an emphasis on audio/visual content. A new BBC navigation bar was introduced as part of the redesign, as well as a change to the coding responsible for the structure of the site. The increase in page resolution meant more space could be added around content, since more viewers have screen resolutions set to 1024 pixels. Smartt was later succeeded by Pete Clifton who was subsequently promoted to Head of BBC News Interactive and replaced by the current editor Steve Herrmann. A restructuring of BBC News starting in 2007 saw the dissolution of BBC News Interactive department; the editorial and management departments joined the new multimedia newsroom along with television and radio news within BBC Television Centre; the development and site design teams are based in BBC White City, both in the White City area.

Features

UK/International Editions

There are two different editions of the site: a UK edition, which gives prominence to UK stories, and an International edition, which prioritises international news. All articles are archived indefinitely and can be retrieved via searching or by browsing the extensive *Special Reports* section, which contains collections of articles relating to major news stories. The previous seven days' top stories were formerly available through the Week at a Glance section of the website.

Internet users with addresses originating from the UK are served the UK edition, all others receive the World edition. As well as pure news articles, the site also contains material to support BBC news, current affairs and factual programmes. The *Magazine* section contains features prompted by current news stories, as well as a number of regular items within the daily *Magazine Monitor* blog with various light-hearted sub-sections including 'Caption Competition', 'Reader's Letters', 'Punorama', quizzes and other humorous items.

A forum, *Have Your Say*, is also a major part of the site, linking with the BBC programme of the same name and promotions on BBC News bulletins. The current system behind the forum was introduced in 2005 to allow or comments to be added to debates and appear in real-time, subject to varying levels of moderation. A more detailed section of the web site is '*Special Reports*, formerly *In Depth*. This brings together news articles by theme or incident and also includes many explanatory articles or diagrams. Since the beginning of May 2007, the BBC News channel has been streamed live on the UK version of the website.

Columnists

BBC News Online has a small number of topic-specific columns written by BBC journalists. Examples include education correspondent Mike Baker's *Mike Baker Weekly* column and technology commentator Bill Thompson's *bill board* (formerly *bill blog*). BBC News Online Science Writer Ivan Noble, diagnosed with a malignant brain tumour in August 2002, shared his experiences of cancer in *Tumour Diary* until his death on 31 January 2005. The use of blogs has also grown with correspondents including Nick Robinson, Robert Peston, Mark Mardell, Justin Webb and Evan Davis, amongst others, making use of them to provide updates on the latest news events. *The Editors' blog* has also seen BBC News editors giving their reasons for editorial decisions, as well as defending criticisms of the BBC. Members of the public are given the opportunity to comment on entries

Embedded Video and Audio

Embedded video using the BBC Embedded Media Player now accompanies many articles. The launch of the BBC iPlayer, with the new Adobe Flash based BBC Embedded Media Player in July 2007 enabled BBC News and Sport Online to change the way it presented video content. Previously the site had delivered online video content using embedded RealPlayer video in pop-up windows branded as the *BBC News Player*.

From March 2008 the BBC began to gradually introduce embedded video using the EMP into individual news articles and onto the front page. The news player also provides constant live streaming of the BBC News channel via the website. This had previously only been viewable in a separate window.

Real-time Information

The site launched a set of semi-official RSS 0.91 syndication feeds in June 2003 and upgraded them to full feed RSS 2.0 in 2008. Each news index has its own RSS feed, including the in-depth sections. The BBC began providing real-time global user information in June 2006.

BBC Newstracker

In 2004 the BBC News website partnered with Moreover Technologies, in a response to the 2003 Graf Report, to provide links from BBC articles to rival publishers. Whilst the BBC does not censor or change results the algorithms used tend to give greater weight to national and international sources over regional or local ones.

Criticism

The site is primarily funded by the television licence, paid by all UK households owning a television set, and used to carry no advertising. The World edition has received some subsidy from the UK's Foreign and Commonwealth Office through its grant-in-aid to the BBC World Service. This has led to complaints of unfair competition from commercial rivals. Others note that large numbers of international visitors enjoy the site at the expense of the UK public, leading to suggestions that foreign users be shown advertising or charged subscription fees when accessing the site.

Proposals to include advertising on the international version of the website were discussed by the BBC Trust in February 2007, but were opposed by BBC journalists, who feared it would weaken public trust in the impartiality of the BBC. In November 2007, the site did start to carry advertising. The advertising consists of large animated banners, which has led to complaints that these make the site's content harder to read. The impartiality of the *Have Your Say* forums has been disputed by organisations such as News Sniffer: moderators are accused of sometimes appearing to promote their own agenda.

Drudge Report

The *Drudge Report* is a conservative news aggregation website. Run by Matt Drudge with the help of Andrew Breitbart, the site consists mainly of links to stories from the United States and international mainstream media about politics, entertainment, and current events as well as links to many columnists. Occasionally, Drudge authors news stories himself based on tips. The *Report* originated in 1996 as a weekly subscriber-based email dispatch. It was most famous for being the first news source to break the Monica Lewinsky scandal to the public after *Newsweek* decided not to publish the story.

Origins

The Drudge Report started as a gossip column focusing on Hollywood and Washington, D.C. Matt Drudge began the email-based newsletter called *Report* from an apartment in Hollywood, California, using his connections with industry and media insiders to break stories, sometimes before they hit the mainstream media. Drudge maintains the website from his home in Miami Beach, Florida, with help from Andrew Breitbart, who assists in story selection and headline writing. Breitbart, who describes himself as "Matt Drudge's bitch", works the afternoon shift at the Drudge Report, as well as running his own website (breitbart.com), and another website providing a conservative support system for people in the Los Angeles entertainment industry.

Drudge, who began his website in 1997 as a supplement to his $10/year email newsletter, received national attention in 1996 when he broke the news that Jack Kemp would be Republican Bob Dole's running mate in the 1996 presidential election. In 1998, Drudge made national waves when he broke the news that *Newsweek* magazine had information on an inappropriate relationship between "a White House intern" and President Bill Clinton (the Monica Lewinsky scandal), but was withholding publication. After Drudge's report, *Newsweek* published the story.

Content

The *Drudge Report* site consists mainly of selected hyperlinks to news websites all over the world, each link carrying a headline written by Drudge or his editors. The linked stories are generally hosted on the external websites of mainstream media outlets. It occasionally includes stories written by Drudge — usually two or three paragraphs in length. They generally concern a story about to be published in a major magazine or newspaper. Drudge occasionally publishes Nielsen, Arbitron, or BookScan ratings, or early election exit polls that are otherwise not made available to the public. The site carries advertisements that generate the site's revenue. The *Drudge Report's* advertising is sold by Vienna, Virginia-based ad firm *Intermarkets*.

In April, 2009, Associated Press announced that it would be examining the fair use doctrine used by sites like Google and *Drudge*

Report to justify the use of AP content without payment. On May 4, 2009, the US Attorney General's office issued a warning to employees in Massachusetts not to visit the *Drudge Report* because of malicious code contained in some of the advertising on the website. The Justice Department also cited other sites such as ESPN.com as having viruses.

Design

The *Drudge Report* was described by Cheryl Woodard, co-founder of *PC*, Macworld, PC World and *Publish* magazines, as "a big, haphazard mishmash of links and photos" and by Dan Rahmel as "popular despite a plain appearance". The *Report* website is simple and, according to Paul Armstrong of *webwithoutwords.com*, retro in feel. Jason Fried of *37signals.com* calls it "one of the best designed sites on the web." It consists of a banner headline and a number of other selected headlines in three columns in monospaced font. Most link to an outside source, usually the online edition of a newspaper, which hosts the story. When no such source is available, either because the story is 'developing' with little known details at the moment or is an exclusive scoop, a special page is created on the *Drudge Report* servers which contain text and possibly images.

There are different importance levels a story could appear as on the site, the rating of which relies on Matt Drudge's editorial discretion. The *Report* almost always holds one major story above the logo, usually just one sentence hyperlinked to the most important story of the day. Other stories surrounding the main headline can be found in the upper left hand side of the page and link to more specific articles dealing with aspects of the headline story.

The standard story, either the headline or links below the logo, are written in black. The stories Drudge considers most important are in red, all under a single major headline in large, bold type. For especially important breaking stories, especially if still emerging, Drudge places art of a flashing red light on the screen. Although the site initially featured very few images, it is now usually illustrated with five or six photographs. Generally the images, like the linked headlines, are hotlinked from other news agencies' servers.

Political Leanings

Matt Drudge has said that he is a conservative, but "more of a populist". The *Drudge Report* website is generally regarded as conservative in tone, and has been referred to in the media as "a conservative news aggregator". More recently Richard Siklos, an editor of Fortune magazine, called the Drudge Report a "conservative bullhorn", the Los Angeles Times labelled Drudge a "well-known conservative warrior", the New York Times referred to him as a "conservative muckraker", and Glenn Greenwald called him a "right-wing hack". Greenwald also wrote that the *Drudge Report* (inter alia) is part of the "Bush/Cheney right-wing noise machine", adding: "Allowing [websites like *Drudge Report,* inter alia] to dominate our political debates and drive media coverage guarantees a decrepit, rotted, and deeply corrupt country.... Their endless lynch mob crusades supplant rational and substantive political debates." Ben Shapiro of townhall.com wrote "The American left can't restrict Internet usage or ban talk radio, so it de-legitimizes these news sources. Ripping alternative news sources as illegitimate is the left's only remaining option — it cannot compete with the right wing in the new media....They call Matt Drudge a muckraker and a yellow journalist."

A 2003 study placed the *Drudge Report* "left of centre". The study was criticised by Mark Liberman and liberal media watchdogs. The authors stated that although "conventional wisdom" asserts that the *Drudge Report* is "relatively conservative", their methodology found it to be "centrist". The authors placed *Drudge Report* in a dead heat with Fox News *Special Report With Brit Hume,* ABC's "Good Morning America", CNN's NewsNight With Aaron Brown" and "NewsHour With Jim Lehrer" as most centrist outlet. The study also noted that "...our data for the Drudge Report was based almost entirely on the articles that the Drudge Report lists on other Web sites... The fact that the Drudge Report appears left of centre is merely a reflection of the overall bias of the media."

Influence

According to Mark Halperin, "Drudge's coverage affects the media's political coverage", effectively steering the media's political coverage towards what Halperin calls "the most salacious aspects of American politics." In *The Way To Win,* a book written by Halperin and John Harris, Drudge is called "the Walter Cronkite of his era." Democratic Party strategist Chris Lehane says "phones start ringing" whenever Drudge breaks a story, and Mark McKinnon, a former media advisor to George W. Bush, said that he checked the site 30–40 times per day. Matt Drudge has been criticized by other media news personalities: Bill O'Reilly twice called Drudge a "threat to democracy" in response to Drudge disclosing his book sales figures, and Keith Olbermann referred to Drudge as "an idiot with a modem".

Drudge (and his website) was labelled one of the "Top 10 anti-Barack Obama conservatives" by the US editor of The Daily Telegraph in February 2009. In addition to the media influence, Drudge Report also has influenced design elements on other sites. Some with opposing view points and some who use the same format of listing news. A left-leaning parody site called Drudge Retort was founded in 1998 as "a send-up of Mr. Drudge's breathless style".

Traffic Statistics

In March, 2008, the Newspaper Association of America listed *The Drudge Report* as having a readership of about 3.5 million with up to 19 visits per person per day. The revisit number is increased by the site's use of an autorefresh script which refreshes the page every three minutes. According to Nielsen NetRatings, *Drudge Report* had 3.4 million unique visitors in February, 2009. On September 25, 2009 Alexa Internet ranked the *Drudge Report* website one month average ranking at 589, up 248 places in 3 months.

Average time spent on the site per user was 3.0 minutes a day. Compete.com showed 2,629,948 unique monthly visitors in April, 2009 — an increase of 20% in one year, and a ranking of 650, down from 630 a year earlier. ComScore logged 2 million uniques to the *Report* in September 2008, and 1.7 million uniques in April, 2009. According to the online advertising company linked to his site, the *Drudge Report* audience is 78 percent male, 60 percent Republican, and 8 percent Democrat. In October, 2006, *Washington Post* editor Leonard Downie, Jr. stated that for bloggers, the "largest driver of traffic is Matt Drudge."

Archives

Many reports from 1995 to early 1997 are available in the Usenet archive provided by Google Groups. A more extensive archive of the website is provided by Drudge Report Archives, which has archives since mid-November 2001 and stores snapshots of the Drudge Report homepage every two minutes.

Notable Stories

Monica Lewinsky Scandal

The Drudge Report attained prominence when it was the first to report what came to be known as the Lewinsky scandal. Drudge published the story on January 17, 1998, after *Newsweek* reportedly turned down the story.

Obama Photo

Drudge published a photo of Barack Obama in Somali tribal dress on February 25, 2008, and reported that the photo had been sent to him by a Clinton campaign staffer. The publication of the photograph resulted in a brief war of words between the Clinton and Obama campaign organizations.

Prince Harry in Afghanistan

On February 28, 2008 Drudge published an article noting that Prince Harry of Wales was serving with his regiment in Afghanistan. Prince Harry was ten weeks into a front-line deployment in Afghanistan that was subject to a voluntary news blackout by the UK press. The blackout was designed to protect Prince Harry and the men serving with him from being specifically targeted by the Taliban. An Australian weekly women's magazine *New Idea* broke the story in January, but it was not followed up at the time. New Idea editors claimed ignorance of any news blackout. Then a German newspaper, the *Berliner Kurier*, published a short piece on February 28, 2008, also before Drudge. Drudge subsequently claimed the report as an exclusive. Chief of the General Staff Sir Richard Dannatt, professional head of the British Army, said: "I am very disappointed that foreign websites have decided to run this story without consulting us". The Prince's tour of duty was prematurely ended, since his unit might be targeted by large scale suicide attacks intended to kill the Prince.

Controversial Stories, Errors and Questions about Sourcing

Exclusives

Research by the media magazine Brill's Content in 1998 cast doubt on the accuracy of the majority of the 'exclusives' claimed by the *Drudge Report.* Of the 51 stories claimed as exclusives from January to September 1998, the magazine found 31 (61%) were actually exclusive stories. Of those, 32% were untrue, 36% were true and the remaining 32% were of debatable accuracy.

Sidney Blumenthal Lawsuit

In 1997, the *Drudge Report* reported that incoming White House assistant Sidney Blumenthal beat his wife and was covering it up. Drudge retracted the story the next day and apologized, saying he was given bad information, but Blumenthal filed a $30 million libel lawsuit against Drudge. After four years, Blumenthal dropped his lawsuit. Blumenthal said the suit had cost him tens of thousands of dollars in legal fees. He agreed to pay $2,500 to Drudge's Los Angeles attorney for travel costs, claiming that Drudge was "backed by unlimited funds from political supporters who use a tax-exempt foundation." The Individual Rights Foundation, led by conservative activist David Horowitz, paid Drudge's legal fees in the Blumenthal lawsuit. A federal judge noted in the judgment that Drudge "is not a reporter, a journalist, or a newsgatherer. He is, as he admits himself, simply a purveyor of gossip."

Alleged John Kerry Intern Scandal

During the 2004 Presidential campaign, Drudge ran a story quoting General Wesley Clark, where Clark claimed that the John Kerry campaign would implode over an intern affair. Drudge reported that other news outlets were investigating the alleged affair. He removed it from the site shortly thereafter when the other news outlets dropped the investigations.

Alleged Bill Clinton Illegitimate Child

In 1999, the *Drudge Report* announced that it had viewed a videotape which was the basis of a *Star Magazine* and *Hard Copy* story. Under the headline, "Woman Names Bill Clinton Father Of Son In Shocking Video Confession", Drudge reported a videotaped "confession" by a former prostitute who claimed that her son was fathered by Bill Clinton. The *Report* stated, "To accuse the most powerful man in the world of being the father of her son is either the hoax of a lifetime, or a personal turmoil that needs resolution. Only two people may know that answer tonight." The claim turned out to be a hoax.

Alleged CNN Reporter Heckling of GOP Senators

On April 1, 2007 Drudge cited an unnamed "official" source saying that CNN reporter Michael Ware had "heckled" Republican Senators McCain and Graham during a live press conference. Drudge reported that:

Ware disputed Drudge's report on CNN April 2, 2007, saying that the story was leaked "by an unnamed official of some kind to a blog", that the story was anonymous, and that no one was willing to put their name to it; he advised people to view the tape. Video hosted by Rawstory shows that Ware did not make a sound nor ask any question during the press conference. The *Drudge Report* did not retract or apologize for the story. Drudge's report was echoed in *The Washington Times*, which carried opinion questioning Ware's trustworthiness, and in many conservative blogs, some of which called for Ware's resignation.

Oprah and Sarah Palin

On September 5, 2008 the Drudge Report reported that Oprah staffers were "sharply divided on the merits of booking Sarah Palin." He said that he obtained the information from an anonymous source. Winfrey responded in a written statement to news outlets that: "The item in today's Drudge Report is categorically untrue. There has been absolutely no discussion about having Sarah Palin on my show.

At the beginning of this presidential campaign when I decided that I was going to take my first public stance in support of a candidate, I made the decision not to use my show as a platform for any of the candidates." Oprah Winfrey's public statement came after she had already used her show to publicly endorse Barack Obama for president. Drudge was accused of planting a false story for political ends by some commentators.

Ashley Todd Attack Hoax

On October 23, 2008, Drudge published an unconfirmed exclusive story regarding Ashley Todd, the 20-year old employee of the College Republican National Committee (CRNC) and John McCain volunteer who had allegedly been attacked by a black male for having a McCain sticker on her car. Drudge reported the story without a link but as 'developing', titling the headline *"Shock: Mccain Volunteer Attacked and Mutilated in Pittsburgh-"B"* carved into 20 yr old Woman's Face". The story set off a "storm of media attention", being quickly picked up by many conservative bloggers and right-wing talk radio show hosts, all citing the Drudge Report as their source.

It was also reported in newspapers and TV both in the US and around the world. The story was confirmed to be a hoax perpetrated by Todd and, according to Talking Points Memo, spread to reporters by McCain's Pennsylvania Communications Director.

Drudge then printed a retraction of the story, including links to the news stories detailing that the attack had been a hoax and that Ashley Todd had performed a similar 'attack' on herself while working for the Ron Paul campaign.

Citizen Journalism

Citizen journalism (also known as "public", "participatory", "democratic" or "street journalism") is the concept of members of the public "playing an active role in the process of collecting, reporting, analysing and disseminating news and information," according to the seminal 2003 report *We Media: How Audiences are Shaping the Future of News and Information.* Authors Bowman and Willis say: "The intent of this participation is to provide independent, reliable, accurate, wide-ranging and relevant information that a democracy requires."

Citizen journalism should not be confused with community journalism or civic journalism, which are practiced by professional journalists, or collaborative journalism, which is practiced by professional and non-professional journalists working together. Citizen journalism is a specific form of citizen media as well as user generated content. Mark Glaser, a freelance journalist who frequently writes on new media issues, said in 2006:

The idea behind citizen journalism is that people without professional journalism training can use the tools of modern technology and the global distribution of the Internet to create, augment or fact-check media on their own or in collaboration with others. For example, you might write about a city council meeting on your blog or in an online forum. Or you could fact-check a newspaper article from the mainstream media and point out factual errors or bias on your blog. Or you might snap a digital photo of a newsworthy event happening in your town and post it online. Or you might videotape a similar event and post it on a site such as YouTube.

In *What is Participatory Journalism?*, J. D. Lasica classifies media for citizen journalism into the following types:

1. Audience participation (such as user comments attached to news stories, personal blogs, photos or video footage captured from personal mobile cameras, or local news written by residents of a community)
2. Independent news and information Websites (Consumer Reports, the Drudge Report)
3. Full-fledged participatory news sites (NowPublic, OhmyNews, DigitalJournal.com, GroundReport)
4. Collaborative and contributory media sites (Slashdot, Kuro5hin, Newsvine)
5. Other kinds of "thin media." (mailing lists, email newsletters)
6. Personal broadcasting sites (video broadcast sites such as KenRadio).

New media theorist Terry Flew states that there are 3 elements "critical to the rise of citizen journalism and citizen media": open publishing, collaborative editing and distributed content. From this perspective, Wikipedia itself is the largest and most successful citizen journalism project, with news often breaking through Wikipedia editors, and stories being maintained as new facts emerge.

History

The idea that average citizens can engage in the act of journalism has a long history in the United States. The modern citizen journalist movement emerged after journalists themselves began to question the predictability of their coverage of such events as the 1988 U.S. presidential election. Those journalists became part of the public, or civic, journalism movement, a countermeasure against the eroding trust in the news media and widespread public disillusionment with politics and civic affairs.

Initially, discussions of public journalism focused on promoting journalism that was "for the people" by changing the way professional reporters did their work. According to Leonard Witt, however, early public journalism efforts were, "often part of 'special projects' that were expensive, time-consuming and episodic. Too often these projects dealt with an issue and moved on. Professional journalists were driving the discussion. They would say, "Let's do a story on welfare-to-work (or the environment, or traffic problems, or the economy)," and then they would recruit a cross-section of citizens and chronicle their points of view. Since not all reporters and editors bought into this form of public journalism, and some outright opposed it, reaching out to the people from the newsroom was never an easy task."

By 2003, in fact, the movement seemed to be petering out, with the Pew Centre for Civic Journalism closing its doors. With today's technology the citizen journalist movement has found new life as the average person can capture news and distribute it globally. As Yochai Benkler has noted, "the capacity to make meaning – to encode and decode humanly meaningful statements – and the capacity to communicate one's meaning around the world, are held by, or readily available to, at least many hundreds of millions of users around the globe." Professor Mary-Rose Papandrea, a constitutional law professor at Boston College, notes in her article, *Citizen Journalism and the Reporter's Privilege,* that:

> *[i]n many ways, the definition of journalist has now come full circle. When the First Amendment was adopted, "freedom of the press" referred quite literally to the freedom to publish using a printing press, rather than the freedom of organized entities engaged in the*

publishing business. The printers of 1775 did not exclusively publish newspapers; instead, in order to survive financially they dedicated most of their efforts printing materials for paying clients. The newspapers and pamphlets of the American Revolutionary era were predominantly partisan and became even more so through the turn of the century. They engaged in little newsgathering and instead were predominantly vehicles for opinion.

The passage of the term "journalism" into common usage in the 1830s occurred at roughly the same time that newspapers, using highspeed rotary steam presses, began mass circulation throughout the eastern United States.

Using the printing press, newspapers could distribute exact copies to large numbers of readers at a low incremental cost. In addition, the rapidly increasing demand for advertising for brand-name products fueled the creation of publications subsidized in large part by advertising revenue. It was not until the late nineteenth century that the concept of the "press" morphed into a description of individuals and companies engaged in an often competitive commercial media enterprise.

Birth of Blogs and the Indymedia Movement

In 1999, activists in Seattle created a response to the WTO meeting being held there. These activists understood the only way they could get into the corporate media was by blocking the streets. And then, the scant 60 seconds of coverage would show them being carted off by the police, but without any context to explain why they were protesting. They knew they had to create an alternative media model. Since then, the Indymedia movement has experienced exponential growth, and IMCs have been created in over 200 cities all over the world. Simultaneously, journalism that was "by the people" began to flourish, enabled in part by emerging internet and networking technologies, such as weblogs, chat rooms, message boards, wikis and mobile computing.

A relatively new development is the use of convergent polls, allowing editorials and opinions to be submitted and voted on. Overtime, the poll converges on the most broadly accepted editorials and opinions. In South Korea, OhmyNews became popular and commercially successful with the motto, "Every Citizen is a Reporter." Founded by Oh Yeon-ho on February 22, 2000, it has a staff of some 40-plus traditional reporters and editors who write about 20% of its content, with the rest coming from other freelance contributors who are mostly ordinary citizens. OhmyNews now has an estimated 50,000 contributors, and has been credited with transforming South Korea's conservative political environment.

In 2001, ThemeParkInsider.com became the first online publication to win a major journalism award for a feature that was reported and written entirely by readers, earning an Online Journalism Award from the Online News Association and Columbia Graduate School of Journalism for its "Accident Watch" section, where readers tracked injury accidents at theme parks and shared accident prevention tips. In February 2003, iBrattleboro.com was launched in Brattleboro, Vermont, becoming one of the first citizen-written news sites in the United States.

In 2004, a citizen journalism website called AssociatedContent.com was launched. The "People's Media Company", as they claim to be, was the first company to offer monetary compensation for their users that publish quality content in the form of articles, videos and audio clips. More recently, Allvoices launched in July 2008. Its CEO, Amra Tareen, is a Muslim American and former venture capitalist who created the site after having done charity work in her native Pakistan. While there she noted there was no central hub on the Internet where anyone, anywhere could witness and then instantly report from their perspective news as it happened.

Allvoices uses a combination of technology and community to vet stories for authenticity and popularity. The site takes contributions from around the world via any Internet-connected device and its contributors frequently break stories before the mainstream media. Allvoices was also the first citizen journalism site to measure the credibility of contributed reports and their authors, providing readers with a gauge launched in March 2009 for assessing the accuracy of news accounts. During the 2004 U.S. presidential election, both the Democratic and Republican parties issued press credentials to citizen bloggers covering the convention, marking a new level of influence and credibility for nontraditional journalists. Some bloggers also began watchdogging the work of conventional journalists, monitoring their work for biases and inaccuracy.

A recent trend in citizen journalism has been the emergence of what blogger Jeff Jarvis terms hyperlocal journalism, as online news sites invite contributions from local residents of their subscription areas, who often report on topics that conventional newspapers tend to ignore. "We are the traditional journalism model turned upside down," explains Mary Lou Fulton, the publisher of the Northwest Voice in Bakersfield, California. "Instead of being the gatekeeper, telling people that what's important to them 'isn't news,' we're just opening up the gates and letting people come on in. We are a better community newspaper for having thousands of readers who serve as the eyes and ears for the Voice, rather than having everything filtered through the views of a small group of reporters and editors."

Who are Citizen Journalists?

According to Jay Rosen, citizen journalists "the people formerly known as the audience," who "*were* on the receiving end of a media system that ran one way, in a broadcasting pattern, with high entry fees and a few firms competing to speak very loudly while the rest of the population listened in isolation from one another— and who *today* are not in a situation like that *at all*.... The people formerly known as the audience are simply the public made realer, less fictional, more able, less predictable."

"Doing citizen journalism right means crafting a crew of correspondents who are typically excluded from or misrepresented by local television news: low-income women, minorities and youth — the very demographic and lifestyle groups who have little access to the media and that advertisers don't want," says Robert Huesca, an associate professor of communication at Trinity University in San Antonio, Texas.

Public Journalism is now being explored via new media such as the use of mobile phones. Mobile phones have the potential to transform reporting and places the power of reporting in the hands of the public. Mobile telephony provides low-cost options for people to set up news operations. One small organization providing mobile news and exploring public journalism is Jasmine News in Sri Lanka.

According to Mark Glaser, during 9/11 many eyewitness accounts of the terrorist attacks on the World Trade Centre came from citizen journalists. Images and stories from citizen journalists with close proximity to the World Trade Centre offered content that played a major role in the story. In 2004, when the 9.1-magnitude underwater earthquake caused a huge tsunami in Banda Aceh Indonesia, news footage from many people who experienced the tsunami was widely broadcast. During the 2009 Iranian election protests the microblog service Twitter played an important role, after foreign journalists had effectivley been "barred from reporting". One of the most outstanding contributors from inside Iran has been persiankiwi.

Criticisms

Citizen journalists may be activists within the communities they write about. This has drawn some criticism from traditional media institutions such as The New York Times, which have accused proponents of public journalism of abandoning the traditional goal of 'objectivity'. Many traditional journalists view citizen journalism with some skepticism, believing that only trained journalists can understand the exactitude and ethics involved in reporting news. See, e.g., Nicholas Lemann, Vincent Maher, and Tom Grubisich.

An academic paper by Vincent Maher, the head of the New Media Lab at Rhodes University, outlined several weaknesses in the claims made by citizen journalists, in terms of the "three deadly E's", referring to ethics, economics and epistemology. This paper has itself been criticized in the press and blogosphere.

An article in 2005 by Tom Grubisich reviewed ten new citizen journalism sites and found many of them lacking in quality and content. Grubisich followed up a year later with, "Potemkin Village Redux." He found that the best sites had improved editorially and were even nearing profitability, but only by not expensing editorial costs. Also according to the article, the sites with the weakest editorial content were able to aggressively expand because they had stronger financial resources.

Another article published on Pressthink examined Backfence, a citizen journalism site with initial three locations in the DC area, which reveals that the site has only attracted limited citizen contributions. The author concludes that, "in fact, clicking through Backfence's pages feels like frontier land-– remote, often lonely, zoned for people but not home to any. The site recently launched for Arlington, Virginia. However, without more settlers, Backfence may wind up creating more ghost towns."

David Simon, a former Baltimore Sun reporter and writer/producer of the popular TV series, "The Wire," criticized the concept of citizen journalism—claiming that unpaid bloggers who write as a hobby cannot replace trained, professional, seasoned journalists. "I am offended to think that anyone, anywhere believes American institutions as insulated, self-preserving and self-justifying as police departments, school systems, legislatures and chief executives can be held to gathered facts by amateurs pursuing the task without compensation, training or for that matter, sufficient standing to make public officials even care to whom it is they are lying to," Simon testified before a Senate committee in May of 2009.

> *"Indeed, the very phrase citizen journalism strikes my ear as nearly Orwellian. A neighbour who is a good listener and cares about people is a good neighbour; he is not in any sense a citizen social worker. Just as a neighbour with a garden hose and good intentions is not a citizen firefighter. To say so is a heedless insult to trained social workers and firefighters."*

Others criticize the formulation of the term "citizen journalism" to describe the concept, as the word "citizen" has a conterminous relation to the nation-state. The fact that many millions of people are considered stateless and often without citizenship (such as refugees or immigrants without papers) limits the concept to those recognised only by governments.

Additionally the global nature of many participatory media initiatives, such as the Independent Media Centre, makes talking of journalism in relation to a particular nation-state largely redundant as its production and dissemination do not recognise national boundaries. Some additional names given to the concept based on this analysis are grassroots media, people's media, or participatory media.

Proponents of Citizen Journalism

- Dan Gillmor, former technology columnist with the *San Jose Mercury News*, is one of the foremost proponents of citizen journalism, and founded a nonprofit, the Centre for Citizen Media, to help promote it.

  The Canadian Broadcasting Corporation's French-language television network has also organized a weekly public affairs program called, "5 sur 5", which has been organizing and promoting citizen-based journalism since 2001. On the program, viewers submit questions on a wide variety of topics, and they, accompanied by staff journalists, get to interview experts to obtain answers to their questions.

- Jay Rosen, a journalism professor at New York University, was one of public journalism's earliest proponents. From 1993 to 1997, he directed the Project on Public Life and the Press, funded by the Knight Foundation and housed at NYU. He also currently runs the PressThink weblog.

Blog

A blog (a contraction of the term "web log") is a type of website, usually maintained by an individual with regular entries of commentary, descriptions of events, or other material such as graphics or video. Entries are commonly displayed in reverse-chronological order. "Blog" can also be used as a verb, meaning *to maintain or add content to a blog.*

Many blogs provide commentary or news on a particular subject; others function as more personal online diaries. A typical blog combines text, images, and links to other blogs, Web pages, and other media related to its topic. The ability for readers to leave comments in an interactive format is an important part of many blogs. Most blogs are primarily textual, although some focus on art (Art blog), photographs (photoblog), videos (Video blogging), music (MP3 blog), and audio (podcasting). Microblogging is another type of blogging, featuring very short posts. As of December 2007, blog search engine Technorati was tracking more than 112,000,000 blogs.

Personal Blogs

The personal blog, an ongoing diary or commentary by an individual, is the traditional, most common blog. Personal bloggers usually take pride in their blog posts, even if their blog is never read. Blogs often become more than a way to just communicate; they become a way to reflect on life or works of art. Blogging can have a sentimental quality. Few personal blogs rise to fame and the mainstream, but some personal blogs quickly garner an extensive following.

A type of personal blog is referred to as "microblogging," which is extremely detailed blogging as it seeks to capture a moment in time. Sites, such as Twitter, allow bloggers to share thoughts and feelings instantaneously with friends and family and is much faster than e-mailing or writing.

Corporate and Organizational Blogs

A blog can be private, as in most cases, or it can be for business purposes. Blogs, either used internally to enhance the communication and culture in a corporation or externally for marketing, branding or public relations purposes are called corporate blogs. Similar blogs for clubs and societies are called club blogs, group blogs, or by similar names; typical use is to inform members and other interested parties of club and member activities.

By Genre

Some blogs focus on a particular subject, such as political blogs, travel blogs (also known as *travelogs*), house blogs, fashion blogs, project blogs, education blogs, niche blogs, classical music blogs, quizzing blogs and legal blogs (often referred to as a blawgs) or dreamlogs.

Two common types of genre blogs are art blogs and music blogs. A blog featuring discussions especially about home and family is not uncommonly called a mom blog. While not a legitimate type of blog, one used for the sole purpose of spamming is known as a Splog.

By Media Type

A blog comprising videos is called a vlog, one comprising links is called a linklog, a site containing a portfolio of sketches is called a sketchblog or one comprising photos is called a photoblog. Blogs with shorter posts and mixed media types are called tumblelogs. Blogs that are written on typewriters and then scanned are called typecast or typecast blogs; see typecasting (blogging). A rare type of blog hosted on the Gopher Protocol is known as a Phlog.

By Device

Blogs can also be defined by which type of device is used to compose it. A blog written by a mobile device like a mobile phone or PDA could be called a moblog. One early blog was Wearable Wireless Webcam, an online shared diary of a person's personal life combining text, video, and pictures transmitted live from a wearable computer and EyeTap device to a web site. This practice of semi-automated blogging with live video together with text was referred to as sousveillance. Such journals have been used as evidence in legal matters.

Community and Cataloguing

The Blogosphere

The collective community of all blogs is known as the *blogosphere*. Since all blogs are on the internet by definition, they may be seen as interconnected and socially networked, through blogrolls, comments, linkbacks (refbacks, trackbacks or pingbacks) and backlinks. Discussions "in the blogosphere" are occasionally used by the media as a gauge of public opinion on various issues. Because new, untapped communities of bloggers can emerge in the space of a few years, Internet marketers pay close attention to "trends in the blogosphere".

Blog Search Engines

Several blog search engines are used to search blog contents, such as Bloglines, BlogScope, and Technorati. Technorati, which is among the most popular blog search engines, provides current information on both popular searches and tags used to categorize blog postings. The research community is working on going beyond simple keyword search, by inventing new ways to navigate through huge amounts of information present in the blogosphere, as demonstrated by projects like BlogScope.

Blogging Communities and Directories

Several online communities exist that connect people to blogs and bloggers to other bloggers, including BlogCatalog and MyBlogLog. Interest-specific blogging platforms are also available. For instance, Blogster has a sizable community of political bloggers among its members.

Blogging and Advertising

It is common for blogs to feature advertisements either to financially benefit the blogger or to promote the blogger's favourite causes. The popularity of blogs has also given rise to "fake blogs" in which a company will create a fictional blog as a marketing tool to promote a product.

Popularity

Researchers have analyzed the dynamics of how blogs become popular. There are essentially two measures of this: popularity through citations, as well as popularity through affiliation (i.e. blogroll). The basic conclusion from studies of the structure of blogs is that while it takes time for a blog to become popular through blogrolls, permalinks can boost popularity more quickly, and are perhaps more indicative of popularity and authority than blogrolls, since they denote that people are actually reading the blog's content and deem it valuable or noteworthy in specific cases.

The blogdex project was launched by researchers in the MIT Media Lab to crawl the Web and gather data from thousands of blogs in order to investigate their social properties. It gathered this information for over 4 years, and autonomously tracked the most contagious information spreading in the blog community, ranking it by recency and popularity. It can therefore be considered the first instantiation of a memetracker. The project is no longer active, but a similar function is now served by tailrank.com.

Blogs are given rankings by Technorati based on the number of incoming links and Alexa Internet based on the Web hits of Alexa Toolbar users. In August 2006, Technorati found that the most linked-to blog on the internet was that of Chinese actress Xu Jinglei. Chinese media Xinhua reported that this blog received more than 50 million page views, claiming it to be the most popular blog in the world. Technorati rated Boing Boing to be the most-read group-written blog.

Blurring with the Mass Media

Many bloggers, particularly those engaged in participatory journalism, differentiate themselves from the mainstream media, while others are members of that media working through a different channel. Some institutions see blogging as a means of "getting around the filter" and pushing messages directly to the public. Some critics worry that bloggers respect neither copyright nor the role of the mass media in presenting society with credible news. Bloggers and other contributors to user-generated content are behind *Time* magazine naming their 2006 person of the year as "you".

Many mainstream journalists, meanwhile, write their own blogs — well over 300, according to CyberJournalist.net's J-blog list. The first known use of a blog on a news site was in August 1998, when Jonathan Dube of The Charlotte Observer published one chronicling Hurricane Bonnie.

Some bloggers have moved over to other media. The following bloggers (and others) have appeared on radio and television: Duncan Black (known widely by his pseudonym, Atrios), Glenn Reynolds (Instapundit), Markos Moulitsas Zúniga (Daily Kos), Alex Steffen (Worldchanging) and Ana Marie Cox (Wonkette). In counterpoint, Hugh Hewitt exemplifies a mass-media personality who has moved in the other direction, adding to his reach in "old media" by being an influential blogger. Equally many established authors, for example Mitzi Szereto have started using Blogs to not only update fans on their current works but also to expand into new areas of writing.

Blogs have also had an influence on minority languages, bringing together scattered speakers and learners; this is particularly so with blogs in Gaelic languages. Minority language publishing (which may lack economic feasibility) can find its audience through inexpensive blogging.

There are many examples of bloggers who have published books based on their blogs, e.g., Salam Pax, Ellen Simonetti, Jessica Cutler,

ScrappleFace. Blog-based books have been given the name blook. A prize for the best blog-based book was initiated in 2005, the Lulu Blooker Prize. However, success has been elusive offline, with many of these books not selling as well as their blogs. Only blogger Tucker Max made the New York Times Bestseller List. The book based on Julie Powell's blog "The Julie/Julia Project" was made into the film *Julie & Julia*, apparently the first to do so.

Legal and Social Consequences

Blogging can result in a range of legal liabilities and other unforeseen consequences.

Defamation or Liability

Several cases have been brought before the national courts against bloggers concerning issues of defamation or liability. U.S. payouts related to blogging totaled $17.4 million by 2009; in some cases these have been covered by umbrella insurance. The courts have returned with mixed verdicts. Internet Service Providers (ISPs), in general, are immune from liability for information that originates with third parties (U.S. Communications Decency Act and the EU Directive 2000/31/EC).

In *Doe v. Cahill*, the Delaware Supreme Court held that stringent standards had to be met to unmask the anonymous posts of bloggers and also took the unusual step of dismissing the libel case itself (as unfounded under American libel law) rather than referring it back to the trial court for reconsideration. In a bizarre twist, the Cahills were able to obtain the identity of John Doe, who turned out to be the person they suspected: the town's mayor, Councilman Cahill's political rival. The Cahills amended their original complaint, and the mayor settled the case rather than going to trial.

In January 2007, two prominent Malaysian political bloggers, Jeff Ooi and Ahiruddin Attan, were sued by pro-government newspaper, The New Straits Times Press (Malaysia) Berhad, Kalimullah bin Masheerul Hassan, Hishamuddin bin Aun and Brenden John a/l John Pereira over an alleged defamation. The plaintiff was supported by the Malaysian government. Following the suit, the Malaysian government proposed to "register" all bloggers in Malaysia in order to better control parties against their interest. This is the first such legal case against bloggers in the country.

In the United States, blogger Aaron Wall was sued by Traffic Power for defamation and publication of trade secrets in 2005. According to Wired Magazine, Traffic Power had been "banned from Google for allegedly rigging search engine results." Wall and other "white hat" search engine optimization consultants had exposed Traffic Power in what they claim was an effort to protect the public. The case was watched by many bloggers because it addressed the murky legal question of who is liable for comments posted on blogs. The case was dismissed for lack of personal jurisdiction, and Traffic Power failed to appeal within the allowed time.

In 2009, a controversial and landmark decision by The Hon. Mr Justice Eady refused to grant an order to protect the anonymity of Richard Horton. In 2009, NDTV issued a legal notice to Indian blogger Chetan Kunte for "abusive free speech" regarding a blog post criticizing their coverage of the Mumbai attacks. The blogger unconditionally withdrew his post, replacing it with legal undertaking and an admission that his post had been "defamatory and untrue" which resulted in several Indian bloggers criticizing NDTV for trying to silence critics.

Employment

Employees who blog about elements of their place of employment raise the issue of employee branding, since their activities can begin to affect the brand recognition of their employer. In general, attempts by employee bloggers to protect themselves by maintaining anonymity have proved ineffective. In late 2004, Ellen Simonetti was fired for what was deemed by her employer, Delta Air Lines, to be inappropriate material on her blog. She subsequently wrote a book based on her blog. Delta Air Lines fired flight attendant Ellen Simonetti because she posted photographs of herself in uniform on an airplane and because of comments posted on her blog "Queen of Sky: Diary of a Flight Attendant" which the employer deemed inappropriate.

This case highlighted the issue of personal blogging and freedom of expression vs. employer rights and responsibilities, and so it received wide media attention. Simonetti took legal action against the airline for "wrongful termination, defamation of character and lost future wages". The suit was postponed while Delta was in bankruptcy proceedings (court docket).

In early 2006, Erik Ringmar, a tenured senior lecturer at the London School of Economics, was ordered by the convenor of his department to "take down and destroy" his blog in which he discussed the quality of education at the school. Mark Cuban, owner of the Dallas Mavericks, was fined during the 2006 NBA playoffs for criticizing NBA officials on the court and in his blog.

Mark Jen was terminated in 2005 after 10 days of employment as an Assistant Product Manager at Google for discussing corporate secrets on his personal blog, then called 99zeros and hosted on the Google-owned Blogger service. He blogged about unreleased products and company finances a week before the company's earnings announcement. He was fired two days after he complied with his employer's request to remove the sensitive material from his blog.

In India, blogger Gaurav Sabnis resigned from IBM after his posts exposing the false claims of a management school, IIPM, led to management of IIPM threatening to burn their IBM laptops as a sign of protest against him. Jessica Cutler, aka "The Washingtonienne", blogged about her sex life while employed as a congressional assistant. After the blog was discovered and she was fired, she wrote a novel based on her experiences and blog: *The Washingtonienne: A Novel*. Cutler is presently being sued by one of her former lovers in a case that could establish the extent to which bloggers are obligated to protect the privacy of their real life associates.

Catherine Sanderson, a.k.a. Petite Anglaise, lost her job in Paris at a British accountancy firm because of blogging. Although given in the blog in a fairly anonymous manner, some of the descriptions of the firm and some of its people were less than flattering. Sanderson later won a compensation claim case against the British firm, however. On the other hand, Penelope Trunk wrote an upbeat article in the *Boston Globe* back in 2006, entitled "Blogs 'essential' to a good career". She was one of the first journalists to point out that a large portion of bloggers are professionals and that a well-written blog can help attract employers.

Political Dangers

Blogging can sometimes have unforeseen consequences in politically sensitive areas. Blogs are much harder to control than broadcast or even print media. As a result, totalitarian and authoritarian regimes often seek to suppress blogs and/or to punish those who maintain them. In Singapore, two ethnic Chinese were imprisoned under the country's anti-sedition law for posting anti-Muslim remarks in their blogs. Egyptian blogger Kareem Amer was charged with insulting the Egyptian president Hosni Mubarak and an Islamic institution through his blog. It is the first time in the history of Egypt that a blogger was prosecuted. After a brief trial session that took place in Alexandria, the blogger was found guilty and sentenced to prison terms of three years for insulting Islam and inciting sedition, and one year for insulting Mubarak. Egyptian blogger Abdel Monem Mahmoud was arrested in April 2007 for anti-government writings in his blog. Monem is a member of the banned Muslim Brotherhood. After expressing opinions in his personal blog about the state of the Sudanese armed forces, Jan Pronk, United Nations Special Representative for the Sudan, was given three days notice to leave Sudan. The Sudanese army had demanded his deportation. In Myanmar, Nay Phone Latt, a blogger, was sentenced to 20 years in jail for posting a cartoon critical of head of state Than Shwe.

Personal Safety

One consequence of blogging is the possibility of attacks or threats against the blogger, sometimes without apparent reason. Kathy Sierra, author of the innocuous blog Creating Passionate Users, was the target of such vicious threats and misogynistic insults that she cancelled her keynote speech at a technology conference in San Diego, fearing for her safety. While a blogger's anonymity is often tenuous, Internet trolls who would attack a blogger with threats or insults can be emboldened by anonymity. Sierra and supporters initiated an online discussion aimed at countering abusive online behaviour and developed a blogger's code of conduct.

History

The term "weblog" was coined by Jorn Barger on 17 December 1997. The short form, "blog," was coined by Peter Merholz, who jokingly broke the word *weblog* into the phrase *we blog* in the sidebar of his blog Peterme.com in April or May 1999.

Shortly thereafter, Evan Williams at Pyra Labs used "blog" as both a noun and verb ("to blog," meaning "to edit one's weblog or to post to one's weblog") and devised the term "blogger" in connection with Pyra Labs' Blogger product, leading to the popularization of the terms.

Origins

Before blogging became popular, digital communities took many forms, including Usenet, commercial online services such as GEnie, BiX and the early CompuServe, e-mail lists and Bulletin Board Systems (BBS). In the 1990s, Internet forum software, such as WebEx, created running conversations with "threads." Threads are topical connections between messages on a metaphorical "corkboard." The modern blog evolved from the online diary, where people would keep a running account of their personal lives. Most such writers called themselves diarists, journalists, or journalers. Justin Hall, who began personal blogging in 1994 while a student at Swarthmore College, is generally recognized as one of the earliest bloggers, as is Jerry Pournelle.

Dave Winer's Scripting News is also credited with being one of the oldest and longest running weblogs. Another early blog was Wearable Wireless Webcam, an online shared diary of a person's personal life combining text, video, and pictures transmitted live from a wearable computer and EyeTap device to a web site in 1994. This practice of semi-automated blogging with live video together with text was referred to as sousveillance, and such journals were also used as evidence in legal matters.

Early blogs were simply manually updated components of common Web sites. However, the evolution of tools to facilitate the production and maintenance of Web articles posted in reverse chronological order made the publishing process feasible to a much larger, less technical, population.

Ultimately, this resulted in the distinct class of online publishing that produces blogs we recognize today. For instance, the use of some sort of browser-based software is now a typical aspect of "blogging". Blogs can be hosted by dedicated blog hosting services, or they can be run using blog software, or on regular web hosting services.

Rise in Popularity

After a slow start, blogging rapidly gained in popularity. Blog usage spread during 1999 and the years following, being further popularized by the near-simultaneous arrival of the first hosted blog tools:

- Bruce Ableson launched Open Diary in October 1998, which soon grew to thousands of online diaries. Open Diary innovated the reader comment, becoming the first blog community where readers could add comments to other writers' blog entries.
- Brad Fitzpatrick started LiveJournal in March 1999.
- Andrew Smales created Pitas.com in July 1999 as an easier alternative to maintaining a "news page" on a Web site, followed by Diaryland in September 1999, focusing more on a personal diary community.
- Evan Williams and Meg Hourihan (Pyra Labs) launched blogger.com in August 1999 (purchased by Google in February 2003).

Political Impact

Since 2002, blogs have gained increasing notice and coverage for their role in breaking, shaping, and spinning news stories. For the first time in the history of modern journalism, the financial and political goals of U.S.-Israeli relations are being analyzed in depth. The Iraq war saw bloggers taking measured and passionate points of view that go beyond the traditional left-right divide of the political spectrum. On 6 December 2002, Josh Marshall's talkingpointsmemo . com blog called attention to U.S. Senator Lott's comments regarding Senator Thurmond. Senator Lott was eventually to resign over the matter.

An early milestone in the rise in importance of blogs came in 2002, when many bloggers focused on comments by U.S. Senate Majority Leader Trent Lott. Senator Lott, at a party honoring U.S. Senator Strom Thurmond, praised Senator Thurmond by suggesting that the United States would have been better off had Thurmond been elected president. Lott's critics saw these comments as a tacit approval of racial segregation, a policy advocated by Thurmond's 1948 presidential campaign. This view was reinforced by documents and recorded interviews dug up by bloggers. Though Lott's comments were made at a public event attended by the media, no major media organizations reported on his controversial comments until after blogs broke the story.

Blogging helped to create a political crisis that forced Lott to step down as majority leader. Similarly, blogs were among the driving forces behind the "Rathergate" scandal. To wit: Dan Rather presented documents (on the CBS show *60 Minutes*) that conflicted with accepted accounts of President Bush's military service record. Bloggers declared the documents to be forgeries and presented evidence and arguments in support of that view. Consequently, CBS apologized for what it said were inadequate reporting techniques. Many bloggers view this scandal as the advent of blogs' acceptance by the mass media, both as a news source and opinion and as means of applying political pressure.

The impact of these stories gave greater credibility to blogs as a medium of news dissemination. Though often seen as partisan gossips, bloggers sometimes lead the way in bringing key information to public light, with mainstream media having to follow their lead.

More often, however, news blogs tend to react to material already published by the mainstream media. Meanwhile, an increasing number of experts blogged, making blogs a source of in-depth analysis.

8

Multimedia Messaging Service

Multimedia Messaging Service, or MMS, is a standard way to send messages that include multimedia content to and from mobile phones. It extends the core SMS (Short Message Service) capability which only allowed exchange of text messages up to 160 characters in length. The most popular use is to send photographs from camera-equipped handsets, although it is also popular as a method of delivering news and entertainment content including videos, pictures, text pages and ringtones. The standard is developed by the Open Mobile Alliance (OMA), although during development it was part of the 3GPP and WAP groups.

History

The immediate predecessor to the MMS is the Japanese picture messaging system Sha-Mail introduced by J-Phone in 2001. It validated the concept of cameraphone users willing to send picture messages from one phone to another. Early MMS deployments were plagued by technical issues and frequent consumer disappointments, such as having sent an MMS message, receiving a confirmation it had been sent, being billed for the MMS message, to find that it had not been delivered to the intended recepient. Pictures would often arrive in the wrong formats, other media elements might be removed such as a video clip arriving without its sound. At the MMS World Congress in 2004 in Vienna, all European mobile operator representatives who had launched MMS, admitted their MMS services were not making money for their networks. Also on all networks at the time, the most common uses were various adult oriented services that had been deployed using MMS. China was one of the early markets to make

MMS a major commercial success partly as the penetration rate of personal computers was modest but MMS-capable cameraphones spread rapidly. The Chairman and CEO of China Mobile said at the GSM Association Mobile Asia Congress in 2009, that MMS in China is now a mature service on par with SMS text messaging.

Europe's most advanced MMS market has been Norway and in 2008 the Norwegian MMS usage level had passed 84% of all mobile phone subscribers. Norwegian mobile subscribers aveage one MMS sent per week. By 2008 worldwide MMS usage level had passed 1.3 billion active users who generated 50 billion MMS messages and produced annual revenues of 26 billion dollars annually.

Technical Description

MMS messages are delivered in a completely different way than SMS. The first step is for the sending device to encode the multimedia content in a fashion similar to sending a MIME e-mail (MIME content formats are defined in the MMS Message Encapsulation specification). The message is then forwarded to the carrier's MMS store and forward server, known as the MMSC. If the receiver is on another carrier, the relay forwards the message to the recipient's carrier using the Internet.

Once the MMSC has received a message, it first determines if the receiver's handset is "MMS capable", that is it supports the standards for receiving MMS. If so, the content is extracted and sent to a temporary storage server with an HTTP front-end. An SMS "control message" containing the URL of the content is then sent to the recipient's handset to trigger the receiver's WAP browser to open and receive the content from the embedded URL. Several other messages are exchanged to indicate status of the delivery attempt.. Before delivering content, some MMSCs also include a conversion service that will attempt to modify the multimedia content into a format suitable for the receiver. This is known as "content adaptation".

If the receiver's handset is not MMS capable, the message is usually delivered to a web based service from where the content can be viewed from a normal internet browser. The URL for the content is usually sent to the receiver's phone in a normal text message. This behaviour is usually known as the 'legacy experience' since content can still be received by a phone number, even if the phone itself does not support MMS. The method for determining whether a handset is MMS capable is not specified by the standards. A database is usually maintained by the operator, and in it each mobile phone number is marked as being associated with a legacy handset or not. It can be a bit hit and miss since customers can change their handset at will and this database is not usually updated dynamically.

E-mail and web-based gateways to the MMS (and SMS) system are common. On the reception side, the content servers can typically receive service requests both from WAP and normal HTTP browsers, so delivery via the web is simple.

For sending from external sources to handsets, most carriers allow MIME encoded message to be sent to the receiver's phone number with a special domain.

Challenges

There are some interesting challenges with MMS that do not exist with SMS:

- *Content adaptation:* Multimedia content created by one brand of MMS phone may not be entirely compatible with the capabilities of the recipients' MMS phone. In the MMS architecture, the recipient MMSC is responsible for providing for *content adaptation* (e.g., image resizing, audio codec transcoding, etc.), if this feature is enabled by the mobile network operator. When content adaptation is supported by a network operator, its MMS subscribers enjoy compatibility with a larger network of MMS users than would otherwise be available.
- *Distribution lists:* Current MMS specifications do not include distribution lists nor methods by which large numbers of recipients can be conveniently addressed, particularly by content providers, called *Value-added service providers* (VASPs) in 3GPP. Since most SMSC vendors have adopted FTP as an ad-hoc method by which large distribution lists are transferred to the SMSC prior to being used in a bulk-messaging SMS submission, it is expected that MMSC vendors will also adopt FTP.
- *Bulk messaging:* The flow of *peer-to-peer* MMS messaging involves several over-the-air transactions that become inefficient when MMS is used to send messages to large numbers of subscribers, as is typically the case for VASPs. For example, when one MMS message is submitted to a very large number of recipients, it is possible to receive a *delivery report* and *read-reply report* for each and every recipient. Future MMS specification work is likely to optimize and reduce the transactional overhead for the bulk-messaging case.

- *Handset Configuration:* Unlike SMS, MMS requires a number of handset parameters to be set. Poor handset configuration is often blamed as the first point of failure for many users. Service settings are sometimes preconfigured on the handset, but mobile operators are now looking at new device management technologies as a means of delivering the necessary settings for data services (MMS, WAP, etc.) via over-the-air programming (OTA).
- *WAP Push:* Few mobile network operators offer direct connectivity to their MMSCs for content providers. This has resulted in many content providers using WAP push as the only method available to deliver 'rich content' to mobile handsets. WAP push enables 'rich content' to be delivered to a handset by specifying the URL (via binary SMS) of a pre-compiled MMS, hosted on a content provider's web server. A consequence is that the receiver who pays WAP per kb or minute (as opposed to a flat monthly fee) pays for receiving the MMS, as opposed to only paying for sending one, and also paying a different rate.

Although the standard does not specify a maximum size for a message, 300 kB is the current recommended size used by networks due to some limitations on the WAP gateway side.

Making of a Multimedia Journalist

Very few words have exerted a strain on modern journalism as "multimedia", which has come to symbolise something akin to next generation reportage. Within the profession it means different things; in other disciplines, such as graphic design, it connotes something wider than the journalism term. ITN may deliver multimedia news, with different elements, but is it multimedia in offering multi-entry, multi faceted news wrapped together to deliver a far richer threaded experience?

So what is multimedia and frankly why should we care? If the user is reliably informed by the news is that not good enough? In a video feature for the the UK Press Gazette, the trailer of which you can find here, I hope to look at that question.

But in the mean time, here's a cursory look at the elements that I believe make up the sum of parts for a multimedia journalist. The key, however is in the application and how a new era of journalists can work together, often as swarms, to provide more indepth, richer, immersive news.

The ff. list some core areas;

- Videojournalism rules
- Paradigm shift
- New Skills
- Appreciate.

Breaking the Rules of Video Journalism

The Videojournalism Manifesto I have been writing provides some guidance to this evolving art.

- I am a video journalist: I crave creativity, loathe that which is predictable. It is my job to look for beyond the headlines and surface story; beyond what may be known as the agenda, trusting my convictions to tell a more expansive story.
- 2. I can move alone in any terrain. Experience is my blanket. Swarming (groups of Vjs coming
- Notes on Videojournalism: "Videojournalism is an advance on television news production-a shift away from the predictable appproach television has stuck to doggedly since its inception.

It is next generation television: story telling in which you are not be bound by the many constraints of traditional news production"

To break the rules, we must try and find out what they are. Vjism has rules, but as Robb Montgomery from Visual Editors would say, "it's less the technology, more the technique.

Understanding there is a Paradigm Shift

One of the biggest threats facing journalism isn't the deludge of new applications and hardware tools on the market; all of which I'd play around with if I had the chance, or even the trend-to-dismiss web 2.0, but the mindset that pre-determines how we perceive journalism. If you can't see the three images above, if you're not prepared to, then you're missing out on the "aha" syndrome.

The very nature of modern journalism is undergoing huge indeterminate changes. Its foundation, core, remains the same, at least for now.

But driven by new soft-hard ware,a maturing web, increasing public-media awareness and zeal for public participation, journalism is changing irrecovably. In New Journalism New Thinking, I expand on the idea that journalism requires new thinking, a paradigm.

The New Thinkers

Others have put their case more eloquently. Here's but a few of my gowing list-some more well known than others.

Here are a few:

- Dan Gillmor
- Jay Rosen
- Adrian Monck
- Andy Dickinson
- Paul Bradshaw
- Michael Rosenblum
- Jemima Kiss
- Peter Ralph
- Jeff Jarvis
- Mindy McAdams.

Knowing there is a New Skillset

These two illustrate the more visible encroachments on journalism via social networks and web 2.0. The whole industry has been turned upside down. The idea of a multimedia journalist, integrating a range of skills, such as videojournalism and blogging, is a reality we're either used to or will soon have to heartliy embrace. So what are some of the fundamentals to becoming a multimedia journalist?

- *Video Journalism now:* Aggressive video produced within hours, here's what you need.
- Final Cut Pro-the trick in FCP use is in its key frames.
- Sound Pro-Film. It's all in the sound.
- After Effects-create incredible film tones.
- Compression technology e.g. Quicktime.
- *Web site CSS build:* Dreaweaver and Photoshop
- writing for SEO, link-rich building and the F-plan.
- *Multi media and Flash:* The cube is inspired by the rubik cube and game theory.

Multimedia Literacy

Multimedia literacy is a new aspect of literacy that is being recognized as technology expands the way people communicate. The concept of Literacy emerged as a measure of the ability to read and write. In modern context, the word means reading and writing at a level adequate for written communication. A more fundamental meaning is now needed to cope with the numerous media in use, perhaps meaning a level that enables one to successfully function at certain levels of a society.

Multimedia is media that utilizes several different content forms to convey information. Several are already a part of the canon of global communication and publication: (text, audio, graphics, animation, video, and interactivity). Multimedia mainly but not exclusively refers to electronic media because content forms such as audio recordings and video footage are delivered electronically.

Other technologies that involve unique forms of literacy such as virtual reality, computer programming and robotics are possible candidates for future inclusion. With widespread use of computers, the basic literacy of 'reading' and 'writing' are often done via a computer, expanding the foundations of literacy to include multimedia. Computer networks, online communities, and the growing need to communicate with machines, challenge the narrower definitions of literacy.

Definition Debate

Critics of the concept of multimedia literacy question whether the term literacy can be extended beyond its original definition. The word technacy may ultimately be more suitable. Others question whether the 'literacy' skills and concepts in multimedia literacy are new at all, being found in the theatre, film, radio etc. for many years. The expansion of basic literacy through history and across geography provides perspective on those seeking to draw hard lines about what literacy is and is not.

Thousands of years ago, a few early cultures invented the skills and technologies of reading and writing. Many languages today still have no written form. Of those with the invention of writing, only a small percentage of the citizens of these early cultures needed literacy. Each culture and time decides its needed technologies of thought and communication. Those who teach in a society respond to these needs. All societies have relatively recently (in the last 200 years) found that traditional literacy is essential. Not all have achieved it yet. Today there is a very rapid growth in forms of literacy, largely due to the arrival of the personal computer and the internet. There was a tipping point in the demand for universal (reading and writing) literacy as an effect of the Industrial Revolution.

Paper, writing instruments and printing also became much cheaper at about this time. Today there is a revolution in the development of new communication media. There is a demand for literate people to become skilled in the new literacies related to the use of a variety of online tools-blogs, social networking, video and audio sharing and so on. The impact of these internet related media is different from that of the earlier multimedia revolution when film and radio became widespread. These media were powerful, but were largely in the hands of a small number of people with the mass of the population being a passive audience. The new media, particularly those described as Web 2.0 tools tend to actively involve the users in responding and creating material.

There is considerable debate in progress about the nature and significance of these new media. Traditionalist educators may argue that the long standing media form of text has and will continue to be the foundation of learning. Others will argue that the new forms are displacing the old forms of literacy and that schools must teach the full range of multimedia literacies..

Changing Digital Technology

As personal computers and their software become more powerful they have the capacity to not only record and edit text, sound, still images, motion pictures and manage interactivity individually, but synthesize all of them onto the same page, screen or viewing, creating new plateaus or forms of composition. Personal computer technology has placed multimedia creation in the hands of any computer user. As multimedia becomes a more prevalent form of communication it is argued that the literacy of 'reading' and 'writing' using multimedia be taught in schools and other education institutions.

The related study of mass media has long been part of the school program in many school systems either as a separate subject option in secondary schools or more often as a part of general literacy learning. Film Study has also been a school subject in many schools for some time using relatively expensive and complicated equipment to make film or video.

The rapid development of multimedia via personal computing means that it is becoming a routine form for a widening group of people not only for just "reading" but for creating the media. The line between mass media and personally authored media is becoming much more blurred if not obliterated.

Some non professional authors on the web already have audiences larger than major commercial publications such as major newspapers and TV stations, whether text based blogs or multimedia podcasts. The sudden emergence of short video as a medium for viewing and authoring on sites such as YouTube has illustrated the very rapid rate of change in this area, and the need to learn new forms of literacy.

In *Datacloud: Toward a New Theory of Online Work*, Johndan Johnson-Eilola describes a specific computer-supported collaboriatin space: The Smart Board. According to Johnson-Eilola, a "Smart Board system provides a 72-inch, rear projection, touchscreen, intelligent whiteboard surface for work". In *Datacloud,* Johnson-Eilola asserts that "[w]e are attempting to understand how users move within information spaces, how users can exist within information spaces rather than merely gaze at them, and how information spaces must be shared with others rather than being private, lived within rather than simply visited".

He explains how the Smart Board system offers an information space that allows his students to engage in active collaboration. He makes three distinct claims regarding the functionality of the technology: 1) The Smart Board allows users to work with large amounts of information, 2) It offers an information space that invites active collaboration, 3) The work produced is often "dynamic and contingent".

Johnson-Eilola further explains that with the Smart Board "...information work becom a bodied experience". Users have the opportunity to engage with—inhabit—the technology by direct manipulation. Moreover, this space allows for more than one user; essentially, it invites multiple users.

Constructivist Learning and Multimedia

Multimedia literacy is a subset of the wider issue of the use of ICT (Information and Communication Technology) in schools. While there is widespread recognition that people need to learn how to use computers effectively in order to function in modern society, there is debate about the nature of that learning. Some see it as a simple but lengthy list of technical skills while others see it as also including recognition of the power of ICT to bring about a major change in learning. Avarim and Talmi identify several groups active in ICT in education, including Technocrats, who see the use of ICT as non-problematic and simply a matter of using the new tools, and Reformists, who see ICT as a major and possibly inexorable agent of change in education. The reformist group see the rapid growth in the use of ICT in schooling occurring in conjunction with the adoption of the constructivist learning theory.(OECD) This theory supports active, hands-on learning. It is related to Cognitive Apprenticeship and the work of Jerome Bruner.

Some educators see ICT as being a major driver of school reform. This reform is towards a more constructivist approach, using related terms such as: student-centred learning, Problem-based learning and experiential education. Others point to the slow pace of such reform and suggest that ICT may support reform but it is by no means inevitable that it will do so. (eLearning europa).

Supporters of ICT as a powerful tool for constructivist learning point to its capacity to provide:

- active and highly motivating engagement with students
- powerful tools to create text, art, music, sound, models, presentations, movies etc. that produce high quality products and remove much of the tedium normally associated with such creation
- an error-forgiving environment in which editing of a product fosters learning by trial and error
- easy communication in text, voice, video
- quick access to information and resources.

Educators are finding, however, that while ICT can provide a technical environment for constructivist learning to occur, there needs to be high quality teaching to develop and sustain an environment that will challenge and inspire students to learn.

Multimedia Literacy in Schools

As pointed out by Will Richardson in his book, Blogs, Wikis, Podcasts, and Other Powerful Web Tools for the Classroom, the very definition of what it means to be literate is evolving due to the explosion of information and technology. While those abilities are still necessary components of literacy, they have become recognized by education professionals as insufficient. Educators today are focused on the paradigm shift from traditional literacy to multiliteracies, a term coined by the New London Group which is based on the assumption that technology impacts the nature of texts, and the way that people use and interact with texts.

A multiliterate person has recently been defined as one who "is flexible and strategic and can understand and use literacy and literate practices with a range of texts and technologies; in socially responsible way; in a socially, culturally, and linguistically diverse world; and to fully participate in life as an active and informed citizen.

Film director George Lucas would approve. As he succinctly put it to Elizabeth Daley, dean of USC's School of Cinema and Television: "In the 21st century, can you honestly tell me that it's not as important for these students to know as much about Hitchcock as they do about Hemingway? Lucas elaborates on this idea in his conversation with Daley:".Well.. I began to realize that the potential for multimedia to enhance the learning process was just astronomical.... I'm a big proponent of a new kind of grammar that goes beyond words.

To tell a story now means grasping a new kind of language, which includes understanding how graphics, color, lines, music and words combine to convey meaning". In this conversation with Elizabeth Daley, Lucas asks: "Don't you think that, in the coming decade, students need to be taught to read and write cinematic language, the language of the screen, the language of sound and image, just as they are now taught to read and write text? Otherwise, won't they be as illiterate as you or I would have been if, on leaving college, we were unable to read and write an essay?".

Not only are multiliteracies becoming recognized as essential for students emerging from school and entering the competitive world of work, but they are also being recognized as important to pedogocial success; research suggests that societal immersion in technology has neurological effects that results in differences in thought from previous generations. Students may become unable to cope effectively with traditional linear learning.

For students to navigate the new media on the World Wide Web, teachers must rethink literacy as they create a participatory culture within learning environments. Eleven core competencies facilitate the engagement of students within the new literacy: play, performance, simulation, appropriation, multi-tasking, distributed cognition, collective intelligence, judgement, transmedia navigation, networking and negotiation. According to Richardson, students will be required post-education to flourish in networked personal learning spaces, and therefore need to be taught a specific set of skills.

First, because anyone can publish content to the Web, students must be taught to be active consumers of information instead of passive acceptance. Second, teachers should teach and model the ways in which ideas and products can be published online. Third, students should be taught to work in collaborative environments, employing communication skills and process. Finally, students should be taught the skills necessary to collect, store, and retrieve relevant information.

Richardson suggests that with teachers using wikis and weblogs, students will be better prepared when put into a real world situation. The more exposure students work have, the more they understand their voices matter. Educator Dawn Reed observed in her classroom that students wished to have their speech perfect because of the wider audience that the internet exposes. Using multimedia technologies also helps teachers get more comfortable and have more confidence in using these Web 2.0 applications. Students really benefit from using multimedia literacy in school; they learn the challenges and benefits of how incorporating technology into everyday lives can build a good foundation for their future will demand. Wikis are a good way for students to learn how to work with others, create a community, and operate in a world that demands the use of information from many different sources.

The following sections provides information on some skills that students may learn to achieve multiliteracy.

Video

Film making has been a major technology and art form for over a century. Personal video making makes use of many but not all of the techniques of professional film making.

Student movie makers need to be familiar with the basic tools and techniques of the art, including familiarity with:

- Camera shots: close up, medium, long shot, pan, fade etc in order to achieve different effects
- Story-boarding: a pictorial frame view of the story line, showing camera views, times and shot sequence which provides the Director with a simple shooting script for a video.
- Editing software replaces tedious and expensive film splicing with digital editing which is quick and forgiving of errors, and allows the insertion of audio tracks in sequence with the video track.
- Sound tracks allow music, sound effects and voice tracks to be added to an existing film.
- The so called Ken Burns Effect, in which the camera pans across a still image allows still images accompanied by a sound track to create quite powerful presentations.

The rise of short videos shared from online services such as YouTube is changing the perception of who makes video and how and why it is viewed. Short and shared online videos have become a major cultural phenomenon in a few years. Their production often breaks most of the 'rules' of how to make video.

There technically quality is sometimes low, but their communication impact high.

Sound

Most people are very familiar with the use of sound as a powerful tool in television, radio and film, but have little experience in using it themselves. Digital recording allows the user much greater opportunity to experiment with the effect of sound features such as:

- Voice tone, pace, pitch
- Music as an influence on mood and atmosphere
- Sound effects that provide enrichment and context to a story.

Robotics

Robotics is the engineering science and technology of robots, and their design, manufacture, application, and structural disposition. Robotics is related to electronics, mechanics, and software. The word robot was introduced to the public by Czech writer Karel Èapek in his play R.U.R. (Rossum's Universal Robots), published in 1920. The first recorded use of the term was by Isaac Asimov in his 1941 science fiction short-story "Liar!"

Origins

Stories of artificial helpers and companions and attempts to create them have a long history, but fully autonomous machines only appeared in the 20th century. The first digitally operated and programmable robot, the Unimate, was installed in 1961 to lift hot pieces of metal from a die casting machine and stack them. Today, commercial and industrial robots are in widespread use performing jobs more cheaply or more accurately and reliably than humans.

They are also employed in jobs which are too dirty, dangerous, or dull to be suitable for humans. Robots are widely used in manufacturing, assembly, and packing; transport; earth and space exploration; surgery; weaponry; laboratory research; safety; and mass production of consumer and industrial goods.

According to the *Oxford English Dictionary*, the word *robotics* was first used in print by Isaac Asimov, in his science fiction short story "Liar!", published in May 1941 in *Astounding Science Fiction.* Asimov was unaware that he was coining the term; since the science and technology of electrical devices is *electronics,* he assumed *robotics* already referred to the science and technology of robots.

However, in some of Asimov's other works, he states that the first use of the word *robotics* was in his short story *Runaround* (Astounding Science Fiction, March 1942). The word *robotics* was derived from the word *robot,* which was introduced to the public by Czech writer Karel Èapek in his play *R.U.R.* which premiered in 1921.

Components of Robots

Structure: The structure of a robot is usually mostly mechanical and can be called a kinematic chain (its functionality being similar to the skeleton of the human body). The chain is formed of links (its bones), actuators (its muscles), and joints which can allow one or more degrees of freedom. Most contemporary robots use open serial chains in which each link connects the one before to the one after it.

These robots are called serial robots and often resemble the human arm. Some robots, such as the Stewart platform, use a closed parallel kinematical chain. Other structures, such as those that mimic the mechanical structure of humans, various animals, and insects, are comparatively rare. However, the development and use of such structures in robots is an active area of research (e.g. biomechanics). Robots used as manipulators have an end effector mounted on the last link. This end effector can be anything from a welding device to a mechanical hand used to manipulate the environment.

Power Source

At present; mostly (lead-acid) batteries are used, but potential power sources could be:

- Pneumatic (compressed gases)
- Hydraulics (compressed liquids)
- Flywheel energy storage
- Organic garbages (through anaerobic digestion)
- Feces (human, animal); may be interesting in a military context as feces of small combat groups may be reused for the energy requirements of the robot assistant
- Still untested energy sources (eg Joe Cell,...)
- Radioactive source (such as with the proposed Ford car of the '50); to those proposed in movies such as Red Planet.

Actuation

Actuators are like the "muscles" of a robot, the parts which convert stored energy into movement. By far the most popular actuators are electric motors, but there are many others, powered by electricity, chemicals, and compressed air.

- *Motors:* The vast majority of robots use electric motors, including brushed and brushless DC on many robots and CNC machines, as their main can specify how much to turn, for more precise control, rather than a "spin and see where it went" approach.
- *Piezo motors:* A recent alternative to DC motors are piezo motors or ultrasonic motors. These work on a fundamentally different principle, whereby tiny piezoceramic elements, vibrating many thousands of times per second, cause linear or rotary motion. There are different mechanisms of operation; one type uses the vibration of the piezo elements to walk the motor in a circle or a straight line. Another type uses the piezo elements to cause a nut to vibrate and drive a screw. The advantages of these motors are nanometer resolution, speed, and available force for their size. These motors are already available commercially, and being used on some robots.
- *Elastic nanotubes:* These are a promising, early-stage experimental technology. The absence of defects in nanotubes enables these filaments to deform elastically by several percent, with energy storage levels of perhaps 10 J/cm for metal nanotubes. Human biceps could be replaced with an 8 mm diameter wire of this material. Such compact "muscle" might allow future robots to outrun and outjump humans.

Sensing

Touch: Current robotic and prosthetic hands receive far less tactile information than the human hand. Recent research has developed a tactile sensor array that mimics the mechanical properties and touch. receptors of human fingertips. The sensor array is constructed as a rigid core surrounded by conductive fluid contained by an elastomeric skin.

Electrodes are mounted on the surface of the rigid core and are connected to an impedance-measuring device within the core. When the artificial skin touches an object the fluid path around the electrodes is deformed, producing impedance changes that map the forces received from the object. The researchers expect that an important function of such artificial fingertips will be adjusting robotic grip on held objects. In 2009, scientists from several European countries and Israel developed a prosthetic hand, called SmartHand, which functions like a real one, allowing patients to write with it, type on a keyboard, play piano and perform other fine movements. The prosthesis has sensors which enable the patient to sense real feeling in its fingertips.

Manipulation

Robots which must work in the real world require some way to manipulate objects; pick up, modify, destroy, or otherwise have an effect. Thus the 'hands' of a robot are often referred to as end effectors, while the arm is referred to as a manipulator. Most robot arms have replaceable effectors, each allowing them to perform some small range of tasks. Some have a fixed manipulator which cannot be replaced, while a few have one very general purpose manipulator, for example a humanoid hand.

- *Mechanical Grippers:* One of the most common effectors is the gripper. In its simplest manifestation it consists of just two fingers which can open and close to pick up and let go of a range of small objects.
- *Vacuum Grippers:* Pick and place robots for electronic components and for large objects like car windscreens, will often use very simple vacuum grippers. These are very simple astrictive devices, but can hold very large loads provided the prehension surface is smooth enough to ensure suction.
- *General purpose effectors:* Some advanced robots are beginning to use fully humanoid hands, like the Shadow Hand, MANUS, and the Schunk hand. These highly dexterous manipulators, with as many as 20 degrees of freedom and hundreds of tactile sensors.

For the definitive guide to all forms of robot endeffectors, their design, and usage consult the book "Robot Grippers".

Locomotion

Rolling robots: For simplicity, most mobile robots have four wheels. However, some researchers have tried to create more complex wheeled robots, with only one or two wheels.

- *Two-wheeled balancing:* While the Segway is not commonly thought of as a robot, it can be thought of as a component of a robot. Several real robots do use a similar dynamic balancing algorithm, and NASA's Robonaut has been mounted on a Segway.

- *Ballbot:* Carnegie Mellon University researchers have developed a new type of mobile robot that balances on a ball instead of legs or wheels. "Ballbot" is a self-contained, battery-operated, omnidirectional robot that balances dynamically on a single urethane-coated metal sphere. It weighs 95 pounds and is the approximate height and width of a person. Because of its long, thin shape and ability to maneuver in tight spaces, it has the potential to function better than current robots can in environments with people.
- *Track Robot:* Another type of rolling robot is one that has tracks, like NASA's Urban Robot, Urbie.

Walking Robots

Walking is a difficult and dynamic problem to solve. Several robots have been made which can walk reliably on two legs, however none have yet been made which are as robust as a human. Many other robots have been built that walk on more than two legs, due to these robots being significantly easier to construct. Hybrids too have been proposed in movies such as I, Robot, where they walk on 2 legs and switch to 4 (arms+legs) when going to a sprint. Typically, robots on 2 legs can walk well on flat floors, and can occasionally walk up stairs. None can walk over rocky, uneven terrain.

Some of the methods which have been tried are:

- *ZMP Technique:* The Zero Moment Point (ZMP) is the algorithm used by robots such as Honda's ASIMO. The robot's onboard computer tries to keep the total inertial forces (the combination of earth's gravity and the acceleration and deceleration of walking), exactly opposed by the floor reaction force (the force of the floor pushing back on the robot's foot). In this way, the two forces cancel out, leaving no moment (force causing the robot to rotate and fall over). However, this is not exactly how a human walks, and the difference is quite apparent to human observers, some of whom have pointed out that ASIMO walks as if it needs the lavatory. ASIMO's walking algorithm is not static, and some dynamic balancing is used. However, it still requires a smooth surface to walk on.
- *Hopping:* Several robots, built in the 1980s by Marc Raibert at the MIT Leg Laboratory, successfully demonstrated very dynamic walking. Initially, a robot with only one leg, and a very small foot, could stay upright simply by hopping. The movement is the same as that of a person on a pogo stick. As

the robot falls to one side, it would jump slightly in that direction, in order to catch itself. Soon, the algorithm was generalised to two and four legs. A bipedal robot was demonstrated running and even performing somersaults. A quadruped was also demonstrated which could trot, run, pace, and bound. For a full list of these robots.

- *Dynamic Balancing or controlled falling:* A more advanced way for a robot to walk is by using a dynamic balancing algorithm, which is potentially more robust than the Zero Moment Point technique, as it constantly monitors the robot's motion, and places the feet in order to maintain stability. This technique was recently demonstrated by Anybots' Dexter Robot, which is so stable, it can even jump. Another example is the TU Delft Flame.
- *Passive Dynamics:* Perhaps the most promising approach utilizes passive dynamics where the momentum of swinging limbs is used for greater efficiency. It has been shown that totally unpowered humanoid mechanisms can walk down a gentle slope, using only gravity to propel themselves. Using this technique, a robot need only supply a small amount of motor power to walk along a flat surface or a little more to walk up a hill. This technique promises to make walking robots at least ten times more efficient than ZMP walkers, like ASIMO.

Other Methods of Locomotion

- *Flying:* A modern passenger airliner is essentially a flying robot, with two humans to manage it. The autopilot can control the plane for each stage of the journey, including takeoff, normal flight, and even landing.[Other flying robots are uninhabited, and are known as unmanned aerial vehicles (UAVs). They can be smaller and lighter without a human pilot onboard, and fly into dangerous territory for military surveillance missions. Some can even fire on targets under command. UAVs are also being developed which can fire on targets automatically, without the need for a command from a human. However these robots are unlikely to see service in the foreseeable future because of the morality issues involved. Other flying robots include cruise missiles, the Entomopter, and the Epson micro helicopter robot. Robots such as the Air Penguin, Air Ray, and Air Jelly have lighter-than-air bodies, propelled by paddles, and guided by sonar. Two robot snakes. Left one has 64 motors (with 2 degrees of freedom per segment), the right one 10.

- *Snaking:* Several snake robots have been successfully developed. Mimicking the way real snakes move, these robots can navigate very confined spaces, meaning they may one day be used to search for people trapped in collapsed buildings. The Japanese ACM-R5 snake robot can even navigate both on land and in water.
- *Skating:* A small number of skating robots have been developed, one of which is a multi-mode walking and skating device, Titan VIII. It has four legs, with unpowered wheels, which can either step or roll. Another robot, Plen, can use a miniature skateboard or rollerskates, and skate across a desktop.
- *Climbing:* Several different approaches have been used to develop robots that have the ability to climb vertical surfaces. One approach mimicks the movements of a human climber on a wall with protrusions; adjusting the center of mass and moving each limb in turn to gain leverage. An example of this is Capuchin,[built by Stanford University, California. Another approach uses the specialised toe pad method of wall-climbing geckoes, which can run on smooth surfaces such as vertical glass. Examples of this approach include Wallbot and Stickybot. A third approach is to mimick the motion of a snake climbing a pole.
- *Swimming:* It is calculated that when swimming some fish can achieve a propulsive efficiency greater than 90%. Furthermore, they can accelerate and maneuver far better than any man-made boat or submarine, and produce less noise and water disturbance.

  Therefore, many researchers studying underwater robots would like to copy this type of locomotion. Notable examples are the Essex University Computer Science Robotic Fish, and the Robot Tuna built by the Institute of Field Robotics, to analyze and mathematically model thunniform motion. The Aqua Penguin, designed and built by Festo of Germany, copies the streamlined shape and propulsion by front "flippers" of penguins. Festo have also built the Aqua Ray and Aqua Jelly, which emulate the locomotion of manta ray, and jellyfish, respectively.

Environmental Interaction and Navigation

Though a significant percentage of robots in commission today are either human controlled, or operate in a static environment, there is an increasing interest in robots that can operate autonomously in a dynamic environment. These robots require some combination of navigation hardware and software in order to traverse their environment. In particular unforeseen events (eg. people and other obstacles that are not stationary) can cause problems or collisions. Some highly advanced robots as ASIMO, EveR-1, Meinü robot have particularly good robot navigation hardware and software.

Also, self-controlled cars, Ernst Dickmanns' driverless car, and the entries in the DARPA Grand Challenge, are capable of sensing the environment well and subsequently making navigational decisions based on this information. Most of these robots employ a GPS navigation device with waypoints, along with radar, sometimes combined with other sensory data such as LIDAR, video cameras, and inertial guidance systems for better navigation between waypoints.

Human-Robot Interaction

If robots are to work effectively in homes and other non-industrial environments, the way they are instructed to perform their jobs, and especially how they will be told to stop will be of critical importance. The people who interact with them may have little or no training in robotics, and so any interface will need to be extremely intuitive. Science fiction authors also typically assume that robots will eventually be capable of communicating with humans through speech, gestures, and facial expressions, rather than a command-line interface. Although speech would be the most natural way for the human to communicate, it is quite unnatural for the robot. It will be quite a while before robots interact as naturally as the fictional C-3PO.

- *Speech recognition:* Interpreting the continuous flow of sounds coming from a human (speech recognition), in real time, is a difficult task for a computer, mostly because of the great variability of speech. The same word, spoken by the same person may sound different depending on local acoustics, volume, the previous word, whether or not the speaker has a cold, etc.. It becomes even harder when the speaker has a different accent. Nevertheless, great strides have been made in the field since Davis, Biddulph, and Balashek designed the first "voice input system" which recognized "ten digits spoken by a single user with 100% accuracy" in 1952. Currently, the best systems can recognize continuous, natural speech, up to 160 words per minute, with an accuracy of 95%.

- *Gestures:* One can imagine, in the future, explaining to a robot chef how to make a pastry, or asking directions from a robot police officer. On both of these occasions, making hand gestures would aid the verbal descriptions. In the first case, the robot would be recognizing gestures made by the human, and perhaps repeating them for confirmation. In the second case, the robot police officer would gesture to indicate "down the road, then turn right". It is quite likely that gestures will make up a part of the interaction between humans and robots. A great many systems have been developed to recognize human hand gestures.
- *Facial expression:* Facial expressions can provide rapid feedback on the progress of a dialog between two humans, and soon it may be able to do the same for humans and robots. Robotic faces have been constructed by Hanson Robotics using their elastic polymer called Frubber, allowing a great amount of facial expressions due to the elasticity of the rubber facial coating and imbedded subsurface motors (servos) to produce the facial expressions. The coating and servos are built on a metal skull. A robot should know how to approach a human, judging by their facial expression and body language. Whether the person is happy, frightened, or crazy-looking affects the type of interaction expected of the robot. Likewise, robots like Kismet and the more recent addition, Nexi can produce a range of facial expressions, allowing it to have meaningful social exchanges with humans.
- *Artificial emotions Artificial emotions can also be imbedded and are composed of a sequence of facial expressions and/or gestures. As can be seen from the movie Final Fantasy:* The Spirits Within, the programming of these artificial emotions is quite complex and requires a great amount of human observation. To simplify this programming in the movie, presets were created together with a special software program. This decreased the amount of time needed to make the film. These presets could possibly be transferred for use in real-life robots.
- *Personality:* Many of the robots of science fiction have a personality, something which may or may not be desirable in the commercial robots of the future. Nevertheless, researchers are trying to create robots which appear to have a personality: i.e. they use sounds, facial expressions, and body language to

try to convey an internal state, which may be joy, sadness, or fear. One commercial example is Pleo, a toy robot dinosaur, which can exhibit several apparent emotions.

Control

The mechanical structure of a robot must be controlled to perform tasks. The control of a robot involves three distinct phases-perception, processing, and action (robotic paradigms). Sensors give information about the environment or the robot itself (e.g. the position of its joints or its end effector). This information is then processed to calculate the appropriate signals to the actuators (motors) which move the mechanical.

The processing phase can range in complexity. At a reactive level, it may translate raw sensor information directly into actuator commands. Sensor fusion may first be used to estimate parameters of interest (e.g. the position of the robot's gripper) from noisy sensor data. An immediate task (such as moving the gripper in a certain direction) is inferred from these estimates. Techniques from control theory convert the task into commands that drive the actuators. At longer time scales or with more sophisticated tasks, the robot may need to build and reason with a "cognitive" model. Cognitive models try to represent the robot, the world, and how they interact. Pattern recognition and computer vision can be used to track objects. Mapping techniques can be used to build maps of the world. Finally, motion planning and other artificial intelligence techniques may be used to figure out how to act. For example, a planner may figure out how to achieve a task without hitting obstacles, falling over, etc.

Autonomy Levels

Control systems may also have varying levels of autonomy.

1. Direct interaction is used for haptic or tele-operated devices, and the human has nearly complete control over the robot's motion.
2. Operator-assist modes have the operator commanding medium-to-high-level tasks, with the robot automatically figuring out how to achieve them.
3. An autonomous robot may go for extended periods of time without human interaction. Higher levels of autonomy do not necessarily require more complex cognitive capabilities. For example, robots in assembly plants are completely autonomous, but operate in a fixed pattern.

An other classification takes in account the interaction between human control and the machine motions.

1. Teleoperation. A human controls each movement, each machine actuator chance is specified by the operator.
2. Supervisory. A human specifies general moves or positions changes and the machine decides specifics movements of its actuators.
3. Task-level autonomy. The operator specifies only the task and the robot manage itself to complain for it.
4. Fully autonomy. The machine will create and complete all its tasks without human interaction.

Dynamics and Kinematics

The study of motion can be divided into kinematics and dynamics. Direct kinematics refers to the calculation of end effector position, orientation, velocity, and acceleration when the corresponding joint values are known. Inverse kinematics refers to the opposite case in which required joint values are calculated for given end effector values, as done in path planning. Some special aspects of kinematics include handling of redundancy (different possibilities of performing the same movement), collision avoidance, and singularity avoidance. Once all relevant positions, velocities, and accelerations have been calculated using kinematics, methods from the field of dynamics are used to study the effect of forces upon these movements.

Direct dynamics refers to the calculation of accelerations in the robot once the applied forces are known. Direct dynamics is used in computer simulations of the robot. Inverse dynamics refers to the calculation of the actuator forces necessary to create a prescribed end effector acceleration. This information can be used to improve the control algorithms of a robot.

In each area mentioned above, researchers strive to develop new concepts and strategies, improve existing ones, and improve the interaction between these areas. To do this, criteria for "optimal" performance and ways to optimize design, structure, and control of robots must be developed and implemented.

Robot Research

Much of the research in robotics focuses not on specific industrial tasks, but on investigations into new types of robots, alternative ways to think about or design robots, and new ways to manufacture them but other investigations, such as MIT's cyberflora project, are almost wholly academic. A first particular new innovation in robot design is the opensourcing of robot-projects. To describe the level of advancement of a robot, the term "Generation Robots" can be used. This term is coined by Professor Hans Moravec, Principal Research Scientist at the Carnegie Mellon University Robotics Institute in describing the near future evolution of robot technology. *First generation* robots, Moravec predicted in 1997, should have an intellectual capacity comparable to perhaps a lizard and should become available by 2010.

Because the *first generation* robot would be incapable of learning, however, Moravec predicts that the *second generation* robot would be an improvement over the *first* and become available by 2020, with an intelligence maybe comparable to that of a mouse.

The *third generation* robot should have an intelligence comparable to that of a monkey. Though *fourth generation* robots, robots with human intelligence, professor Moravec predicts, would become possible, he does not predict this happening before around 2040 or 2050. The second is Evolutionary Robots. This is a methodology that uses evolutionary computation to help design robots, especially the body form, or motion and behavior controllers. In a similar way to natural evolution, a large population of robots is allowed to compete in some way, or their ability to perform a task is measured using a fitness function. Those that perform worst are removed from the population, and replaced by a new set, which have new behaviors based on those of the winners. Over time the population improves, and eventually a satisfactory robot may appear.

This happens without any direct programming of the robots by the researchers. Researchers use this method both to create better robots. and to explore the nature of evolution. Because the process often requires many generations of robots to be simulated, this technique may be run entirely or mostly in simulation, then tested on real robots once the evolved algorithms are good enough. Currently, there are about 1 million industrial robots toiling around the world, and Japan is the top country having high density of utilizing robots in its manufacturing industry.

Education and Training

Robotics is a common undergraduate area of study. Some universities offer degrees in robotics. Robots recently became a popular tool in raising interests in computing for middle and high school students. First year computer science courses at several universities were developed which involves the programming of a robot instead of the traditional software engineering based coursework. Some Master courses in the field of Robotics are also offered.

Employment in Robotics

As the number of robots increases, robotics-related jobs grow. Some jobs require existing job skills, such as building cables, assembling parts, and testing.

Healthcare

Script Pro manufactures a robot designed to help pharmacies fill prescriptions that consist of oral solids or medications in pill form. The pharmacist or pharmacy technician enters the prescription information into its information system. The system, upon determining whether or not the drug is in the robot, will send the information to the robot for filling. The robot has 3 different size vials to fill determined by the size of the pill. The robot technician, user, or pharmacist determines the needed size of the vial based on the tablet when the robot is stocked. Once the vial is filled it is brought up to a conveyor belt that delivers it to a holder that spins the vial and attaches the patient label. Afterwards it is set on another conveyor that delivers the patient's medication vial to a slot labeled with the patient's name on an LED read out. The pharmacist or technician then checks the contents of the vial to ensure it's the correct drug for the correct patient and then seals the vials and sends it out front to be picked up. The robot is a very time efficient device that the pharmacy depends on to fill prescriptions.

McKesson's Robot RX is another healthcare robotics product that helps pharmacies dispense thousands of medications daily with little or no errors. The robot can be ten feet wide and thirty feet long and can hold hundreds of different kinds of medications and thousands of doses. The pharmacy saves many resources like staff members that are otherwise unavailable in a resource scarce industry. It uses an electromechanical head coupled with a pneumatic system to capture each dose and deliver it to its either stocked or dispensed location. The head moves along a single axis while it rotates 180 degrees to pull the medications. During this process it uses barcode technology to verify its pulling the correct drug. It then delivers the drug to a patient specific bin on a conveyor belt. Once the bin is filled with all of the drugs that a particular patient needs and that the robot stocks, the bin is then released and returned out on the conveyor belt to a technician waiting to load it into a cart for delivery to the floor.

Technacy

Technacy is the ability to understand, skillfully apply and communicate creative and 'balanced' technological solutions that are based on understanding the contextual factors involved. The Australian meaning of technacy is as a theoretical 'model' of technological activity. It implies a deep (critical) knowledge of the nature of technologies as systems, or phenomena or simply as a comprehensive prowess in specific technologies, especially if understood in the context of their application.

It is that ability to show an holistic understanding of technology, and make rounded judgements for effective and usually sustainable technological solutions. Not to be confused with technological literacy, which has a variety of meanings world-wide from skilled use of computers, to the ability to know and use the technical language for a Technological Genre (eg Australian NSW Board of Studies definition), to a broad scientific and technological orientation of knowledge as suggested by the International Technology Education Association(ITEA)'s definition or via the Wiki entry on Technological literacy.

Technacy, in Australian literature, is the name of a specific theoretical framework for understanding technological activity whereas Technological Literacy, as noted above, is not based on a theoretical framework, but rather is used as a broad expression for a range of ideas around technology and associated interpretations of desired capabilities. To this end they are complementary concepts.

Technate people study the context of a technological problem in a comprehensive way before selecting the knowledge, tools and resources needed to progress a solution. This comprehensive assessment is critical to the success of the solution. Generally, being technate is demonstrating the ability to develop 'balanced' solutions based on a collection of key ideas within the context. Therefore, technate people successfully solve technological problems-whether in computing or product design-as they have clearly considered the purpose and context for the end use of the developed solution.

Literacy, Numeracy, Technacy-Comparative Metaphors

Technacy is to the study of technologies, as literacy is to the study of languages, and numeracy is to the study of mathematics. As with literacy, where there are functional levels to being literate (signing your name, basic reading and comprehension) to sophisticated levels (powerful and effective poetry, comprehension of complex constructs in meaning and context), so too in technacy there are functional levels to being technate (skilled and knowledgeable in use of basic tools for a job, use of basic software to perform a task) to sophisticated levels (design and develop or evaluate appropriate technology solutions that are sustainable for specific and complex contexts in place or time).

And like literacy where there are various "text types" to master (such as narrative, transactional, procedural and persuasive texts, recounts, reports and explanations), so too in technacy there are various Technological Genre of technology knowledge that may be mastered (such as Information and Communication Technologies, Timber Technologies, Metal technologies, Composite based Technologies (plastics), Electrical technologies, Food Technologies, Textiles Technologies, or Human Management Systems as technologies and so on). These Technological Genre are commonly presented in the form of trades and technical faculties in schools, colleges and universities.

Technacy Guidelines

The Australian Federal Government has set a target for this capability across all K-12 and teacher education. It asserts that all technological activity always, whether it is immediately apparent or not, contains the following:

1. task purpose and context factors: normally difficult to control in the first instance and includes temporal (time based) and contingency factors;
2. agent(s) of the task: usually seen as human contribution of knowledge, technique, organisation, skill, process, values, etc. The agent is normally, but not exclusively, the human contribution (sometimes labelled 'Human Factors' or simply "People");
3. at least one physical or abstract 'tool' being used: either devices/ instruments or 'manipulators' such as algorithms or systems;
4. at least one resource material or data being manipulated by the above tool: includes such things as materials drawn from the eco-environment, data, or objects shaped by the 'tools'.

However, the notion of technacy neither implies good or bad design, but rather, models the essential elements inherent in all technological activity; at any scale of complexity, or at any time historically. It therefore suggests that good or bad design can be explained through analysis of the four technacy elements and the interactions of those elements.

It offers a basic framework for tasks that may include:

- planning what to address in technological research,
- educational experiences,
- evaluating situations from a technological perspective or,
- creating innovative solutions in new contexts or purposes or by way of mixing Technological Genre.

Propositions

1. Critical Technacy, is the deep, methodical and rational examination of technology as a phenomenon.
2. All technological activity integrates the above four elements as a minimum system. Thus, no technological activity is possible with less than the four elements being engaged as a minimum system.
3. All technology choices are value laden and context dependent, and as such, technology transfer problems can occur when a solution intended for one context and purpose is not appropriate for a different context and purpose
4. Validation of technological knowledge progresses by way of Context Criteria and Purpose Achievement: adhoc, *"I know because it works, against the defined context criteria"*
5. Given that technological knowledge integrates the agent (people), the tools and the eco-resource, towards a purpose with contextual criteria to meet, technological actions necessarily inherit ethical/moral criteria. Technacy necessitates ethical, moral & affect considerations, even if blithely ignored.
6. The context and purpose criteria basis of validating if something 'works', implies that Deep Technological Expertise, in any Genre, is driven by experience in optimising the scope of context criteria measures to be used for the scale of the purpose set. Under-estimating or over-estimating the scope of context criteria to be used may invalidate the claim *"I know because it works"*.
7. The above four elements of technacy interact in a deliberate logical way, and not in an arbitrary or disassociated way.
8. The above four elements are paradoxically both resource and constraints to the functionality of the system

9. The four minimum elements form the basis of Technological Genre: eg, the Genre of Textiles technology contains typical and specific tools, materials, and human factors for a purpose and context, that is different from the genre of information technology.
10. All events and things can be viewed from a technological perspective, by studying the four elements and their interactions, as a minimum system. However, a technological (technacy) perspective may not be the optimum framework for understanding every event or item under study. Use the technacy perspective appropriately, normally, for understanding the possible technological aspect of any event or item to be studied.
11. Innovations often merge different Technological Genre.
12. The four elements of the technacy theory form a fractal system where any one of them can be a product of another technacy system, and where the product of any technacy system can be an element of a new technacy system. This simple repeating pattern is a 'model' for explaining both the basic underlining structure of technological activity, and also its complexity and seemingly unlimited scope of manifestations.
13. Complex connected technological systems, whether digital like the internet, or industrial like human settlements, tend to form Scale-free_network characteristics.
14. All technologies and technological systems tend to display inherent logical functionality. A great deal of these logical functions are based on the physical sciences and are usually the result of design.

Australian Origin

Technology transfer into remote Australian, largely traditional, Indigenous communities has raised serious concerns about the way mainstream discourse perceives technologies as values neutral and not context specific.

A national Indigenous Technology research agency created the concept in 1986 to help communicate the understanding that all technologies are based on a fundamental system of interdependent factors. Understanding this system, or technacy, is to know technologies wholly, and as such, offers engineers, designers and policy makers a more robust framework for transference of technologies across cultures or into other contexts.

Web 2.0

The term "Web 2.0" (2004–present) is commonly associated with web applications that facilitate interactive information sharing, interoperability, user-centered design and collaboration on the World Wide Web. Examples of Web 2.0 include web-based communities, hosted services, web applications, social-networking sites, video-sharing sites, wikis, blogs, mashups and folksonomies. A Web 2.0 site allows its users to interact with other users or to change website content, in contrast to non-interactive websites where users are limited to the passive viewing of information that is provided to them.

The term is closely associated with Tim O'Reilly because of the O'Reilly Media Web 2.0 conference in 2004. Although the term suggests a new version of the World Wide Web, it does not refer to an update to any technical specifications, but rather to cumulative changes in the ways software developers and end-users use the Web. Whether Web 2.0 is qualitatively different from prior web technologies has been challenged by World Wide Web inventor Tim Berners-Lee, who called the term a "piece of jargon" — precisely because he intended the Web to embody these values in the first place.

History: From Web 1.0 to 2.0

The term "Web 2.0" was coined in 1999. Darcy DiNucci in her article "Fragmented Future", writes: The Web we know now, which loads into a browser window in essentially static screenfulls, is only an embryo of the Web to come. The first glimmerings of Web 2.0 are beginning to appear, and we are just starting to see how that embryo might develop. The Web will be understood not as screenfulls of text and graphics but as a transport mechanism, the either through which interactivity happens. It will [...] appear on your computer screen, [...] on your TV set [...] your car dashboard [...] your cell phone [...] hand-held game machines [...] maybe even your microwave oven.

Her use of the term deals mainly with Web design and aesthetics; she argues that the Web is "fragmenting" due to the widespread use of portable Web-ready devices. Her article is aimed at designers, reminding them to code for an ever-increasing variety of hardware. As such, her use of the term hints at – but does not directly relate to – the current uses of the term. The term did not resurface until 2003. These authors focus on the concepts currently associated with the term where, as Scott Dietzen puts it, "the Web becomes a universal, standards-based integration platform".

In 2004, the term began its rise in popularity when O'Reilly Media and MediaLive hosted the first Web 2.0 conference. In their opening remarks, John Batelle and Tim O'Reilly outlined their definition of the "Web as Platform", where software applications are built upon the Web as opposed to upon the desktop. The unique aspect of this migration, they argued, is that "customers are building your business for you". They argued that the activities of users generating content (in the form of ideas, text, videos, or pictures) could be "harnessed" to create value. O'Reilly et al contrasted Web 2.0 with what they called "Web 1.0". They associated Web 1.0 with the business models of Netscape and the Encyclopedia Britannica Online. For example,

Netscape framed "the web as platform" in terms of the old software paradigm: their flagship product was the web browser, a desktop application, and their strategy was to use their dominance in the browser market to establish a market for high-priced server products. Control over standards for displaying content and applications in the browser would, in theory, give Netscape the kind of market power enjoyed by Microsoft in the PC market.

Much like the "horseless carriage" framed the automobile as an extension of the familiar, Netscape promoted a "webtop" to replace the desktop, and planned to populate that webtop with information updates and applets pushed to the webtop by information providers who would purchase Netscape servers. In short, Netscape focused on creating software, updating it on occasion, and distributing it to the end users. O'Reilly contrasts this with Google, a company which does not focus on producing software such as a browser but instead focuses on providing a service based on data. The data here, of course, are the links Web page authors make between sites. Google exploits this user-generated content to offer Web search based on reputation through its "Page Rank" algorithm. Unlike software, which undergoes scheduled releases, a service such as Google is constantly updated, a process called "the perpetual beta".

O'Reilly's Web 2.0 conferences have been held every year since 2004, attracting entrepreneurs, large companies, and technology reporters. In terms of the lay public, the term Web 2.0 was largely championed by bloggers and by technology journalists, culminating in the 2006 TIME magazine Person of The Year – "You". That is, TIME selected the masses of users who were participating in content creation on social networks, blogs, wikis, and media sharing sites.

The cover story author Lev Grossman explains: It's a story about community and collaboration on a scale never seen before. It's about the cosmic compendium of knowledge Wikipedia and the million-channel people's network YouTube and the online metropolis MySpace. It's about the many wresting power from the few and helping one another for nothing and how that will not only change the world, but also change the way the world changes.

Since that time, Web 2.0 has found a place in the lexicon; the Global Language Monitor recently declared it to be the one-millionth English word.

Characteristics

Web 2.0 websites allow users to do more than just retrieve information. They can build on the interactive facilities of "Web 1.0" to provide "Network as platform" computing, allowing users to run software-applications entirely through a browser. Users can own the data on a Web 2.0 site and exercise control over that data.

These sites may have an "Architecture of participation" that encourages users to add value to the application as they use it. The concept of eb-as-participation-platform captures many of these characteristics. Bart Decrem, a founder and former CEO of Flock, calls Web 2.0 the "participatory Web" and regards the Web-as-information-source as Web 1.0.

The impossibility of excluding group-members who don't contribute to the provision of goods from sharing profits gives rise to the possibility that rational members will prefer to withhold their contribution of effort and free-ride on the contribution of others.

This requires what is sometimes called Radical Trust by the management of the website. According to Best, the characteristics of Web 2.0 are: rich user experience, user participation, dynamic content, metadata, web standards and scalability. Further characteristics, such as openness, freedom and collective intelligence by way of user participation, can also be viewed as essential attributes of Web 2.0.

Technology Overview

Web 2.0 draws together the capabilities of client-and server-side software, content syndication and the use of network protocols. Standards-oriented web browsers may use plugins and software extensions to handle the content and the user interactions. Web 2.0 sites provide users with information storage, creation, and dissemination capabilities that were not possible in the environment now known as

"Web 1.0". Web 2.0 websites typically include some of the following features and techniques. Andrew McAfee used the acronym SLATES to refer to them:

Search: Finding information through keyword search.

Links: Connects information together into a meaningful information ecosystem using the model of the Web, and provides low-barrier social tools.

Authoring: The ability to create and update content leads to the collaborative work of many rather than just a few web authors. In wikis, users may extend, undo and redo each other's work. In blogs, posts and the comments of individuals build up over time.

Tags: Categorization of content by users adding one-word descriptions to facilitate searching, without dependence on pre-made categories. This is referred to as "folksonomy".

Extensions: Software that makes the Web an application platform as well as a document server.

Signals: The use of syndication technology such as RSS to notify users of content changes.

While SLATES forms the basic framework of Enterprise 2.0, it does not contradict all of the higher level Web 2.0 design patterns and business models. And in this way, the new Web 2.0 report from O'Reilly is quite effective and diligent in interweaving the story of Web 2.0 with the specific aspects of Enterprise 2.0. It includes discussions of self-service IT, the long tail of enterprise IT demand, and many other consequences of the Web 2.0 era in the enterprise. The report also makes many sensible recommendations around starting small with pilot projects and measuring results, among a fairly long list.

How it Works: The client-side/web browser technologies typically used in Web 2.0 development are Asynchronous JavaScript and XML (Ajax), Adobe Flash, and JavaScript/Ajax frameworks such as Yahoo! UI Library, Dojo Toolkit, MooTools, and jQuery. Ajax programming uses JavaScript to upload and download new data from the web server without undergoing a full page reload.

To permit the user to continue to interact with the page, communications such as data requests going to the server are separated from data coming back to the page (asynchronously). Otherwise, the user would have to routinely wait for the data to come back before they can do anything else on that page, just as a user has to wait for a page to complete the reload. This also increases overall performance of the site, as the sending of requests can complete quicker independent of blocking and queuing required to send data back to the client.

The data fetched by an Ajax request is typically formatted in XML or JSON (JavaScript Object Notation) format, two widely used structured data formats. Since both of these formats are natively understood by JavaScript, a programmer can easily use them to transmit structured data in their web application. When this data is received via Ajax, the JavaScript program then uses the Document Object Model (DOM) to dynamically update the web page based on the new data, allowing for a rapid and interactive user experience. In short, using these techniques, Web designers can make their pages function like desktop applications. For example, Google Docs uses this technique to create a Web-based word processor.

Adobe Flash is another technology often used in Web 2.0 applications. As a widely available plugin independent of W3C (World Wide Web Consortium, the governing body of web standards and protocols), standards, Flash is capable of doing many things which are not currently possible in HTML, the language used to construct web pages. Of Flash's many capabilities, the most commonly used in Web 2.0 is its ability to play audio and video files.

This has allowed for the creation of Web 2.0 sites such as YouTube, where video media is seamlessly integrated with standard HTML. In addition to Flash and Ajax, JavaScript/Ajax frameworks have recently become a very popular means of creating Web 2.0 sites. At their core, these frameworks do not use technology any different from JavaScript, Ajax, and the DOM.

What frameworks do is smooth over inconsistencies between web browsers and extend the functionality available to developers. Many of them also come with customizable, prefabricated 'widgets' that accomplish such common tasks as picking a date from a calendar, displaying a data chart, or making a tabbed panel.

On the server side, Web 2.0 uses many of the same technologies as Web 1.0. Languages such as PHP, Ruby, ColdFusion, Perl, Python, and ASP are used by developers to dynamically output data using information from files and databases. What has begun to change in Web 2.0 is the way this data is formatted.

In the early days of the internet, there was little need for different websites to communicate with each other and share data. In the new "participatory web", however, sharing data between sites has become an essential capability. To share its data with other sites, a web site must be able to generate output in machine-readable formats such as XML, RSS, and JSON.

When a site's data is available in one of these formats, another website can use it to integrate a portion of that site's functionality into itself, linking the two together. When this design pattern is implemented, it ultimately leads to data that is both easier to find and more thoroughly categorized, a hallmark of the philosophy behind the Web 2.0 movement.

Usage: The popularity of the term Web 2.0, along with the increasing use of blogs, wikis, and social networking technologies, has led many in academia and business to coin a flurry of 2.0s, including Library 2.0, Social Work 2.0, Enterprise 2.0, PR 2.0, Classroom 2.0, Publishing 2.0, Medicine 2.0, Telco 2.0, Travel 2.0, Government 2.0, and even Porn 2.0. Many of these 2.0s refer to Web 2.0 technologies as the source of the new version in their respective disciplines and areas. For example, in the Talis white paper "Library 2.0: The Challenge of Disruptive Innovation", Paul Miller argues

Blogs, wikis and RSS are often held up as exemplary manifestations of Web 2.0. A reader of a blog or a wiki is provided with tools to add a comment or even, in the case of the wiki, to edit the content. This is what we call the Read/Write web.Talis believes that Library 2.0 means harnessing this type of participation so that libraries can benefit from increasingly rich collaborative cataloguing efforts, such as including contributions from partner libraries as well as adding rich enhancements, such as book jackets or movie files, to records from publishers and others.

Here, Miller links Web 2.0 technologies and the culture of participation that they engender to the field of library science, supporting his claim that there is now a "Library 2.0". Many of the other proponents of new 2.0s mentioned here use similar methods.

Of course, not much time passed before "Web 3.0" was coined. Definitions of Web 3.0 vary. Amit Agarwal argues that it is the Semantic Web. Andrew Keen, author of The Cult of the Amateur, argues that Web 3.0 is the return of experts and authorities to the Web.

For example, he points to Bertelsman's deal with the German Wikipedia to produce an edited print version of that encyclopedia. CNN Money's Jessi Hempel simply argues that Web 3.0 is Web 2.0 but with a profitable business model.

Criticism

Critics of the term claim that "Web 2.0" does not represent a new version of the World Wide Web at all, but merely continues to use so-called "Web 1.0" technologies and concepts.

First, techniques such as AJAX do not replace underlying protocols like HTTP, but add an additional layer of abstraction on top of them.

Second, many of the ideas of Web 2.0 had already been featured in implementations on networked systems well before the term "Web 2.0" emerged.

Amazon.com, for instance, has allowed users to write reviews and consumer guides since its launch in 1995, in a form of self-publishing. Amazon also opened its API to outside developers in 2002. Previous developments also came from research in computer-supported collaborative learning and computer-supported cooperative work and from established products like Lotus Notes and Lotus Domino, all phenomena which precede Web 2.0.

But perhaps the most common criticism is that the term is unclear or simply a buzzword. For example, in a podcast interview, Tim Berners-Lee described the term "Web 2.0" as a "piece of jargon": "Nobody really knows what it means...If Web 2.0 for you is blogs and wikis, then that is people to people. But that was what the Web was supposed to be all along."

Other critics labeled Web 2.0 "a second bubble" (referring to the Dot-com bubble of circa 1995–2001), suggesting that too many Web 2.0 companies attempt to develop the same product with a lack of business models.

For example, *The Economist* has dubbed the mid-to late-2000s focus on Web companies "Bubble 2.0". Venture capitalist Josh Kopelman noted that Web 2.0 had excited only 53,651 people (the number of subscribers at that time to TechCrunch, a Weblog covering Web 2.0 startups and technology news), too few users to make them an economically viable target for consumer applications.

Although Bruce Sterling reports he's a fan of Web 2.0, he thinks it is now dead as a rallying concept. Critics have cited the language used to describe the hype cycle of Web 2.0 as an example of Techno-utopianist rhetoric.

In terms of Web 2.0's social impact, critics such as Andrew Keen argue that Web 2.0 has created a cult of digital narcissism and amateurism, which undermines the notion of expertise by allowing anybody, anywhere to share – and place undue value upon – their own opinions about any subject and post any kind of content regardless of their particular talents, knowledgeability, credentials, biases or possible hidden agendas.

He states that the core assumption of Web 2.0, that all opinions and user-generated content are equally valuable and relevant, is misguided and is instead "creating an endless digital forest of mediocrity: uninformed political commentary, unseemly home videos, embarrassingly amateurish music, unreadable poems, essays and novels", also stating that Wikipedia is full of "mistakes, half truths and misunderstandings".

9

Tools and Toys of New Media

Reporters, editors and photographers all store data digitally. Even if it's just your list of contacts, learn to manage your data electronically to maximize its usefulness in the future. And open up your reporting to harness the power of the public. As disruptive as Web sites have been to the traditional publishing and broadcasting model, we ain't seen nothin' yet. The digital landscape is awash in change. Before you learn the basic skills that will allow you to participate in the digital revolution, it's important for you to look at the lay of the land through a broad lens. New and evolving technology and gadgets have changed—and will continue to change—the markets that news operations are aiming to serve.

I will start with information about some tools you should be using and then discuss tools you should understand that others are using. Not everyone wants to watch movies on their cell phones, but there are some very simple tools and practices you should adopt as you become digitally literate.

Tools you should be Using

Vanity searching: If you're in a position to hire others, you have almost certainly added Google and Yahoo! to the screening process. Conducting a Web search of a prospective job candidate is a common step in the early sorting process and the results can be revealing. A 2006 survey conducted by CareerBuilder found that, of hiring managers who used Web searches to research job candidates, 51 percent have eliminated a candidate based on what they found. If they searched a social networking site like MySpace or Facebook, the results were more ominous: 63 percent did not hire the person based on what they found. What does this mean for you? Before you apply for a new job, do some vanity searching in both Google and Yahoo! Make sure there aren't any compromising photos or inappropriate material. And if you're a recent college grad, better check MySpace and Facebook, too. Just because you've never posted a picture of some wild times at a party doesn't mean that no one else has. (If you find something, hopefully you can contact the "friend" who posted it and ask that it be removed.)

Flash drives and memory cards: Remember floppy disks? You probably have a stack of them at home or work, yet you never use them anymore. That's because they hold such a small amount of data—1.4MB—that they're just not practical. Think about it this way: A floppy disk could hold one, maybe two, digital photos. Today's digital landscape relies on small devices with huge amounts of storage. USB flash drives (for text) and memory cards like compact flash (CF) or secure digital (SD) (for digital photos or added game memory) can store hundreds or thousands of megabytes. And, like most technology, the prices on these devices have dropped precipitously since they hit the mainstream. A 1GB flash drive cost as much as $100 in 2004. In 2006, the same drive cost as little as $19. As a result, as many as 150 million flash drives were expected to be sold in 2006.

What does this mean for you? If you work with text, you can feasibly back up all your documents on a flash drive every time you log off your computer. It's quick and easy and, as the saying goes, there are two kinds of computer users: Those who back up their data, and those who will.

Another useful application for flash drives is the transfer of large files. If you have photos or a honkin' PDF that you want to send to someone in the newsroom, give the e-mail server a rest and copy it to a flash drive. The recipient can download it in a few seconds and your IT department will thank you for not clogging the server with several MBs of an attachment. Flash drives have a bright future, too. In September 2006, the USB Flash Drive Alliance announced it will endorse a new generation of "smart" drives that will allow users to run active programs from flash drives. So in addition to document and image storage, the new flash drives will have your Web browser with all your bookmarks, your instant messaging program with all your buddies, your games and more, all encrypted to keep it safe. So wherever you are in the world, you could use any computer and it would be just like using the one at your home or office.

Mobile 2.0

Now that you understand a little more about Web 2.0—and you're reading about Journalism 2.0—it's time to introduce Mobile 2.0. The next generation of wireless connectivity to mobile phones will allow regular cell phones, smart phones, BlackBerries and other devices to connect to the Internet via a high-speed network. Data will transfer as much as 10 times faster, according to some reports, which will make video, music, games and e-mail convenient to anyone, anywhere.

In effect, this is like going from a dial-up Internet connection to a high-speed hookup like the one you have at work.

Even before the third generation (commonly referred to as 3G) saturates the market, mobile delivery is a great opportunity for local publishers and broadcasters. Calendar listings, sports scores, news and weather updates are all within the regular operation of most local news publishing operations. Delivering them to mobile phones and other portable devices is the next logical step. Look at the market: There are 200 million mobile phone users in the U.S. and 70 percent are Web-enabled; 35 percent of those who have the Web option are "regular" users.

- The Weather Channel has 4.8 million paying subscribers a month for its mobile service.
- ABC/Disney has 2 million subscribers at $15 a month delivering ring tones, voice tones, wallpapers and video clips.

You should be aware that dozens of companies are working hard to make what is happening now obsolete, so to preview the promise of any of these technologies would be like predicting the future. Some of these new technologies will gain critical mass and change the world of communications, but, if I knew which ones, I would be a venture capitalist instead of a journalist.

What does this mean for you? The push for immediacy will continue as news operations master breaking news on a Web site and move to present breaking news on mobile devices. It also means a broadening of the scope of information that will be considered worthy of an immediate update, meaning all types of information and news (sports, business, entertainment) will be part of the mobile equation.

iPod: The Slim, Sleek, 800-pound Gorilla

One gadget that has already changed the media landscape is the Apple iPod. By describing the capabilities and uses of the iPod here, I mean to include any of the MP3 players on the market with video capability. No other device has changed the media landscape like Apple's player and iTunes stores.

As of November 2006, Apple had sold nearly 60 million iPods in the five-year life of the gadget, with 36 million sales in the past 12 months. According to Piper Jaffray & Co. research released in October 2006, the iPod owns 79 percent of the market share for digital media players. And talk about a youth market. Other Piper Jaffray research on teenagers found that 72 percent own an MP3 player and 79 percent of those specifically own an iPod. Almost half of the 1,000 students surveyed expect to buy a new media player within a year, and 76 percent of those prefer the iPod.

Some mainstream media companies are responding to this growing market. In September 2006, ABC News began creating a daily 15-minute newscast, separate from "ABC World News," frequently using the same anchor, Charles Gibson. The "World News Webcast" is available through the Web site at 3 p.m. ET and ready to download on iTunes about an hour later. There were more than 5 million downloads in both September and October, 2006. Newspapers such as the Roanoke Times in Virginia and the Naples Daily News in Florida began "vodcasting" in 2006. Each paper has built a studio for recording and producing video segments and each is making those shows available for download to an iPod or viewable on the Web site. National Public Radio, meanwhile, serves more than 6 million downloads of its podcasts each month. What does this mean for you? Every news organization is likely to try adding video to its mix very soon (if it hasn't already). If you can be an early adopter and find a way to incorporate video into your beat or your specialty, you will have a leg up on the competition.

'Other' Wireless

Some people actually still connect to the wireless Internet with a laptop computer. OK, that's being too flip, since laptops are still the primary vehicle for people to use with the Internet, but when you see what's happening with iPods and cell phones, it's easy to forget. Hitting a coffee shop with your laptop and paying a few bucks to connect to the Internet is one of the most popular ways to work wirelessly these days. But that business model doesn't look promising. Independent coffee shops, restaurants, car dealers, rock-climbing gyms and all sorts of other small businesses now offer free Wi-Fi access, too. And the field is only getting more crowded.

- Many cities are working on municipal Wi-Fi systems to bring free wireless Internet access to a concentrated area like a downtown.
- Special cards provided by the major cell phone companies insert into most laptops and allow wireless connection to the Internet from anywhere there's cell phone coverage. Users pay for the card—usually less than $100—then pay a monthly service fee for unlimited connectivity. A new service, called EV-DO, offers broadband-like speeds.
- A company called Clearwire, founded by Craig McCaw, who built one of the first cell phone companies, is launching in several U.S. cities. It offers standard wireless service or a special modem-like device that can be plugged into a laptop or desktop computer for more reliable service at a higher speed. The idea is that you could pay for one service that would go with you anywhere, so Clearwire would be your provider at home, at the local coffee shop, or wherever. You would use this external modem to connect at home or take it into coffee shop and use it instead of paying six bucks for a T-Mobile hook-up. It's like having your home Internet connection anywhere.

What does this mean for you? The online audience served by breaking-news updates throughout the day will continue to grow. Thought of as the "at-work" audience for much of the digital age, potential readers of news updates will grow as wireless Internet service becomes free and ubiquitous. Combined with Mobile 2.0 gadgets and services and the continued mainstream adoption of downloaded material on iPods, the opportunities for news companies to reach customers digitally will continue to explode.

Get your "mojo" on: The increasing adoption of mobile communication technology not only changes the way audiences receive the news, but also opens up new ways to report it. Mobile journalists—or "mojos"—are becoming more common at TV news stations and even popping up at newspapers. Also known as backpack journalists, these multidimensional dynamos can carry an assortment of tools into the field to report the news in a fully multimedia manner. A laptop with wireless Internet connection, a video camera (that also shoots still photos) and an audio recorder are the basic pieces of equipment that allow journalists to produce news stories or blog posts, photos, video, or audio for a story. Yahoo!'s Kevin Sites is the best-known backpack journalist working today. Sites travelled to war-torn countries around the world to tell the stories of those most affected by calamity, and his regular feature, In The Hot Zone, on Yahoo! News claimed 2 million readers a week in 2006.

The News-Press in Fort Myers, Fla., meanwhile, dispatched several "mojos" into the field every day to report hyperlocal news close to home. These new era reporters have no desks and rarely a specific assignment outside of a geographical area to visit. They drive around their area and perform a modern version of that "old shoe leather reporting." They also do marketing, handing out fliers to educate people about the news organization's online services. Frank Ahrens of The Washington Post profiled the News-Press mojos in December 2006 (and shot this photo of Kevin Myron in his car). "Their guiding principle: A constantly updated stream of intensely local, fresh Web content—regardless of its traditional news value—is key to building online and newspaper readership." Mojos are still an experiment, but if nothing else, they show how flexible—and mobile—journalists in the future can be when it comes to covering and reporting news.

Digital Audio and Podcasting

Eventually you will be asked to capture audio to go with your story (if you haven't been already). Learn the basics of gathering natural sound, recording an interview and editing the clip (with free software) in this chapter. A challenge for many reporters is to capture in words a story's particular sights and sounds. Photographs usually solve the visual end of this equation. Now, with the advent of cheap digital audio recorders, reporters can bring readers even closer to the story by enhancing their reporting with audio clips.

The Basics: Audio Formats

It's helpful to have an understanding of digital file formats as you get started. If you download or listen to audio on a Web site, then it is probably in a compressed format so that it downloads faster. You're probably familiar with some of the formats, like MP3 and Windows Media. It's not necessary for you to know the technical differences between them, just know what you're dealing with. Here's a glance at the most prevalent formats of digital audio.

Compressed (on Web sites);

- MP3 (most universal)
- WMA (Windows Media)
- Real (Real Audio)

- MPEG-4 (QuickTime)
- MPEG-4 AAC (iTunes).

Uncompressed (not found on Web sites)

- WAV (pronounced "wave")
- AIFF (Apple's standard format).

Your goal should be to provide audio clips in MP3 format for your readers. Why? Because virtually any computer can play an MP3. Programs like iTunes, Windows Media Player or Real Player can play them, too, but they can't play the other proprietary formats. For example, you can't play a Windows Media file in iTunes or a Real Media file in Windows Media Player, but you can play an MP3 on any of them.

Identifying Opportunities

If you are a reporter, interviewing people is what you do. Sure, you can transcribe the best quotes for print but does that really provide a thorough and complete report? Did one of your sources elaborate on an important topic, which you then paraphrased to avoid a long quote? Did someone say something with emotion or feeling or uniqueness that doesn't transfer to text? Most news articles can be improved with the addition of audio clips. A newspaper reporter can easily produce audio clips on more than half of the stories he or she turns in, based on the subject matter alone. That may sound too ambitious if you haven't edited and published audio for the Web before. But once you do it a couple of times, it will become second nature. The first step is to toss that microcassette machine from the 1990s and get yourself a digital recorder.

Buying A Recorder

Like most digital tools, there are plenty of options on the market today and deciding which one is right for you starts with a basic question: How much can you afford to spend? You can buy a new digital recorder for as little as $50, but if you spend even a little bit more you can dramatically improve your capacity to participate in this game. And, of course, if you spend even more you will go from "entry level" to "professional" in no time.

The key points to consider include recording time, digital file format and compatibility with your computer, ease of use and transferring files, and quality of recording. Let's look at a few options in different price levels and evaluate them on these aspects. Important note: You might be tempted to buy a $50 version because, hey, it says it's a digital recorder. But unless you can transfer the files from the recorder to your computer, you will be unable to get the files onto a Web site where readers can listen to them. So it would be like writing a story on a computer and not being able to send it to your editor.

Using A Microphone

While using an external mike can be an extra nuisance during an interview, the added sound quality is well worth the effort. There are basically two types of external microphones: A standard mike with a cord, and a wireless or lavalier mike. Let's take a look at the advantage both have to offer and also explore the best way to record telephone calls digitally.

A standard mike with a cord is helpful if you are interviewing more than one person at a time or you want to include your voice on the audio clip so listeners can hear the full interview instead of just selected quotes. It is also the best way to gather natural, or environmental, sound, which can be spliced into the audio segment to enhance the listening experience.

Gathering natural sound is not the same as background noise. Interviews should be done in a setting that allows the voices to be recorded without interruption. Separate from the interview session, however, it's always a good idea to search for those sounds that will help describe the setting. Are there power tools being used? Is it a noisy office with lots of chatter and phones ringing? Is it an outside setting where you can hear the bugs and the birds?

If there is natural sound to be had, take just a few minutes and record it—without anyone talking. "You might feel silly just standing there holding your mike in the air, but when you get back to edit your stuff, you'll be glad you have it," said Kirsten Kendrick, a reporter and morning host on KPLU radio, an NPR affiliate in Seattle and Tacoma. You should record natural sound in uninterrupted 15-second increments. That way you'll avoid the problem of not having enough to use in editing. You can always make a clip shorter by cutting it but you can't make it longer, so make sure the material you're working from is long enough to cut from.

Assignment

Find the NPR station near you or listen online from NPR's Web site. The public radio broadcasters do a masterful job of weaving natural sound into their reports. And as a listener, you get a better sense of the setting for the story when you hear what it really sounds like. A wireless or lavalier mike is most helpful when your goal is to capture the voice and words of one person and you're "in the field." While they might be intimidating at first, wireless mikes are really very simple.

There are two halves: A battery pack and miniature mike on a cord that clips on the person you want to record (this sends the signal), and a battery pack and cord that goes into your recording device (this receives the signal).

Here's how to get started:

1. Clip the mike on the lapel of your subject and give them the battery pack to put in their pocket. Don't forget to turn the device on!
2. Connect the receiver pack to your recording device, turn it on, and put it in your pocket or purse or handbag. Then operate your recorder as you normally would: Hit the record button when you're ready and pause button if there's a break in the action.

Recording with Your Computer

To record a phone call digitally, you'll need another piece of equipment: A telephone recording control unit that sells at Radio Shack for $25. Many journalists already use one of these to record phone calls to their analog microcassette tape recorder. And those same journalists probably have an unruly jungle of tapes on their desk or in a drawer that is unlikely to produce the tape from six months ago that someone might need. (NOTE: In some states it's illegal to record someone on the phone without their express permission.)

That's one reason to go digital—organization. With the Radio Shack device you can record directly to your computer, which makes it easy to store files in an organized fashion. And going through the "tape" is easier on a computer since most playback programs like Windows Media Player have slider bars that allow you to quickly go from the beginning of a recording to the end.

Your hardware is ready. Now you need software to manage and edit the sound files with your computer. There are literally hundreds of options for audio software, ranging from Adobe Audition (the choice for most radio professionals, $349) to Audacity and JetAudio, popular free downloads that work great.

No matter which audio software you use, there are a few basic settings on your computer to check before starting your first recording:

- File name: You will either need to select File-> New and create a file or choose where on your system this new file will be created. Either way you need to think about what to call your file. This is a good time to come up with a standard file naming convention that will serve you for months and years to come. Include the date and the name of the person you'll be talking to, so an interview on Valentine's Day with Paris Hilton would be named "021407hilton." It's also helpful to create new folders by year or month for more organization.
- Format: You should record in WAV format so your files are uncompressed and, therefore, of the highest quality. You can convert the files to MP3 (Audacity and JetAudio can both do this) once they're edited for publishing on the Web. You only need to worry about this when recording directly into your computer, not when using a digital recorder.
- Input/Mike level: Make sure the software is set to capture data via microphone input. Then find the setting that adjusts the microphone level and set it to about 70 percent of the possible level.

Assignment: Now call a friend and record the call for a trial run. Save the file with your new naming convention. Play it back to make sure it sounds good.

Editing Your Audio

It's unlikely you'll ever publish an entire session online. Just like you don't publish entire interviews in text, you need to edit your audio to make sure the best stuff is not obscured by less compelling, less important or repetitive content. Editing audio is remarkably similar to editing text, so you shouldn't be intimidated when approaching this task. First, acquire the audio file if it's still on your recording device. Connect the digital recorder to your computer through USB and drag the file(s) you need into a folder or onto the desktop. Important note: Most—but not all—digital recorders come with a USB cord that connects to a computer to make this easy (simply plug the cord into the recorder, then connect it to the computer through a USB port). The cheapest recorders, however, do not interface with computers, making them much less useful.

Launch your audio-editing software. Ideally, the program should be easy to use and export files in MP3 format. If you use a PC or a Windows machine, Audacity and JetAudio are excellent free options.

Let's go through the editing process with Audacity since it appears to be the most prevalent free software in use today.

Editing with Audacity

1. Use File-> Open and open the audio file
2. *Crop out the bad stuff:* Think about how users would best appreciate the content—in one full serving or broken up into smaller bites. Highlight areas that represent unwanted ums, ahs, mouth noises and lip smacking. Then simply hit DELETE. Also crop out silence and any small talk at the beginning and end.
3. *Make it stereo:* Some files will be mono, not stereo, meaning you'll only hear the audio in one side of your headphones. You want to make it stereo so the sound file will play in both sides of speakers and headphones, instead of just one. To make it stereo, click on the Audio Track label next to an upside down triangle. Then select Split Stereo Track from the drop-down menu. Then copy the region that you've edited by highlighting it and using Edit-> Copy. Then click into the lower window and use Edit-> Paste.
4. *Export the file:* Convert your audio edit into a compressed, ready-for-online publishing MP3. Just go to File and select Export as MP3. Ignore the meta data interface (Author, Description, etc.) unless you're doing a podcast.

Assignment: Record your own voice as a test. Count from 1-10 into a microphone and capture it digitally. Then edit your take. Highlight the section where you say "3" and select Edit-> Cut. Then move the cursor to after the "6" and select Edit-> Paste. Repeat a few more times with other numbers. This will give you a feel for how the sound waves represent words and sounds and also show you how easy it is to edit audio.

Using Time Points for Speed

Most newspaper journalists will do what they know first—use the audio to get quotes so they can write their story before they edit the audio for online publishing. That's great. But think about the audio editing you will do next as you listen to the entire take. If you make a note of the time when a good quote plays, you'll save loads of time when you go back to edit the take for the good stuff.

All audio-editing software programs feature convenient time track marks, so if your interview's best quote occurred 10 minutes into the interview, you write "10:00" next to the quote in your notebook. Then go directly to the 10-minute mark on the track when you're ready to edit and you've saved yourself 9 minutes, 59 seconds.

Ready for Podcasting

Podcasting is the distribution of audio files over the Internet using RSS subscription. The files can be downloaded to mobile devices such as MP3 players or played on personal computers. The term podcast, (Playable On Demand + broadcast) can mean both the content and the method of delivery. Podcasters' Web sites also may offer direct download of their files, but the subscription feed of automatically delivered new content is what distinguishes a podcast from a simple download. Usually, the podcast features one type of "show" with new episodes available either sporadically or at planned intervals such as daily or weekly.

Podcasting with video files is often referred to as vodcasting (video + podcasting). It works the same, but includes video. If you download a vodcast on an MP3 player that doesn't have a video screen, you will still be able to hear the audio. In format, podcasts are similar to conventional radio programming with a host or hosts interviewing a subject, playing music or introducing pre-recorded audio stories. So it's no surprise that National Public Radio produces some of the most popular podcasts online.

The San Francisco Chronicle was producing two dozen podcasts as of January 2007 on topics as diverse as the San Francisco 49ers football team, wine and movies. Listening to podcasts in iTunes: If you have iTunes, finding and listening to podcasts is simple. Just click the Podcasts link in the left menu, then click Podcasts directory on the bottom of the screen. Search by category or most popular. Click Subscribe if you'd like to add a podcast to your collection and it will automatically update any time there is new content.

Setting up a podcast: If you know you will have regular audio files on a specific topic to offer to readers, setting up a podcast will make organizing and publishing the audio convenient for you and your readers. A good example is a sports beat writer who records interviews with coaches and players and wants to offer them to readers. Setting up a podcast will allow a reader to subscribe and automatically receive new files as they become available. Creating a podcast that others can subscribe to is easy and free—if you have an RSS feed set up. Go to iTunes and click on the Submit a podcast logo or use another service like Podcast Alley.

Functions of Communication

Mass media has a prominent role to play in modern society. It can bring about radical changes and improve social situation as it influences our social, civil, cultural, political, economic and aesthetic outlook.Modernization has converted media into an indispensable feature of human activity. However, factors like age, education, economic condition, personal needs and availability of proper components decide the quantum and frequency of media use. This is evident from the fact that most media centres are located in urban areas. The majority of consumers of media products are also concentrated in and around cities and towns. It is rightly said that media use is an index of development.

The greater the use, the higher will be the level of education. As social beings, humans are sustained by mutual interactions, exchange of ideas, information and views with the fellow beings. Illiteracy, which is nothing but absence of education and information is a stumbling block for any aspect of development-social, economic, political, cultural and even spiritual. Media has become the harbinger of development through the removal of these roadblocks and the provision of information and knowledge. In a democratic country like India, the ultimate power lies with the people. But a democratic society needs vigilant and informed people who are able to see through the gimmicks of political parties and politicians. Media creates such valuable citizens.Besides, media has done much good to society by exposing various scams, scandals, frauds, embezzlements and many other cases of corruption leading to initiation of enquiries and other processes of prosecution against the perpetrators of these crimes.

History is witness that press has been instrumental in putting an end to atrocities and bringing the downfall of ruthless dictators. In India, vernacular press did the job of uniting people against the oppressive British rule and triggered its end in the country. However, media too suffers from some pitfalls, growing consumerism and materialism have adversely impacted our media. The partisan attitude, sectarian outlook and biased individualism in some sections of media are a testimony that media too is susceptible to harmful influences. Often, in fierce rivalries, ethics of journalism are thrown out of the window to settle old scores. Running after opportunistic gains is another malady our media suffers from. The incidents of throwing are against the ethics of media. Deliberately creating sensational stuff to attract with reality-is another tactic that media must avoid.

It is said that big minds discuss issues but small or swallow minds discuss/attack persons. The significance of communication for human life cannot be overestimated. This is true because beyond the physical requirements of food and shelter man needs to communicate with his/ her fellow human beings. This urge for communication is a primal one and in our contemporary civilization a necessity for survival. That is to say without communication no society can exist, much less develop and survive. For the existence as well as the organization of every society communication is a fundamental and vital process.

Mass Communication and the Mass Media

Among the four identified forms of communication is mass communication, which deals with messages addressed from one to many persons mediated by elements in mass media such as radio, television, film, newspaper, magazine, book etc. Fortunately and not boastfully I can say that since the early 1970s when I became a trained teacher, I have been involved with all the elements of mass media except film. In the 1970s I was writing for radio and television (news commentaries, reflections, and news reports as well as poems and youth programs) in Ghana and the most popular newspaper in Ghana-the Daily Graphic.

By 1980 I had become a regular contributor to the Network Africa program on the B.B.C. World Service. My love for the mass media sent me to the Kwame Nkrumah University of Science and Technology (KNUST) in Kumasi, Ghana to do a degree program in Publishing Management (Book Industry) from 1989 to 1992. I specialized in editing and marketing and worked as an editor for the newsletter of the Department of Book Industry as well as an assistant editor for the students? magazine published by KNUST. Above all, I single-handedly initiated and published a church quarterly paper-the Southern Trumpet-for the S.D.A. Church in South Ghana for almost ten years before leaving Ghana in 1995 for further studies at the University of Toronto in Canada. Since 1998 that I joined the editorial board of the dynamic community newspaper-the Ghanaian News-published monthly in Toronto I have served in the capacities of assistant editor and contributing editor till now. I have therefore come a long way living through the bad and good days of the mass communicator associated with the print media, especially newspapers. The joy of disseminating good news, the anxiety of hitting scoops in news reporting, the embarrassment of the printer?s devil, which causes elementary errors in published articles and the wild attacks on opinions expressed in the mass media! My contribution to the discourse on the role of the mass media in community development is authentic since I understand the nitty-gritty of being a mass communicator.

Mass communication is the technological means of sending information, ideas and opinions from a mass communicator to a complex audience. It is also defined as comprising the institutions and techniques by which specialized groups such as broadcasters, film producers and publishers employ technological devices to disseminate symbolic content to large heterogeneous and widely disperse audience. Mass communicators are impersonal. They are part of the institutions they work for and should not be blamed personally for what comes from the institutions. The credibility of the message is not for the individual communicator, but for the institution or the organization that sends it. Thus, mass communication deals with collective sender. For example, a newspaper is not produced by only one person.

The newspaper is the end results of collective efforts of reporters, editors, type-setters, proofreaders, designers and printers. These must be well-trained persons. It is, however, sad to admit that the mass media have been infiltrated by some unqualified persons as well as some unscrupulous individuals with their own political agendas other than to serve the communities they are supposed to educate, inform, entertain and mobilize for development. Hence, the establishment of media commissions in most democratic and civilized communities! Institutions and organizations engaged in mass communication anywhere must be weary of such persons. The other important area of notice is that mass communication deals with the concept of mass audience. Here, there is no common motivation. Audience do not act together. They belong to different classes-different education and socio-economic status. The message communicated in the mass media is open to the public and everyone has access to it provided she/he has the mass communication technological device as well as understands the language in which the message is sent.

10

Categorization of Multimedia

Multimedia may be broadly divided into linear and non-linear categories. Linear active content progresses without any navigational control for the viewer such as a cinema presentation. Non-linear content offers user interactivity to control progress as used with a computer game or used in self-paced computer based training. Hypermedia is an example of non-linear content. Multimedia presentations can be live or recorded. A recorded presentation may allow interactivity via a navigation system. A live multimedia presentation may allow interactivity via an interaction with the presenter or performer.

Movie Theater

A typical multiplex (AMC Promenade 16 in Woodland Hills, Los Angeles, United States). Most movie theaters are commercial operations catering to the general public, who attend by purchasing a ticket. The movie is projected with a movie projector onto a large projection screen at the front of the auditorium. Some movie theaters are now equipped for digital cinema projection, removing the need to create and transport a physical film print.

Spelling and Alternative Terms

Outside of North America, most English-speaking countries use the term *cinema*. Both terms, as well as their derivative adjectives "cinematic" and "kinematic," ultimately derive from the Greek -Ohio, "movement." In these areas the term "theatre" is usually restricted to live-performance venues. In the United States, the customary spelling is "theater", but the National Association of Theatre Owners uses the spelling "theatre" to refer to a movie theater. Colloquial expressions, mostly used for cinemas collectively, include *the silver screen*, *the big screen* (contrasted with the "small screen" of television) and (in the United Kingdom) *the pictures*, *the flicks*, and *the flea pit*. A "screening room" usually refers to a small facility for viewing movies, often for the use of those involved in the production of motion pictures, or in large private residences.

History

The Gateway Theatre in Jefferson Park, Chicago was a Movie Palace for the Balaban and Katz theater chain. The theater's Baroque spire is a replica of the Royal Castle in Warsaw.

Before 1900

The first public exhibition of projected motion pictures in the United States was at Koster and Bial's Music Hall on 34th Street in New York City on April 23, 1896. However, the first "storefront theater" in the US dedicated exclusively to showing motion pictures was Vitascope Hall, established on Canal Street, New Orleans, Louisiana June 26, 1896—it was converted from a vacant store.

A crucial factor was Thomas Edison's decision to sell a small number of Vitascope Projectors as a business venture in April-May 1896. In the basement of the new Ellicott Square Building, Main Street, Buffalo, New York, Mitchell Mark and his brother Moe Mark added what they called Edison's Vitascope Theater (entered through Edisonia Hall), which they opened to the general public on October 19, 1896 in collaboration with Rudolph Wagner, who had moved to Buffalo after spending several years working at the Edison laboratories. This 72-seat, plush theater was designed from scratch solely to show motion pictures.

Terry Ramseye, in his book, *A Million and One Nights* (1926), notes that this "was one of the earliest permanently located and exclusively motion-picture exhibitions." According to the *Buffalo News*, "There were seats for about 90 persons and the admission was three cents. Feeble, flickering films of travel scenes were the usual fare."

This November 7, 1897 ad shows the actual programming of Vitascope Theater, one of the first motion picture theaters specially built for that purpose. In its first year, 200,000 people attended. It was in Buffalo, New York. However, during the rest of this period, between 1891-1900, films did not achieve much popularity.

Many older movie theaters, such as the River Oaks Theatre in Houston, Texas, have been restored and play arthouse movies; newer multiplexes in the areas with restored theaters show first run films. Other older movie theaters, such as the Texas Theatre in Dallas, Texas, have been deemed historically significant and undergone restoration. The Texas Theater is shown here in 2008 with replica marquee and appears as it did in 1963 when Lee Harvey Oswald was arrested on the premises. The building today hosts live theater.

1900-1919

The first permanent structure designed for screening of movies in the state of California was Tally's Electric Theater, completed in 1902 in Los Angeles. Tally's theater was a storefront within a larger building, but apparently purpose-built as a movie theater. *The Great Train Robbery* (1903), which was 12 minutes in length, would also give the film industry a boost.

In 1905, Pittsburgh movie theater owners Harry Davis and John Harris also established the first of what would become a popular form of movie theaters spread throughout the country, which were five-cent nickelodeon movies. In 1906, Montreal opened one of the first movie theatres in the world.

The previous oldest oldest movie theatre still in action today according to the Guinness World Records belonged to the Pionier Cinema which opened as the Helios on the 26 September 1909 in Szczecin, Poland (at the time of the opening it was Stettin, Germany). Nevertheless, this position was beaten in 2008 when the owners of the *Korsør Biograf Teater* in Korsør, Denmark, discovered that they actually operated a movie theater that opened in August 1908. They were accepted into the Guinness Book of World Records as the oldest still operating movie theater the same year (to appear in the 2010 edition of the book).

In 1912, the Picture House, in Clevedon, England, opened with a charity film performance to raise funds for the victims of the Titanic disaster, and has been showing films continuously since. The 1913 opening of the Regent Theater in New York City signalled a new respectability for the medium, and the start of the two-decade heyday of American cinema design.

The million dollar Mark Strand Theater at 47th Street and Broadway in New York City opened in 1914 by Mitchell Mark was the archetypical movie palace. The ornate Al Ringling Theater was the very first "Movie Palace" it was built in Baraboo, WI by Al Ringling, one of the founders of the Ringling Bros. Circus for the then incredible sum of $100,000.00.

In 1915, the movie *The Birth of a Nation* would also pave way for feature films. By 1915, feature films were so successful that the five cent ticket admission prices would expand to ten cents, hence ending the era of nickelodeon movie theaters. Later, Los Angeles promoter Sid Grauman continued the trend of theatre-as-destination with his ornate "Million Dollar Theatre", using the same design firm as Ringling (the MDT was the first to signify its primary use for motion pictures with the "theatre" spelling), and opened on Broadway in downtown Los Angeles in 1918.

Post 1920s : Modern Era

In the next ten years, as movie revenues exploded, independent promoters and movie studios (who owned their own proprietary chains until an antitrust ruling in 1948) raced to build the most lavish, elaborate, attractive theatres. These forms morphed into a unique architectural genre—the movie palace—a unique and extreme architectural genre which boasted a luxurious design, a giant screen, and, beginning in 1953, stereophonic sound. The movie chains were also among the first industries to install air conditioning systems which gave the theatres an additional lure of comfort in the summer period.

Several movie studios achieved vertical integration by acquiring and constructing theatre chains. The so-called "Big Five" theatre chains of the 1920s and 1930s were all owned by studios: Paramount, Warner, Loews (which owned Metro-Goldwyn-Mayer), Fox, and RKO. All were broken up as a result of the U.S. Supreme Court's ruling in the 1948 *United States v. Paramount Pictures, Inc.* anti-trust case. In the 1970s, porn theatres became ubiquitous in some areas. However, the introduction of the low-cost VHS video system for home televisions has decommissioned many porno cinemas as well as many 'second-run' theatres.

People can pay to watch movies at home after a few short months following their theatrical release, through cable television or streamed from the Internet: pay-per-view (PPV) and video on demand (VOD). Initially, home video contributed to an industry wide slump in the late 1980s, not to mention the decline of the 'Dollar Cinema' (where first-run films are pulled from circulation to play at reduced rates for the remainder of their run). The theater industry responded by building larger auditoriums with stadium seating layouts, installing more screens (to allow for more variety and more show times), upgrading sound systems and installing more amenities and higher-quality food and drink. The growing popularity of high-definition television sets, along with HD DVD and Blu-ray Disc players may also contributed to the decline in cinema attendance, although there seems to be little evidence of this at the moment. By June 12, 2009; all US television stations will be broadcast in the digital format. This could also affect US movie theaters.

3D

3-D film is a system ofpresenting film images so that they appear to the viewer to be three-dimensional. Visitors usually borrow or keep special glasses to wear while watching the film. Depending on the system used, these are typically polarized glasses. Three Dimensional films use two images channelled, respectively, to the right and left eyes to simulate depth by using 3-D glasses with red and blue lenses (anaglyph), polarized (linear and circular), and other techniques.

3-D glasses deliver the proper image to the proper eye and make the image appear to "pop-out" at the viewer and even follow the viewer when he/she moves so viewers relatively see the same image.

Most 3-D films are shown in amusement parks and even "4-D" techniques are used when certain effects such as spraying of water, movement of seats, and other effects are used to simulate actions seen on the screen. The earliest 3-D films were presented in the 1920s. There have been several "waves" of 3D film distribution, most notably in the 1950s when they were promoted as a way to offer audiences something that they could not see at home on television. Still the process faded quickly and as yet has never been more than a periodic novelty in film presentation. Currently, films are again being presented in cinemas in 3-D, in the IMAX 3D system and in digital 3-D, such as is used in the animated films of Disney/Pixar.

In 2009, Ben Walters suggested that film exhibitors are now more interested in 3-D film. The number of 3-D screens in theaters is increasing (Real D company expects 15,000 screens worldwide in 2010). 3-D films also encourage exhibitors to adopt digital cinema. One incentive for 3-D screens is that although ticket sales decline, revenues from 3-D tickets grow.

Imax

IMAX is a system using film with more than ten times the frame size of a 35 mm film to produce image quality far superior to conventional film. IMAX theaters use an oversized screen as well as special projectors. Invented by a Canadian company, the first permanent IMAX theater was at Ontario Place in Toronto, Ontario.

Design

Traditionally a movie theater, like a stage theater, consists of a single auditorium with rows of comfortable seats, as well as a foyer area containing a box office for buying tickets, a counter and/or self-service facilities for buying snacks and drinks, and washrooms. Stage theaters are sometimes converted into movie theatres by placing a screen in front of the stage and adding a projector; this conversion may be permanent, or temporary for purposes such as showing arthouse fare to an audience accustomed to plays. The familiar characteristics of relatively low admission and open seating can be traced to Samuel Roxy Rothafel, an early movie theater impresario. Many of these early theatres contain a balcony, an elevated level across the auditorium above the theater's rearmost seats. The rearward main floor "loge" seats were sometimes larger, softer, and more widely spaced and sold for a higher price.

In conventional low pitch viewing floors the preferred seating arrangement is to use staggered rows. While a less efficient use of floor space this allows a somewhat improved sight line between the patrons seated in the next row toward the screen, provided they do not lean toward one another.

"Stadium seating," popular in modern multiplexes, actually dates back to the 1920s. The 1922 Princess Theatre in Honolulu, Hawaii featured "stadium seating," sharply raked rows of seats extending from in front of the screen back towards the ceiling. It gives patrons a clear sight line over the heads of those seated in front of them. Modern "stadium seating" was utilized in IMAX theatres, which have very tall screens, beginning in the early 1970s. Among recent stadium-style movie theaters in the United States is the AMC Grand in Dallas, Texas, which opened in 1995.

Rows of seats are divided by one or more aisles so that there are seldom more than 20 seats in a row. This allows easier access to seating, as the space between rows is very narrow. Depending on the angle of rake of the seats, the aisles have steps. In older theaters, aisle lights were often built into the end seats of each row to help patrons find their way in the dark. Since the advent of stadium theaters with stepped aisles, each step in the aisles may be outlined with small lights to prevent patrons from tripping in the darkened theater.

Multiplexes and Megaplexes

Canada was the first country in the world to have a two-screen theater. The Elgin Theatre in Ottawa became the first venue to offer two film programs on different screens in 1957 when Canadian theater-owner Nat Taylor converted the dual screen theater into one capable of showing two different films simultaneously. Later in the USA, other purpose-built two-screen theaters opened in the mid to late-1960's, such as the Martin's Westgate Cinemas in East Point, Ga.(1965).

Taylor is credited as inventor of the multiplex or cineplex, and later founded the Cineplex Odeon Corporation, opening the 18-screen Toronto Eaton Centre Cineplex, the world's largest at the time, in Toronto, Canada. Stanley Durwood of American Multi-Cinema (now AMC Theatres) pioneered what would become the *multiplex* in 1963 after realizing that he could operate several attached auditoriums with the same staff needed for one through careful management of the start times for each movie.

Since that time multiple-screen theatres have become the norm, and many existing venues have been retrofitted so that they have multiple auditoriums. A single foyer area is shared among them. In the 1970s many large 1920s movie palaces were converted into multiple screen venues by dividing their large auditoriums, and sometimes even the stage space, into smaller theaters. In most markets, nearly all single-screen theatres (sometimes referred to as a "Uniplex") have gone out of business, the ones remaining are generally used for arthouse films, eg the Crest Theatre in downtown Sacramento, California, small scale productions, film festivals or other presentations. Because of the late development of multiplexes, the term "cinema" or "theater" may refer either the whole complex or a single auditorium, and sometimes "screen" is used to refer to an auditorium.

A popular film may be shown on multiple screens at the same multiplex, which reduces the choice of other films but offers more choice of viewing times or a greater number of seats to accommodate patrons. Two or three screens may be created by dividing up an existing cinema (as Durwood did with his Roxy in 1964), but newly built multiplexes usually have at least six to eight screens, and often as many as twelve, fourteen or even sixteen.

Although definitions vary, a large multiplex with 20 or more screens is usually called a megaplex however in the United Kingdom this was a brand name for large Virgin Cinema (later UGC). The first megaplex is generally considered to be the Kinepolis in Brussels,

Belgium, which opened in 1988 with 25 screens and a seating capacity of 7,500. The first theatre in the U.S. built from the ground up as a megaplex was the AMC Grand 24 in Dallas, Texas, which opened in May 1995, while the first megaplex in the U.S. based on an expansion of an existing facility was Studio 28 in Grand Rapids, Michigan, which reopened in November 1988 with 20 screens and a seating capacity of 6,000.

Drive-in

A drive-in movie theatre is basically an outdoor parking area with a screen at one end and a projection booth at the other. Moviegoers drive into the parking spaces which are sometimes sloped upwards at the front to give a more direct view of the movie screen. Films are usually viewed through the car windscreen (windshield) although some people prefer to sit on the hood of the car.

Sound is either provided through portable loudspeakers located by each parking space, or is broadcast on an FM radio frequency, to be played through the car's stereo system. Because of their outdoor nature, drive-ins usually only operate seasonally, and after sunset. Drive-in movie theatres are mainly found in the United States, where they were especially popular in the 1950s and 1960s. Once numbering in the thousands, about 400 remain in the U.S. today. In some cases, multiplex or megaplex theatres were built on the sites of former drive-in theatres.

Other Venues

Some outdoor movie theatres are just cleared areas where the audience sits upon chairs or blankets and watch the movie on a temporary screen, or even the wall of a convenient building. Colleges and universities have often sponsored film screenings in lecture halls. The formats of these screenings include 35 mm, 16 mm, DVD, VHS, and even 70 mm in rare cases. Some alternative methods of showing films have been popular in the past. In the 1980s the introduction of VHS cassettes made possible video-salons, small rooms where visitors viewed the film on a large TV. These establishments were especially popular in the Soviet Union, where official distribution companies were slow to adapt to changing demand, and so movie theatres could not show popular Hollywood and Asian films.

In 1967 the British government launched seven custom built mobile cinema units for use as part of the Ministry of Technology campaign to raise standards. Using a very futuristic look these 27 seat cinema vehicles were designed to attract attention. They were built on a Bedford SB3 chassis with a custom Coventry Steel Caravan extruded aluminium body. Films are also commonly shown on airliners in flight, using large screens in each cabin or smaller screens for each group of rows or each individual seat; the airline company sometimes charges a fee for the headphones needed to hear the films's sound. Films are sometimes also shown on trains, such as the Auto Train.

The smallest purpose-built cinema in operation is the Cinema dei Piccoli in Villa Borghese, Rome, Italy. The Cinema dei Piccoli was built by Alfredo Annibali in 1934 in the park of Villa Borghese, and today covers an area of 71.52 m^2 (769.83 sq ft). Originally called the Topolino Cinema (after Mickey Mouse), the movie theatre used a Path-Baby 9.5 mm movie projector, bed sheets for the screen and played 78's for background music. Restored in 1991, the cinema now has 63 seats, a 5 × 2.5 m (16.4 × 8.2 ft) screen, stereo sound and air conditioning. It is mentioned in the *Guinness Book of Records.*

Programming

Movie theaters may be classified by the type of movies or when they are shown:

- *First-run theater*: A theater that runs primarily mainstream film fare from the major film companies and distributors, during the initial new release period of each film.
- *Second-run* or *discount theater*: A theater that runs films that have already shown in the first-run theaters and presented at a lower ticket price. (These are sometimes known as dollar theaters or "Cheap Seats".) This form of cinema is diminishing in viability owing to the increasingly shortened intervals before the films' home video release, called the video window.
- *Repertoire/repertory theater* or *arthouse*: A theater that presents more alternative and art films as well as second-run and classic films (often known as an "Independent Cinema" in the UK).
- An *adult theater* or *sex theater* specializes in showing pornographic movies. Such movies are rarely shown in other theaters.
- IMAX theaters can show conventional movies, but the major benefits of the IMAX system are only available when showing movies filmed using it. While a few mainstream feature films have been produced in IMAX, IMAX movies are often documentaries featuring spectacular natural scenery, and may be limited to the 45-minute length of a single reel of IMAX film.

Presentation

Usually an admission is for one feature film. Sometimes two feature films are sold as one admission (double feature), with a break in between. Separate admission for a short subject is rare; it is either an extra before a feature film or part of a series of short subjects sold as one admission (this mainly occurs at film festivals). Historically, many movie theatres presented a number of shorter items in addition to the feature film. This might include a newsreel, live-action comedy short films, documentary short films, musical short films, and/or cartoon shorts (many classic cartoons series such as the *Looney Tunes* and *Mickey Mouse* shorts were created for this purpose). Examples of this kind of programming are available on certain DVD releases of two of the most famous films starring Errol Flynn, *Captain Blood* and *The Adventures of Robin Hood* as a special feature arrangement designed to recreate that kind of filmgoing experience. Some theatres ran on *continuous showings*, where the same items would repeat throughout the day, with patrons arriving and departing at any time rather than having distinct entrance and exit cycles. Newsreels gradually became obsolete by the 1960s with the rise of television news, and most material now shown prior to a feature film is of a commercial or promotional nature.

A typical modern theatre presents commercial advertising shorts, then movie trailers, and then the feature film. Advertised start times are usually for the entire program or session, not the feature itself; thus people who want to avoid commercials and/or trailers would opt to enter later. This is easiest and causes the least inconvenience when it is not crowded, and/or one is not very choosy about where one wants to sit. If one has a ticket for a specific seat one is formally assured of that, but it is still inconvenient and disturbing to find and claim it during the commercials and trailers, unless it is near an aisle.

Some movie theaters have some kind of break during the presentation. There may also be a break between the introductory material and the feature. Some countries such as the Netherlands have a tradition of incorporating an intermission in regular feature presentations, though many theaters have now abandoned that tradition, while in North America this is very rare, and usually limited to special circumstances involving extremely long movies. During the closing credits many people leave, some stay until the end. Usually the lights are switched on after the credits, sometimes already during them. Some films show additional scenes while the credits are rolling.

Until the multiplex era, prior to showtime, the screen would typically be covered by the traditional curtain which would be drawn for the feature. Some theaters, lacking a curtain, occupied the screen with slides of some form of abstract art. Currently, in multiplexes, theater chains often feature a continuous slideshow between showings featuring a loop of movie trivia, promotional material for the theater chains (such as encouraging patrons to purchase gift vouchers and group rates, or buy foyer retail offers), or advertising for local and national businesses.

Advertisements for Fandango and other convenient methods of purchasing tickets is often shown. Also prior to showing the film, reminders, in varying forms would be shown concerning theater etiquette (no smoking, no talking, no littering, removing crying babies, etc) and in recent years, added reminders to silence mobile phones.

Some well-equipped theaters have "interlock" projectors which allow two or more projectors and sound units to be run in unison by connecting them electronically or mechanically. This set up can be used to project two prints in sync (for dual-projector 3-D) or to "interlock" one or more sound tracks to a single film. Sound interlocks were used for stereophonic sound systems before the advent of magnetic film prints. Fantasound (developed by RAC in 1940 for Disney's Fantasia) was an early interlock system. Likewise, early stereophonic films such as *This is Cinerama* and *House of Wax* utilized a separate, magnetic oxide-coated film to reproduce up to six or more tracks of stereophonic sound.

DTS uses a time code printed on and read off of the film to synchronize with a CD-ROM in the sound track, allowing multi-channel soundtracks or foreign language tracks. This is not considered a projector interlock, however.

This practice is most common with so-called blockbuster movies. Regal Entertainment Group, Reading Cinemas, Pacific Theatres and AMC Theatres are some theatres that interlock films.

Live Broadcasting to Movie Theaters

Sometimes movie theaters provide digital projection of a live broadcast of an opera, concert, or other performance or event. For example, there are regular live broadcasts to movie theaters of Metropolitan Opera performances, with additionally limited repeat showings.

Pricing and Admission

In order to obtain admission to a movie theater, the prospective theater-goer must usually purchase a ticket, which may be for an arbitrary seat ("open" or "free" seating, first-come, first-served) or for a specific one (allocated seating). Movie theaters in North America generally have open seating. Cinemas in Europe can have free seating or numbered seating. Some theatres in Mexico offer numbered seating, in particular, Cinepolis VIP.

In the case of numbered seating systems the attendee can often pick seats from a screen; sometimes the attendee cannot see the screen and has to make a choice based on still available seats. In the case of free seats, already seated customers may be forced by staff to move one or more places for the benefit of an arriving couple or group wanting to sit together. In 2008, the average price for a movie ticket in the United States was $7.18.

The price of a ticket may be discounted during off-peak times e.g. for matinées, and higher at busy times, typically evenings and/or weekends. In Australia and Canada, when this practice is used, it is traditional to offer the lower prices for Tuesday for all showings, one of the slowest days of the week in the movie theatre business, which has led to the nickname "cheap Tuesday." Sometimes tickets are cheaper on Monday, or on Sunday morning.

Almost all movie theaters employ economic price discrimination: tickets for youth, students, and seniors are typically cheaper. Large theater chains, such as AMC Theaters, also own smaller theaters that show "second runs" of popular films, at reduced ticket prices. Movie theaters in India and other developing countries employ price discrimination in seating arrangement: seats closer to the screen cost less, while the ones farthest from the screen cost more. Some movie theaters and chains sell passes for unlimited entrance to regular showings. Some examples:

- *Pathé Unlimited Card (PUC)* for the chain of 12 multi-and megaplex theatres of Pathé in the Netherlands (100 screens), for €18/month; there are 15,000 pass holders (April 2006)
- *Cineville Pass* for 13 Amsterdam movie theaters (almost all movie theaters except those of Pathé) for € 17.50 per month.
- *Groninger Filmkaart* for €20/month for the two movie theaters Must See Euroborg (10 screens) and Images (3 screens) in Groningen

- *Unlimited Card* for the chain of movie theaters of Cineworld (formerly UGC) in the UK and Ireland, for £16.50/month, or £13.50 excluding those in London's West End-tickets can only be purchased on the day of the showing.
- *Carte Le Pass* for the chain of movie theatres of Pathé/Gaumont in 40 French cities (with a total of 790 screens), for 19.80 euro/month
- *UGC Illimité* passes for all UGC movie theaters in France, for 18 euro/month, and an entrance fee of 30 euro.
- *UGC Unlimited* passes for the four UGC movie theaters in Belgium, for 15 euro/month
- *SF Movie Passport* pass for all the movies shown in SF Group theaters in Thailand, valid for a month for one person and one showing per movie, at the price of 800 baht or eqv USD 20
- *Membresía Club Cinépolis* $125 Pesos(10USD)/month for the regular membership grants access to all the facilities across México for unlimited viewing. 1 Year of forced membership is required. There are also VIP and double memberships.

Note that in Thailand there is the restriction of one viewing per movie, while in the Netherlands one can see any movie as many times as one wants as is the case with the Cineworld UK pass.

Luxury Screens

Cinemas in city centres are increasingly offering luxury seating with services like complimentary refills of soft drinks and popcorn, a bar, reclining leather seats and service bells. The Vue Cinema chain is a good example of a large-scale offering of such a service, called "Gold Class" and similarly Britains largest cinema chain ODEON have gallery areas in some of their bigger cinemas where there is a separate foyer area with a bar and unlimited snacks. Another example is the Warren theaters located in Wichita, Kansas and Moore, Oklahoma. Also the AMC Theater chain has re outfitted some of its theaters in Olathe, Kansas and Kansas City, Missouri and Atlanta, Georgia with a new concept called "Fork and Screen" and also even more high-end is the "Cinema Suites".

Age Restrictions

Admission to a movie may also be restricted by a motion picture rating system. According to such systems, children or teenagers below a certain age may be forbidden access to theaters showing certain movies, or only admitted when accompanied by a parent or other adult. In some jurisdictions a rating may legally impose this on movie theaters. Furthermore, where movie theaters do not have this legal obligation, they may enforce restrictions on their own.

Accordingly, a movie theater may either not be allowed to program an unrated film, or voluntarily refrain from that. In the US many mainstream movie theaters do not even show movies rated NC-17 ("No one 17 and under admitted"). Often, instead, an edited R-rated version ("Restricted. Persons under 17 are not admitted unless accompanied by parent or adult guardian.") is shown.

Ticket Check; Movie Hopping

In some movie theater complexes, the theaters are arranged such that tickets are checked at the entrance into the entire plaza, rather than before each theater. This has led to *movie hopping*, also called *theater hopping* and *plexing*, the practice of buying a ticket for one film and illicitly attending additional showings within the complex without buying the required tickets. Younger patrons may also use this practice to enter auditoriums showing age-restricted movies. While not illegal, people caught theater hopping are generally forced to leave the movie theater. At a theater with a sold-out show there is often an additional ticket check, to make sure that everybody with a ticket for that show can find a seat.

Revenue

Movie studios/film distributors in the U.S. traditionally drive hard bargains entitling them to as much as 100% of the gross ticket revenue during the first weeks (and then the balance changes in 10% increments at an undetermined time).

Movie Theater Culture

Movie theaters are associated with dating, popcorn and expensive treats. It is rather common that people throw and leave their garbage on the floor in a movie theater.

Intimacy

Sometimes couples go to a movie theater for the additional reason that it provides the possibility of intimacy, where the dark provides some privacy (with additional privacy in the back-row). This kind of intimacy is considered by some a lesser form of public display of affection. This applies in particular for young people who still live with their parents, and these parents tend to monitor and/or forbid certain activities, and in the case of other social or even legal problems with public displays of affection. Compared with being together in a room without other people, it may also be reassuring for one or both of the couple (and for parents) that the intimacy is necessarily limited.

Arm rests pose a hindrance to intimacy for some people. Some theaters have love seats: seats for two without an armrest in the middle. The most modern theaters have movable armrests throughout the theater that when down can hold a food container as well as act as an armrest or partition between the seats and when up allow closer contact between the couple. Some theaters such as the Parkway in Oakland, California have sofas for greater comfort.

Foyer Area, Food and Drinks

Movie theaters usually sell various snack foods and drinks at retail counters or kiosks. Sometimes it can be a self-service where one pays at the counter till, and/or a coin-operated machines. Sometimes the area of sale is more like a self-service shop or kiosk (it is not suitable for consuming the goods), and one pays at the check-out between the shop and the area with the screens.

The facilities for buying snacks and drinks often represent the theater's primary source of profit since most of the ticket revenue goes to the film distributor (and onward to the movie studio). Some movie theaters forbid eating and drinking inside the viewing room (restricting such activities to the foyer), while others encourage it by fitting cup holders on the arm rests (on the front side of the arm rests of one's own chair, or the back side of the arm rests in front) and selling large portions of popcorn and soft drinks; also in that case bringing one's own food and drinks may be forbidden.

Retail is currently a huge area of expansion with many companies in the U.S. offering a wider range of snacks, including hot dogs and nachos. Many theaters have embraced the "brew and view" concept, serving alcoholic beverages, in addition to snacks and popcorn.

Some movie theaters such as the Alamo Drafthouse offer full restaurant service at one's seat, though this is not as widespread. McMenamins is a chain of restaurant/brewpub establishments in the U.S. states of Oregon and Washington, many of which have full movie theaters.

Some movie theaters feature a wider selection than simply snacks and popcorn. These "dine-in" theaters allow patrons to purchase "meals" (ranging from pizza slices to hamburgers and more) that can be consumed while watching the movie.

Business Practice Controversies

- *Advertising*-Many filmgoers complain about commercial advertising shorts, arguing that their absence would be one of the main advantages of going to a movie theater. Other critics such as Roger Ebert have expressed concerns that these advertisements, plus an excessive number of movie trailers, could lead to pressure to restrict the preferred length of the feature films themselves to facilitate playing schedules. So far, the theatre companies have typically been highly resistant to these complaints, citing the need for the supplementary income. Some chains like Famous Players and AMC Theatres have compromised with the commercials restricted to being shown before the scheduled start time for the trailers and the feature film. Individual theaters within a chain also sometimes adopt this policy.
- *Presentation*-Another major recent concern is that the dramatic improvements in stereo sound systems have led to cinemas playing the soundtracks of presented films at unacceptably high volume levels. Usually, the trailers are presented at a very high sound level, presumably to overcome the sounds of a busy crowd. The sound is not adjusted downward for a sparsely occupied theater, and some patrons employ earplugs for the trailer period. Volume is normally adjusted based on the projectionist's judgment of a high or low attendance. The film is usually shown at a lower volume level than the trailers. In response to audience complaints, a manager at a Cinemark theater in California explained that the studios set trailer sound levels, not the theater.
- *Piracy*-In recent years, cinemas have started to show warnings, before the movie starts, against using cameras and camcorders during the movie (camming). These warnings threaten customers with being removed from the cinema and arrested by the police. This example was shown at cinemas in the United Kingdom:

  You are not permitted to use any camera or recording equipment in this cinema. This will be treated as an attempt to breach copyright. Any person doing so can be ejected and such articles may be confiscated by the police. We ask the audience to be vigilant against any such activity and report any matters arousing suspicion to cinema staff. Thank you.

Some theaters (including those with IMAX stadiums) have detectors at the doors to pick up recording smugglers. At particularly anticipated showings, theatres may employ night vision equipment to detect a working camera during a screening. In some jurisdictions this is illegal unless the practice has been announced to the public in advance.

- *Crowd control*-As movie theaters have grown into multiplexes and megaplexes, crowd control has become a major concern. An overcrowded megaplex can be rather unpleasant, and in an emergency can be extremely dangerous (indeed, "shouting fire in a crowded theater" is the standard example in American English of how to cause unnecessary panic). Therefore, all major theater chains have implemented crowd control measures. The most well-known measure is the ubiquitous holdout line which prevents ticket holders for the next showing of that weekend's most popular movie from entering the building until their particular auditorium has been cleared out and cleaned. Since the 1980s, some theater chains (especially AMC Theatres) have developed a policy of co-locating their theaters in shopping centers (as opposed to the old practice of building stand-alone theaters). They deliberately build lobbies and corridors that cannot hold as many people as the auditoriums, thus making holdout lines necessary. In turn, ticket holders may be enticed to shop or eat while stuck outside in the holdout line. However, given the fact that rent is based on floor area, the practice of having a smaller lobby is somewhat understandable.

Personal Computer Game

A personal computer game (also known as a computer game or PC game) is a game played on a personal computer, rather than on a video game console or arcade machine. Computer games have evolved from the simple graphics and gameplay of early titles like *Spacewar!*, to a wide range of more visually advanced titles.

PC games are created by one or more game developers, often in conjunction with other specialists (such as game artists) and either published independently or through a third party publisher. They may then be distributed on physical media such as DVDs and CDs, as Internet-downloadable, possibly freely redistributable, software, or through online delivery services such as Direct2Drive and Steam. PC games often require specialized hardware in the user's computer in order to play, such as a specific generation of graphics processing unit or an Internet connection for online play, although these system requirements vary from game to game.

History

Early Growth: *Spacewar!*, developed for the PDP-1 in 1961, is often credited as being the first ever computer game. The game consisted of two player-controlled spaceships maneuvering around a central star, each attempting to destroy the other. Although personal computers only became popular with the development of the microprocessor, mainframe and minicomputers, computer gaming has existed since at least the 1960s. One of the first computer games was developed in 1961, when MIT students Martin Graetz and Alan Kotok, with MIT employee Steve Russell, developed *Spacewar!* on a PDP-1 computer used for statistical calculations.

The first generation of PC games were often text adventures or interactive fiction, in which the player communicated with the computer by entering commands through a keyboard. The first text-adventure, *Adventure,* was developed for the PDP-11 by Will Crowther in 1976, and expanded by Don Woods in 1977. By the 1980s, personal computers had become powerful enough to run games like *Adventure,* but by this time, graphics were beginning to become an important factor in games. Later games combined textual commands with basic graphics, as seen in the SSI Gold Box games such as *Pool of Radiance,* or *Bard's Tale.*

By the mid-1970s, games were developed and distributed through hobbyist groups and gaming magazines, such as *Creative Computing* and later *Computer Gaming World.* These publications provided game code that could be typed into a computer and played, encouraging readers to submit their own software to competitions. Microchess was one of the first games for microcomputers which was sold to the public. First sold in 1977, Microchess eventually sold over 50,000 copies on cassette tape.

Industry Crash

As the video game market became flooded with poor-quality cartridge games created by numerous companies attempting to enter the market, and over-production of high profile releases such as the Atari 2600 adaptation of *E.T.* and Pacman grossly underperformed, the popularity of personal computers for education rose dramatically. In 1983, consumer interest in console video games dwindled to historical lows, as interest in computer games rose.

The effects of the crash were largely limited to the console market, as established companies such as Atari posted record losses over subsequent years. Conversely, the home computer market boomed, as sales of low-cost color computers such as the Commodore 64 rose to record highs and developers such as Electronic Arts benefited from increasing interest in the platform. The console market experienced a resurgence in the United States with the release of the Nintendo Entertainment System. In Europe, computer gaming continued to boom for many years after.

New Genres

Increasing adoption of the computer mouse, driven partially by the success of games such as the highly successful *King's Quest* series, and high resolution bitmap displays allowed the industry to include increasingly high-quality graphical interfaces in new releases. Meanwhile, the Commodore Amiga computer achieved great success in the market from its release in 1985, contributing to the rapid adoption of these new interface technologies.

Further improvements to game artwork were made possible with the introduction of the first sound cards, such as AdLib's Music Synthesizer Card, in 1987. These cards allowed IBM PC compatible computers to produce complex sounds using FM synthesis, where they had previously been limited to simple tones and beeps. However, the rise of the Creative Labs Sound Blaster card, which featured much higher sound quality due to the inclusion of a PCM channel and digital signal processor, led AdLib to file for bankruptcy in 1992.

The year before, id Software had produced one of the first first-person shooter games, *Hovertank 3D*, which was the company's first in their line of highly influential games in the genre. There were other companies that made fps shooters such as *Day of the Viper* from the company Accolade made in 1989. Id Software went on to develop *Wolfenstein 3D* in 1992, which helped to popularize the genre, kick-starting a genre that would become one of the highest-selling in modern times. The game was originally distributed through the shareware distribution model, allowing players to try a limited part of the game for free but requiring payment to play the rest, and represented one of the first uses of texture mapping graphics in a popular game, along with *Ultima Underworld.*

While leading Sega and Nintendo console systems kept their CPU speed at 3-7 MHz, the 486 PC processor ran much faster, allowing it to perform many more calculations per second. The 1993 release of

Doom on the PC was a breakthrough in 3D graphics, and was soon ported to various game consoles in a general shift toward greater realism. In the same time frame, games such as Myst took advantage of the new CD-ROM delivery format to include many more assets (sound, images, video) for a richer game experience.

Many early PC games included extras such as the peril-sensitive sunglasses that shipped with *The Hitchhiker's Guide to the Galaxy.* These extras gradually became less common, but many games were still sold in the traditional over-sized boxes that used to hold the extra "feelies". Today, such extras are usually found only in Special Edition versions of games, such as Battlechests from Blizzard.

Contemporary Gaming

By 1996, the rise of Microsoft Windows and success of 3D console titles such as *Super Mario 64* sparked great interest in hardware accelerated 3D graphics on the IBM PC compatible, and soon resulted in attempts to produce affordable solutions with the ATI *Rage*, Matrox *Mystique* and Silicon Graphics *ViRGE.* Tomb Raider, which was released in 1996, was one of the first third person shooter games and was praised for its revolutionary graphics. As 3D graphics libraries such as DirectX and OpenGL matured and knocked proprietary interfaces out of the market, these platforms gained greater acceptance in the market, particularly with their demonstrated benefits in games such as *Unreal.* However, major changes to the Microsoft Windows operating system, by then the market leader, made many older MS-DOS-based games unplayable on Windows NT, and later, Windows XP (without using an emulator, such as DOSbox). The faster graphics accelerators and improving CPU technology resulted in increasing levels of realism in computer games. During this time, the improvements introduced with products such as ATI's Radeon R300 and N Video's GeForce 6 Series have allowed developers to increase the complexity of modern game engines. PC gaming currently tends strongly toward improvements in 3D graphics.

Unlike the generally accepted push for improved graphical performance, the use of physics engines in computer games has become a matter of debate since announcement and 2005 release of the N Video's PhysX PPU, ostensibly competing with middleware such as the Havok physics engine. Issues such as difficulty in ensuring consistent experiences for all players, and the uncertain benefit of first generation PhysX cards in games such as *Tom Clancy's Ghost Recon Advanced Warfighter* and *City of Villains*, prompted arguments over the value of such technology. Similarly, many game publishers began to experiment with new forms of marketing. Chief among these alternative strategies is episodic gaming, an adaptation of the older concept of expansion packs, in which game content is provided in smaller quantities but for a proportionally lower price. Titles such as *Half-Life 2: Episode One* took advantage of the idea, with mixed results rising from concerns for the amount of content provided for the price.

PC Game Development

Game development, as with console games, is generally undertaken by one or more game developers using either standardized or proprietary tools. While games could previously be developed by very small groups of people, as in the early example of Wolfenstein 3D, many popular computer games today require large development teams and budgets running into the millions of dollars.

PC games are usually built around a central piece of software, known as a game engine, that simplifies the development process and enables developers to easily port their projects between platforms. Unlike most consoles, which generally only run major engines such as Unreal Engine 3 and RenderWare due to restrictions on homebrew software, personal computers may run games developed using a larger range of software. As such, a number of alternatives to expensive engines have become available, including open source solutions such as Crystal Space, OGRE and DarkPlaces.

User-Created Modifications

The multi-purpose nature of personal computers often allows users to modify the content of installed games with relative ease. Since console games are generally difficult to modify without a proprietary software development kit, and are often protected by legal and physical barriers against tampering and homebrew software, it is generally easier to modify the personal computer version of games using common, easy-to-obtain software. Users can then distribute their customised version of the game (commonly known as a *mod*) by any means they choose.

The inclusion of map editors such as UnrealEd with the retail versions of many games, and others that have been made available online such as GtkRadiant, allow users to create modifications for games easily, using tools that are maintained by the games' original developers. In addition, companies such as id Software have released the source code to older game engines, enabling the creation of entirely new games and major changes to existing ones. Modding had allowed much of the community to produce game elements that would not normally be provided by the developer of the game, expanding or modifying normal gameplay to varying degrees. One notable example is the Hot Coffee mod for the PC port of *Grand Theft Auto: San Andreas*, which enables access to an abandoned sex minigame by modifying the game's data file.

Distribution

Physical distribution: Computer games are typically sold on standard storage media, such as compact discs, DVD, and floppy disks. These were originally passed on to customers through mail order services, although retail distribution has replaced it as the main distribution channel for video games due to higher sales. Different formats of floppy disks were initially the staple storage media of the 1980s and early 1990s, but have fallen out of practical use as the increasing sophistication of computer games raised the overall size of the game's data and program files.

The introduction of complex graphics engines in recent times has resulted in additional storage requirements for modern games, and thus an increasing interest in CDs and DVDs as the next compact storage media for personal computer games. The rising popularity of DVD drives in modern PCs, and the larger capacity of the new media (a single-layer DVD can hold up to 4.7 gigabytes of data, more than five times as much as a single CD), have resulted in their adoption as a format for computer game distribution. To date, CD versions are still offered for most games, while some games offer both the CD and the DVD versions.

Shareware: Shareware marketing, whereby a limited or demonstration version of the full game is released to prospective buyers without charge, has been used as a method of distributing computer games since the early years of the gaming industry and was seen in the early days of Tanarus as well as many others. Shareware games generally offer only a small part of the gameplay offered in the retail product, and may be distributed with gaming magazines, in retail stores or on developers' websites free of charge.

In the early 1990s, shareware distribution was common among fledging game companies such as Apogee Software, Epic Megagames and id Software, and remains a popular distribution method among smaller game developers. However, shareware has largely fallen out of favour among established game companies in favour of traditional retail marketing, with notable exceptions such as Big Fish Games and PopCap Games continuing to use the model today.

Online Delivery: With the increased popularity of the Internet, online distribution of game content has become more common. Retail services such as Direct2Drive and Download.com allow users to purchase and download large games that would otherwise only be distributed on physical media, such as DVDs, as well as providing cheap distribution of shareware and demonstration games. Companies such as Real Networks provide a service that allows other websites to use their game catalog and ecommerce backend to publish their own game download distribution sites. Real powers dozens of sites from channels on major portals to upstarts like Game-Downloads.Net. Other services, allow a subscription-based distribution model in which users pay a monthly fee to download and play as many games as they wish.

The Steam system, developed by Valve Corporation, provides an alternative to traditional online services. Instead of allowing the player to download a game and play it immediately, games are made available for "pre-load" in an encrypted form days or weeks before their actual release date. On the official release date, a relatively small component is made available to unlock the game. Steam also ensures that once bought, a game remains accessible to a customer indefinitely, while traditional mediums such as floppy disks and CD-ROMs are susceptible to unrecoverable damage and misplacement. The user would however depend on the Steam servers to be online to download its games. According to the terms of service for Steam, Valve has no obligation to keep the servers running. Therefore, if the Valve Corporation shut down, so would the servers. (although they have said that if that event were to happen they'd make it so Steam games would no longer require authorization, it should be noted they are not obligated to do so though).

PC Game Genres: The real-time strategy genre, which accounts for more than a quarter of all PC games sold, has found very little success on video game consoles, with releases such as Starcraft 64 failing in the marketplace. Strategy games tend to suffer from the design of console controllers, which do not allow fast, accurate movement.

PC Gaming Technology

An exploded view of a modern personal computer:

1. Display
2. Motherboard

3. CPU (Microprocessor)
4. Primary storage (RAM)
5. Expansion cards (graphics cards, etc)
6. Power supply
7. Optical disc drive
8. Secondary storage (Hard disk)
9. Keyboard
10. Mouse.

Hardware

Modern computer games place great demand on the computer's hardware, often requiring a fast central processing unit (CPU) to function properly. CPU manufacturers historically relied mainly on increasing clock rates to improve the performance of their processors, but had begun to move steadily towards multi-core CPUs by 2005. These processors allow the computer to simultaneously process multiple tasks, called threads, allowing the use of more complex graphics, artificial intelligence and in-game physics. Similarly, 3D games often rely on a powerful graphics processing unit (GPU), which accelerates the process of drawing complex scenes in realtime. GPUs may be an integrated part of the computer's motherboard, the most common solution in laptops, or come packaged with a discrete graphics card with a supply of dedicated Video RAM, connected to the motherboard through either an AGP or PCI-Express port. It is also possible to use multiple GPUs in a single computer, using technologies such as Nevada's Scalable Link Interface and ATI's CrossFire.

Sound cards are also available to provide improved audio in computer games. These cards provide improved 3D audio and provide audio enhancement that is generally not available with integrated alternatives, at the cost of marginally lower overall performance. The Creative Labs SoundBlaster line was for many years the *de facto* standard for sound cards, although its popularity dwindled as PC audio became a commodity on modern motherboards.

Physics processing units (PPUs), such as the Nevada PhysX (formerly AGEIA PhysX) card, are also available to accelerate physics simulations in modern computer games. PPUs allow the computer to process more complex interactions among objects than is achievable using only the CPU, potentially allowing players a much greater degree of control over the world in games designed to use the card.

Virtually all personal computers use a keyboard and mouse for user input. Other common gaming peripherals are a headset for faster communication in online games, joysticks for flight simulators, steering wheels for driving games and gamepads for console-style games.

Software

Computer games also rely on third-party software such as an operating system (OS), device drivers, libraries and more to run. Today, the vast majority of computer games are designed to run on the Microsoft Windows OS. Whereas earlier games written for MS-DOS would include code to communicate directly with hardware, today Application programming interfaces (APIs) provide an interface between the game and the OS, simplifying game design. Microsoft's DirectX is an API that is widely used by today's computer games to communicate with sound and graphics hardware. OpenGL is a cross-platform API for graphics rendering that is also used. The version of the graphics card's driver installed can often affect game performance and gameplay. It is not unusual for a game company to use a third-party game engine, or third-party libraries for a game's AI or physics.

Multiplayer

Local Area Network Gaming

Multiplayer gaming was largely limited to local area networks (LANs) before cost-effective broadband Internet access became available, due to their typically higher bandwidth and lower latency than the dial-up services of the time. These advantages allowed more players to join any given computer game, but have persisted today because of the higher latency of most Internet connections and the costs associated with broadband Internet.

LA gaming typically requires two or more personal computers, a router and sufficient networking cables to connect every computer on the network. Additionally, each computer must have a network card installed or integrated onto its motherboard in order to communicate with other computers on the network. Optionally, any LAN may include an external connection to the Internet.

Online Games

Online multiplayer games have achieved popularity largely as a result of increasing broadband adoption among consumers. Affordable high-bandwidth Internet connections allow large numbers of players to play together, and thus have found particular use in massively multiplayer online RPGs, Tanarus and persistent online games such as World War II Online.

Although it is possible to participate in online computer games using dial-up modems, broadband internet connections are generally considered necessary in order to reduce the latency between players (commonly known as "lag"). Such connections require a broadband-compatible modem connected to the personal computer through a network interface card (generally integrated onto the computer's motherboard), optionally separated by a router.

Online games require a virtual environment, generally called a "game server." These virtual servers inter-connect gamers, allowing real time, and often fast paced action. To meet this subsequent need, Game Server Providers (GSP) have become increasingly more popular over the last half decade. While not required for all gamers, these servers provide a unique "home," fully customizable (such as additional modifications, settings, etc)-giving the end gamers the experience they desire. Today there are over 510,000 game servers hosted in North America alone.

Emulation

Emulation software, used to run software without the original hardware, are popular for their ability to play legacy video games without the consoles or operating system for which they were designed. The operating system emulators include DOSBox, a DOS emulator which allows playing games developed originally for this operating system and thus not compatible with a modern day OS. Console emulators such as NESticle and MAME are relatively commonplace, although the complexity of modern consoles such as the Xbox or Playstation makes them far more difficult to emulate, even for the original manufacturers. Most emulation software mimics a particular hardware architecture, often to an extremely high degree of accuracy. This is particularly the case with classic home computers such as the Commodore 64, whose software often depends on highly sophisticated low-level programming tricks invented by game programmers and the demoscene.

Controversy

PC games have long been a source of controversy, particularly related to the violence that has become commonly associated with video gaming in general. The debate surrounds the influence of objectionable content on the social a... ment of minors, with organisations such as the American ...ological Association concluding that video game violence increa... a concern that prompted a further investig...hildren's aggression, Disease Control in September 2006. ... by the Center for

Industry groups have responded by noting th...esponsibility of parents in governing their children's activities, while ...tempts in the United States to control the sale of objectionable games ...ve generally been found unconstitutional.

Video game addiction is another cultural aspect of gaming to draw criticism as it can have a negative influence on health and on social relations. The problem of addiction and its health risks seems to have grown with the rise of Massively Multiplayer Online Role Playing Games (MMORPGs). Alongside the social and health problems associated with computer game addiction have grown similar worries about the effect of computer games on education.

E-Learning

E-learning (or electronic learning or eLearning) encompasses forms of technology-enhanced learning (TEL) or very specific types of TEL such as online or Web-based learning. Nevertheless, the term does not have a universally accepted definition and there are divides in the e-learning industry about whether a technology-enhanced system can be called e-learning if there is no set pedagogy as some argue e-learning is: "pedagogy empowered by digital technology".

The term *e-learning* is ambiguous to those outside the e-learning industry, and even within its diverse disciplines it has different meanings to different people. For instance in companies, it often refers to the strategies that use the company network to deliver training courses to employees and lately in most Universities, e-learning is used to define a specific mode to attend a course or program of study where the students rarely or never meet face-to-face, nor access on-campus educational facilities, because they study online.

Goals and Benefits of E-Learning

E-Learning can provide benefits for the organizations and individuals involved.

1. Improved performance: A 12-year meta-analysis of research by the U.S. Department of Education found that higher education students in online learning generally performed better than those in face-to-face courses.

2. Increased acc... nstructors of the highest calibre can share their knowl... across borders, allowing students to attend courses ac... physical, political, and economic boundaries. Recogniz... perts have the opportunity of making information availabl... ternationally, to anyone interested at minimum costs. ... example, the MIT OpenCourseWare program has made ... bstantial portions of that university's curriculum and lect... es available for free online.
3. C...venience and flexibility to learners: in many contexts, ...earning is self-paced and the learning sessions are available 24x7. Learners are not bound to a specific day/time to physically attend classes. They can also pause learning sessions at their convenience. The High technology is not necessary for all online courses. Basic internet access, audio, and video capabilities are common requirements.
4. To develop the skills and competencies needed in the 21st century, in particular to ensure that learners have the digital literacy skills required in their discipline, profession or career Bates (2009) states that a major argument for e-learning is that it enables learners to develop essential skills for knowledge-based workers by embedding the use of information and communications technologies within the curriculum. He also argues that using e-learning in this way has major implications for course design and the assessment of learners.

Market

The worldwide e-learning industry is estimated to be worth over thirty-eight (38) billion euros according to conservative estimates, although in the European Union only about 20% of e-learning products are produced within the common market. Developments in internet and multimedia technologies are the basic enabler of e-learning, with consulting, content, technologies, services and support being identified as the five key sectors of the e-learning industry.

Higher Education

By 2006, nearly 3.5 million students were participating in online learning at institutions of higher education in the United States. According to the Sloan Foundation reports. There has been an increase of around 12-14 per cent per year on average in enrollments for fully online learning over the five years 2004-2009 in the US post-secondary system, compared with an average of approximately 2 per cent increase per year in enrollments overall.

Allen and Seamen (2009) claim that almost a quarter of all students in post-secondary education were taking fully online courses in 2008, and a report by Ambient Insight Research suggests that in 2009, 44 per cent of post-secondary students in the USA were taking some or all of their courses online, and projected that this figure would rise to 81 per cent by 2014. Thus it can be seen that e-learning is moving rapidly from the margins to being a predominant form of post-secondary education, at least in the USA.

Many higher education, for-profit institutions, now offer online classes. By contrast, only about half of private, non-profit schools offer them. The Sloan report, based on a poll of academic leaders, says that students generally appear to be at least as satisfied with their online classes as they are with traditional ones. Private institutions may become more involved with online presentations as the cost of instituting such a system decreases. Properly trained staff must also be hired to work with students online. These staff members need to understand the content area, and also be highly trained in the use of the computer and Internet. Online education is rapidly increasing, and online doctoral programs have even developed at leading research universities.

History

In its first 10 years (1995-2005), e-learning was often focused on using the internet to replicate the instructor-led experience of classroom teaching (e-learning 1.0.) Content was designed to lead a learner through the content, providing a wide and ever-increasing set of interactions, online discussion, experiences, assessments, and simulations.

Learning 2.0

The term Learning 2.0 is used to refer to new ways of thinking about e-learning inspired by the emergence of Web 2.0. From an e-Learning 2.0 perspective, conventional e-learning systems were based on instructional packets that were delivered to students using Internet technologies. The role of the student consisted in learning from the readings and preparing assignments. Assignments were evaluated by the teacher. In contrast, the new e-learning places increased emphasis on social learning and use of social software such as blogs, wikis, podcasts and virtual worlds such as *Second Life*. This phenomenon has also been referred to as Long Tail Learning.

Learning 2.0, by contrast to e-learning 1.0 is built around collaboration. Learning 2.0 assumes that knowledge (as meaning and understanding) is socially constructed. Learning takes place through conversations about content and grounded interaction about problems and actions. Advocates of social learning claim that one of the best ways to learn something is to teach it to others.

However, it should be noted that many early online courses, such as those developed by Murray Turoff and Roxanne Hiltz in the 1970s and 80s at the New Jersey Institute of Technology, courses at the University of Guelph in Canada, the British Open University, and the online distance courses at the University of British Columbia (where Web CT, now incorporated into Blackboard Inc. was first developed), have always made heavy use of online discussion between students. Also, from the start, practitioners such as Heroism (1995) have put heavy emphasis on the use of learning networks for knowledge construction, long before the term e-learning, let alone e-learning 2.0, was even considered.

There is also an increased use of virtual classrooms (online presentations delivered live) as an online learning platform and classroom for a diverse set of education providers such as Minnesota State Colleges and Universities and Sachem School District. In addition to virtual classroom environments, social networks have become an important part of E-learning 2.0. Social networks have been used to foster online learning communities around subjects as diverse as test preparation and language education. Mobile Assisted Language Learning (MALL) is a term used to describe using handheld computers or cell phones to assist in language learning.

11

Internet Protocol

layers

TCP/IP is a two-layer programme. The higher layer, Transmission Control Protocol, manages the assembling of a message or file into smaller packets that are transmitted over the Internet and received by a TCP layer that reassembles the packets into the original message.

The lower layer, Internet Protocol, handles the address part of each packet so that it gets to the right destination. Each gateway computer on the network checks this address to see where to forward the message. Even though some packets from the same message are routed differently than others, they'll be reassembled at the destination.

TCP/IP uses the client/server model of communication in which a computer user (a client) requests and is provided a service (such as sending a Web page) by another computer (a server) in the network. TCP/IP communication is primarily point-to-point, meaning each communication is from one point (or host computer) in the network to another point or host computer. TCP/IP and the higher-level applications that use it are collectively said to be "stateless" because each client request is considered a new request unrelated to any previous one (unlike ordinary phone conversations that require a dedicated connection for the call duration). Being stateless frees network paths so that everyone can use them continuously. (Note that the TCP layer itself is not stateless as far as any one message is concerned. Its connection remains in place until all packets in a message have been received.) Many Internet users are familiar with the even higher layer application protocols that use TCP/IP to get to the Internet. These include the World Wide Web's Hypertext Transfer

Protocol (HTTP), the File Transfer Protocol (FTP), Telnet (Telnet) which lets you logon to remote computers, and the Simple Mail Transfer Protocol (SMTP). These and other protocols are often packaged together with TCP/IP as a "suite."

Personal computer users with an analog phone modem connection to the Internet usually get to the Internet through the Serial Line Internet Protocol (SLIP) or the Point-to-Point Protocol (PPP). These protocols encapsulate the IP packets so that they can be sent over the dial-up phone connection to an access provider's modem.

User Datagram

Protocols related to TCP/IP include the User Datagram Protocol (UDP), which is used instead of TCP for special purposes. Other protocols are used by network host computers for exchanging router information. These include the Internet Control Message Protocol (ICMP), the Interior Gateway Protocol (IGP), the Exterior Gateway Protocol (EGP), and the Border Gateway Protocol (BGP).

An increasing number of people are using the Internet and, many for the first time, are using the tools and utilities that at one time were only available on a limited number of computer systems (and only for really intense users!). One sign of this growth in use has been the significant number of Transmission Control Protocol/Internet Protocol (TCP/IP) and Internet books, articles, courses, and even TV shows that have become available in the last several years; there are so many such books that publishers are reluctant to authorize more because bookstores have reached their limit of shelf space! This memo provides a broad overview of the Internet and TCP/IP, with an emphasis on history, terms, and concepts. It is meant as a brief guide and starting point, referring to many other sources for more detailed information. TCP and IP were developed by a Department of Defence (DOD) research project to connect a number different networks designed by different vendors into a network of networks (the "Internet"). It was initially successful because it delivered a few basic services that everyone needs (file transfer, electronic mail, remote logon) across a very large number of client and server systems.

Network in army

The Army puts out a bid on a computer and DEC wins the bid. The Air Force puts out a bid and IBM wins. The Navy bid is won by Unisys. Then the President decides to invade Grenada and the armed forces discover that their computers cannot talk to each other. The

DOD must build a "network" out of systems each of which, by law, was delivered by the lowest bidder on a single contract.

The Internet Protocol was developed to create a Network of Networks (the "Internet"). Individual machines are first connected to a LAN (Ethernet or Token Ring). TCP/IP shares the LAN with other uses (a Novell file server, Windows for Workgroups peer systems). One device provides the TCP/IP connection between the LAN and the rest of the world.

To insure that all types of systems from all vendors can communicate, TCP/IP is absolutely standardized on the LAN. However, larger networks based on long distances and phone lines are more volatile. In the US, many large corporations would wish to reuse large internal networks based on IBM's SNA. In Europe, the national phone companies traditionally standardize on X.25.

However, the sudden explosion of high speed microprocessors, fibre optics, and digital phone systems has created a burst of new options: ISDN, frame relay, FDDI, Asynchronous Transfer Mode (ATM). New technologies arise and become obsolete within a few years. With cable TV and phone companies competing to build the National Information Superhighway, no single standard can govern citywide, nationwide, or worldwide communications.

The original design of TCP/IP as a Network of Networks fits nicely within the current technological uncertainty. TCP/IP data can be sent across a LAN, or it can be carried within an internal corporate SNA network, or it can piggyback on the cable TV service. Furthermore, machines connected to any of these networks can communicate to any other network through gateways supplied by the network vendor.

Addresses

On top of these local or vendor specific network addresses, TCP/IP assigns a unique number to every workstation in the world. This "IP number" is a four byte value that, by convention, is expressed by converting each byte into a decimal number (0 to 255) and separating the bytes with a period. For example, the PC Lube and Tune server is 130.132.59.234.

An organization begins by sending electronic mail to Hostmaster@INTERNIC.NET requesting assignment of a network number. It is still possible for almost anyone to get assignment of a number for a small "Class C" network in which the first three bytes identify the network and the last byte identifies the individual computer. The author followed this procedure and was assigned the numbers 192.35.91.* for a network of computers at his house. Larger organizations can get a "Class B" network where the first two bytes identify the network and the last two bytes identify each of up to 64 thousand individual workstations. Yale's Class B network is 130.132, so all computers with IP address 130.132.*.* are connected through Yale.

The organization then connects to the Internet through one of a dozen regional or specialized network suppliers. The network vendor is given the subscriber network number and adds it to the routing configuration in its own machines and those of the other major network suppliers.There is no mathematical formula that translates the numbers 192.35.91 or 130.132 into "Yale University" or "New Haven, CT." The machines that manage large regional networks or the central Internet routers managed by the National Science Foundation can only locate these networks by looking each network number up in a table.

There are potentially thousands of Class B networks, and millions of Class C networks, but computer memory costs are low, so the tables are reasonable. Customers that connect to the Internet, even customers as large as IBM, do not need to maintain any information on other networks. They send all external data to the regional carrier to which they subscribe, and the regional carrier maintains the tables and does the appropriate routing.

New Haven is in a border state, split 50-50 between the Yankees and the Red Sox. In this spirit, Yale recently switched its connection from the Middle Atlantic regional network to the New England carrier. When the switch occurred, tables in the other regional areas and in the national spine had to be updated, so that traffic for 130.132 was routed through Boston instead of New Jersey. The large network carriers handle the paperwork and can perform such a switch given sufficient notice. During a conversion period, the university was connected to both networks so that messages could arrive through either path.

Subnets

Although the individual subscribers do not need to tabulate network numbers or provide explicit routing, it is convenient for most Class B networks to be internally managed as a much smaller and simpler version of the larger network organizations. It is common to subdivide the two bytes available for internal assignment into a one byte department number and a one byte workstation ID. The enterprise network is built using commercially available TCP/IP router boxes. Each router has small tables with 255 entries to translate the one byte department number into selection of a destination Ethernet connected to one of the routers. Messages to the PC Lube and Tune server (130.132.59.234) are sent through the national and New England regional networks based on the 130.132 part of the number. Arriving at Yale, the 59 department ID selects an Ethernet connector in the C& IS building. The 234 selects a particular workstation on that LAN. The Yale network must be updated as new Ethernets and departments are added, but it is not effected by changes outside the university or the movement of machines within the department.

IP Routers

There is concept of a session with a preselected path for all traffic. Consider a company with facilities in New York, Los Angeles, Chicago and Atlanta. It could build a network from four phone lines forming a loop (NY to Chicago to LA to Atlanta to NY). A message arriving at the NY router could go to LA via either Chicago or Atlanta. The reply could come back the other way.

There is no correct answer. Traffic could be routed by the "clockwise" algorithm (go NY to Atlanta, LA to Chicago). The routers could alternate, sending one message to Atlanta and the next to Chicago. More sophisticated routing measures traffic patterns and sends data through the least busy link. If one phone line in this network breaks down, traffic can still reach its destination through a roundabout path. After losing the NY to Chicago line, data can be sent NY to Atlanta to LA to Chicago. This provides continued service though with degraded performance. This kind of recovery is the primary design feature of IP.

The loss of the line is immediately detected by the routers in NY and Chicago, but somehow this information must be sent to the other nodes. Otherwise, LA could continue to send NY messages through Chicago, where they arrive at a "dead end." Each network adopts some Router Protocol which periodically updates the routing tables throughout the network with information about changes in route status. If the size of the network grows, then the complexity of the routing updates will increase as will the cost of transmitting them. Building a single network that covers the entire US would be unreasonably complicated. Fortunately, the Internet is designed as a Network of Networks. This means that loops and redundancy are built into each regional carrier. The regional network handles its own problems and reroutes messages internally. Its Router Protocol updates the tables in its own routers, but no routing updates need to propagate from a regional carrier to the NSF spine or to the other regions (unless, of course, a subscriber switches permanently from one region to another).

Ibm design

IBM designs its SNA networks to be centrally managed. If any error occurs, it is reported to the network authorities. By design, any error is a problem that should be corrected or repaired. IP networks, however, were designed to be robust. In battlefield conditions, the loss of a node or line is a normal circumstance. Casualties can be sorted out later on, but the network must stay up. So IP networks are robust. They automatically (and silently) reconfigure themselves when something goes wrong. If there is enough redundancy built into the system, then communication is maintained.

In 1975 when SNA was designed, such redundancy would be prohibitively expensive, or it might have been argued that only the Defence Department could afford it. Today, however, simple routers cost no more than a PC. However, the TCP/IP design that, "Errors are normal and can be largely ignored," produces problems of its own.

Data traffic is frequently organized around "hubs," much like airline traffic. One could imagine an IP router in Atlanta routing messages for smaller cities throughout the Southeast. The problem is that data arrives without a reservation. Airline companies experience the problem around major events, like the Super Bowl. Just before the game, everyone wants to fly into the city. After the game, everyone wants to fly out. Imbalance occurs on the network when something new gets advertised. Adam Curry announced the server at "mtv.com" and his regional carrier was swamped with traffic the next day. The problem is that messages come in from the entire world over high speed lines, but they go out to mtv.com over what was then a slow speed phone line.

Occasionally a snow storm cancels flights and airports fill up with stranded passengers. Many go off to hotels in town. When data arrives at a congested router, there is no place to send the overflow. Excess packets are simply discarded. It becomes the responsibility of the sender to retry the data a few seconds later and to persist until it finally gets through. This recovery is provided by the TCP component of the Internet protocol. TCP was designed to recover from node or line failures where the network propagates routing table changes to all router nodes. Since the update takes some time, TCP is slow to initiate recovery. The TCP algorithms are not tuned to optimally handle packet loss due to traffic congestion. Instead, the traditional Internet response to traffic problems has been to increase the speed of lines and equipment in order to say ahead of growth in demand.

TCP treats the data as a stream of bytes. It logically assigns a sequence number to each byte. The TCP packet has a header that says, in effect, "This packet starts with byte 379642 and contains 200 bytes of data." The receiver can detect missing or incorrectly sequenced packets. TCP acknowledges data that has been received and retransmits data that has been lost. The TCP design means that error recovery is done end-to-end between the Client and Server machine. There is no formal standard for tracking problems in the middle of the network, though each network has adopted some ad hoc tools.

TCP/IP and Internet

For additional information and insight, readers are urged to read two excellent histories of the Internet: *Casting The Net: From ARPANET to INTERNET and beyond...* by Peter Salus and *Where Wizards Stay Up Late: The Origins of the Internet* by Katie Hafner and Mark Lyon.

Evolution

While the Internet today is recognized as a network that is fundamentally changing social, political, and economic structures, and in many ways obviating geographic boundaries, this potential is merely the realization of predictions that go back nearly forty years.

In a series of memos dating back to August 1962, J.C.R. Licklider of MIT discussed his "Galactic Network" and how social interactions could be enabled through networking. The Internet certainly provides such a national and global infrastructure and, in fact, interplanetary Internet communication has already been seriously discussed.

Prior to the 1960s, what little computer communication existed comprised simple text and binary data, carried by the most common telecommunications network technology of the day; namely, circuit switching, the technology of the telephone networks for nearly a hundred years. Because most data traffic is bursty in nature (*i.e.*, most of the transmissions occur during a very short period of time), circuit switching results in highly inefficient use of network resources.

The fundamental technology that makes the Internet work is called *packet switching*, a data network in which all components (*i.e.*, hosts and switches) operate independently, eliminating single point-of-failure problems. In addition, network communication resources appear to be dedicated to individual users but, in fact, statistical multiplexing and an upper limit on the size of a transmitted entity result in fast, economical networks.

In the 1960s, packet switching was ready to be discovered. In 1961, Leonard Kleinrock of MIT published the first paper on packet switching theory (and the first book on the subject in 1964). In 1962, Paul Baran of the Rand Corporation described a robust, efficient, store-and-forward data network in a report for the U.S. Air Force.

At about the same time, Donald Davies and Roger Scantlebury suggested a similar idea from work at the National Physical Laboratory (NPL) in the U.K. The research at MIT (1961-1967), RAND (1962-1965), and NPL (1964-1967) occurred independently and the principal researchers did not all meet together until the Association for Computing Machinery (ACM) meeting in 1967. The term *packet* was adopted from the work at NPL.

The modern Internet began as a U.S. Department of Defence (DoD) funded experiment to interconnect DoD-funded research sites in the U.S. The 1967 ACM meeting was also where the initial design for the so-called ARPANET — named for the DoD's Advanced Research Projects Agency (ARPA) — was first published by Larry Roberts. In December 1968, ARPA awarded a contract to Bolt Beranek and Newman (BBN) to design and deploy a packet switching network with a proposed line speed of 50 kbps.

In September 1969, the first node of the ARPANET was installed at the University of California at Los Angeles (UCLA), followed monthly with nodes at Stanford Research Institute (SRI), the University of California at Santa Barbara (UCSB), and the University of Utah. With four nodes by the end of 1969, the ARPANET spanned the continental U.S. by 1971 and had connections to Europe by 1973. The original ARPANET gave life to a number of protocols that were new to packet switching.

One of the most lasting results of the ARPANET was the development of a user-network protocol that has become the standard interface between users and packet switched networks; namely, ITU-T (formerly CCITT) Recommendation X.25. This "standard" interface encouraged BBN to start Telenet, a commercial packet-switched data service, in 1974; after much renaming, Telenet became a part of Sprint's X.25 service.

The initial host-to-host communications protocol introduced in the ARPANET was called the Network Control Protocol (NCP). Over time, however, NCP proved to be incapable of keeping up with the growing network traffic load. In 1974, a new, more robust suite of communications protocols was proposed and implemented throughout the ARPANET, based upon the Transmission Control Protocol (TCP) for end-to-end network communication.

But it seemed like overkill for the intermediate gateways (what we would today call *routers*) to needlessly have to deal with an end-to-end protocol so in 1978 a new design split responsibilities between a pair of protocols; the new Internet Protocol (IP) for routing packets and device-to-device communication (*i.e.*, host-to-gateway or gateway-to-gateway) and TCP for reliable, end-to-end host communication. Since TCP and IP were originally envisioned functionally as a single protocol, the protocol suite, which actually refers to a large collection of protocols and applications, is usually referred to simply as *TCP/IP*.

TCP IP Versions

The original versions of both TCP and IP that are in common use today were written in September 1981, although both have had several modifications applied to them (in addition, the IP version 6, or IPv6, specification was released in December 1995). In 1983, the DoD mandated that all of their computer systems would use the TCP/IP protocol suite for long-haul communications, further enhancing the scope and importance of the ARPANET.

In 1983, the ARPANET was split into two components. One component, still called ARPANET, was used to interconnect research/development and academic sites; the other, called MILNET, was used to carry military traffic and became part of the Defence Data Network. That year also saw a huge boost in the popularity of TCP/IP with its inclusion in the communications kernel for the University of California s UNIX implementation, 4.2BSD (Berkeley Software Distribution) UNIX. In 1986, the National Science Foundation (NSF) built a backbone network to interconnect four NSF-funded regional supercomputer centers and the National Center for Atmospheric Research (NCAR). This network, dubbed the NSFNET, was originally intended as a backbone for other networks, not as an interconnection mechanism for individual systems.

Furthermore, the "Appropriate Use Policy" defined by the NSF limited traffic to non-commercial use. The NSFNET continued to grow and provide connectivity between both NSF-funded and non-NSF regional networks, eventually becoming the backbone that we know today as the Internet.

Although early NSFNET applications were largely multiprotocol in nature, TCP/IP was employed for interconnectivity (with the ultimate goal of migration to Open Systems Interconnection).

The NSFNET originally comprised 56-kbps links and was completely upgraded to T1 (1.544 Mbps) links in 1989. Migration to a "professionally-managed" network was supervised by a consortium comprising Merit (a Michigan state regional network headquartered at the University of Michigan), IBM, and MCI. Advanced Network and Services, Inc.

(ANS), a non-profit company formed by IBM and MCI, was responsible for managing the NSFNET and supervising the transition of the NSFNET backbone to T3 (44.736 Mbps) rates by the end of 1991. During this period of time, the NSF also funded a number of regional Internet service providers (ISPs) to provide local connection points for educational institutions and NSF-funded sites.

In 1993, the NSF decided that it did not want to be in the business of running and funding networks, but wanted instead to go back to the funding of research in the areas of supercomputing and high-speed communications.

In addition, there was increased pressure to commercialize the Internet; in 1989, a trial gateway connected MCI, CompuServe, and Internet mail services, and commercial users were now finding out about all of the capabilities of the Internet that once belonged exclusively to academic and hard-core users! In 1991, the Commercial Internet Exchange (CIX) Association was formed by General Atomics, Performance Systems International (PSI), and UUNET Technologies to promote and provide a commercial Internet backbone service. Nevertheless, there remained intense pressure from non-NSF ISPs to open the network to all users.

It is worth saying a few words about the NAPs. The NSF provided major funding for the four NAPs mentioned above but they needed to have additional customers to remain economically viable. Some companies — such as then-Metropolitan Fibre Systems (MFS) — decided to build other NAP sites. One of MFS' first sites was MAE-East, where "MAE" stood for "Metropolitan Area Ethernet."

MAE-East was merely a point where ISPs could interconnect which they did by buying a router and placing it at the MAE-East facility. The original MAE-East provided a 10 Mbps Ethernet LAN to interconnect the ISPs' routers, hence the name. The Ethernet LAN was eventually replaced with a 100 Mbps FDDI ring and the "E" then became "Exchange." Over the years, MFS/MCI Worldcom has added sites in San Jose, CA (MAE-West), Los Angeles, Dallas, and Houston.

Other companies also operate their own NAPs. Savvis, for example, operates an international Internet service and has built more than a dozen private NAPs in North America. Many large service providers go around the NAPs entirely by creating bilateral agreement whereby the directly route traffic coming from one network and going to the other. Before their merger in 1998, for example, MCI and LDDS Worldcom had more than 10 DS-3 (44.736 Mbps) lines interconnecting the two networks.

The North American Network Operators Group (NANOG) provides a forum for the exchange of technical information and the discussion of implementation issues that require coordination among network service providers. Meeting three times a year, NANOG is an essential element in maintaining stable Internet services in North America. Initially funded by the NSF, NANOG currently receives funds from conference registration fees and vendor donations.

In 1988, meanwhile, the DoD and most of the U.S. Government chose to adopt OSI protocols. TCP/IP was now viewed as an interim, proprietary solution since it ran only on limited hardware platforms and OSI products were only a couple of years away. The DoD mandated that all computer communications products would have to use OSI protocols by August 1990 and use of TCP/IP would be phased out. Subsequently, the U.S. Government OSI Profile (GOSIP) defined the set of protocols that would have to be supported by products sold to the federal government and TCP/IP was not included.

Despite this mandate, development of TCP/IP continued during the late 1980s as the Internet grew. TCP/IP development had always been carried out in an open environment (although the size of this open community was small due to the small number of ARPA/NSF sites), based upon the creed "We reject kings, presidents, and voting. We believe in rough consensus and running code" [*Dave Clark, M.I.T.*]. OSI products were still a couple of years away while TCP/IP became, in the minds of many, the real open systems interconnection protocol suite.

It is not the purpose of this memo to take a position in the OSI vs. TCP/IP debate (although it is absolutely clear that TCP/IP offers the primary goals of OSI; namely, a universal, non-proprietary data communications protocol. In fact, TCP/IP does far more than was ever envisioned for OSI — or for TCP/IP itself, for that matter). But before TCP/IP prevailed and OSI sort of dwindled into nothingness, many efforts were made to bring the two communities together. The ISO Development Environment (ISODE) was developed in 1990, for example, to provide an approach for OSI migration for the DoD. ISODE software allows OSI applications to operate over TCP/IP. During this same period, the Internet and OSI communities started to work together to bring about the best of both worlds as many TCP and IP features started to migrate into OSI protocols, particularly the OSI Transport Protocol class 4 (TP4) and the Connectionless Network Layer Protocol (CLNP), respectively.

Finally, a report from the National Institute for Standards and Technology (NIST) in 1994 suggested that GOSIP should incorporate TCP/IP and drop the "OSI-only" requirement. [NOTE:Some industry observers have pointed out that OSI represents the ultimate example of a *sliding window*; OSI protocols have been "two years away" since about 1986.]

None of this is meant to suggest that the NSF isn't funding Internet-class research networks anymore. That is just the function of Internet2, a consortium of nearly 400 universities, corporations, and non-profit research oriented organizations working in partnership to develop and deploy advanced network applications and technologies for the next generation Internet. Goals of Internet2 are to create a leading edge network capability for the national research community, enable the development of new Internet-based applications, and to quickly move these new network services and applications to the commercial sector.

Growth

The ARPANET started with four nodes in 1969 and grew to just under 600 nodes before it was split in 1983. The NSFNET also started with a modest number of sites in 1986. After that, the network experienced literally exponential growth. Internet growth between 1981 and 1991 is documented in "Internet Growth (1981-1991)".

The Internet Software Consortium hosts the Internet Domain Survey (with technical support from Network Wizards, who originated the survey). According to their chart, the Internet had nearly 30 million reachable hosts by January 1998 and over 56 million by July 1999. Dedicated residential access methods, such as cable modem and asymmetrical digital subscriber line (ADSL) technologies, are undoubtedly the reason that this number has shot up to over 171 million by January 2003.

During the boom-1990s, the Internet was growing at a rate of about a new network attachment every half-hour, interconnecting hundreds of thousands of networks. It was estimated that the Internet was doubling in size every ten to twelve months and traffic was doubling every 100 days (for 1000% annual growth). For the last several year, the number of nodes has been growing at a rate of about 50% annually and traffic continues to keep pace with that growth.

And what of the original ARPANET? It grew smaller and smaller during the late 1980s as sites and traffic moved to the Internet, and was decommissioned in July 1990. Cerf and Kahn ("Selected ARPANET Maps," *Computer Communications Review*, October 1990) re-printed a number of network maps documenting the growth (and demise) of the ARPANET.

Domain Names and IP Addresses

Although not directly related to the administration of the Internet for operational purposes, the assignment of Internet domain names (and IP addresses) is the subject of some controversy and a lot of current activity. Internet hosts use a hierarchical naming structure comprising a top-level domain (TLD), domain and subdomain (optional), and host name. The IP address space, and all TCP/IP-related numbers, have historically been managed by theInternet Assigned Numbers Authority (IANA).

Domain names are assigned by the TLD naming authority; until April 1998, the Internet Network Information Center (InterNIC) had overall authority of these names, with NICs around the world handling non-U.S. domains. The InterNIC was also responsible for the overall coordination and management of the Domain Name System (DNS), the distributed database that reconciles host names and IP addresses on the Internet.

The InterNIC is an interesting example of the recent changes in the Internet. Since early 1993, Network Solutions, Inc. (NSI) operated the registry tasks of the InterNIC on behalf of the NSF and had exclusive registration authority for the*.com.org.net*, and*.edu* domains.

NSI's contract ran out in April 1998 and was extended several times because no other agency was in place to continue the registration for those domains. In October 1998, it was decided that NSI would remain the sole administrator for those domains but that a plan needed to be put into place so that users could register names in those domains with other firms.

In addition, NSI's contract was extended to September 2000, although the registration business was opened to competition in June 1999. Nevertheless, when NSI's original InterNIC contract expired, IP address assignments moved to a new entity called theAmerican Registry for Internet Numbers (ARIN). (And NSI itself was purchased by VeriSign in March 2000.)

The newest body to handle governance of global Top Level Domain (gTLD) registrations is the Internet Corporation for Assigned Names and Numbers (ICANN). Formed in October 1998, ICANN is the organization designated by the U.S. National Telecommunications and Information Administration (NTIA) to administer the DNS. Although surrounded in some early controversy (which is well beyond the scope of this paper!), ICANN has received wide industry support. ICANN has created several Support Organizations (SOs) to create policy for the administration of its areas of responsibility, including domain names (DNSO), IP addresses (ASO), and protocol parameter assignments (PSO).

In April 1999, ICANN announced that five companies had been selected to be part of this new *competitive* Shared Registry System for the.com.net, and.org domains. The concept was that these five organizations could accept applications for names in these gTLD name spaces, with final approval by ICANN. By the end of 1999, ICANN had added an additional 29 registrars and there are several hundred registrars accredited by ICANN today. Definitive ICANN registrar accreditation information can be found at the ICANN-Accredited Registrars page.

Other top-level domain names use the two-letter country codes defined in ISO standard 3166; *munnari.oz.au*, for example, is the address of the 1990's Internet gateway to Australia and *myo.inst.keio.ac.jp* is a host at the Science and Technology Department of Keio University in Yokohama, Japan. Other ISO 3166-based domain country codes are *ca* (Canada), *de* (Germany), *es* (Spain), *fr* (France), *gb* (Great Britain) [NOTE: For some historical reasons, the TLD.*gb* is rarely used; the TLD.*uk* (United Kingdom) seems to be preferred although UK is not an official ISO 3166 country code.], *ie* (Ireland), *il* (Israel), *mx* (Mexico), and *us* (United States). It is important to note that there is not necessarily any correlation between a country code and where a host is actually physically located.

In addition, some countries allow their country codes to be used for other, commercial purposes. *E.g.*, the " Web site" domain.*ws* actually belongs to the country of Samoa and the tv.com domain belongs to the country of Tuvalu. One of the most authoritative and up-to-date listings can be found at the "Domain name registries around the world" page maintained by UNINETT Norid AS.

The host name *www.latimes.com*, for example, is assigned to a computer named *www* (probably, but not necessarily, a Web server) at the Los Angeles Times (*latimes*), within the commercial gTLD (*com*). The host name *mail.sover.net* refers to a host (*mail*) in the SoverNet domain (*sover*) within the network provider gTLD (*net*). Guidelines for selecting host names is the subject of RFC 1178.

There are several registries responsible for blocks of IP addresses and domain naming policies around the globe. The American Registry for Internet Numbers (ARIN), was originally responsible for the Americas (western hemisphere) and parts of Africa. In 2002, the Latin American and Caribbean Internet Addresses Registry (LACNIC) was officially recognized and now covers Central and South America, as well as some Caribbean nations. TheAfrican Regional Internet Registry (AfriNIC)has responsibility for sub-Sahara Africa. At this time, ARIN only covers North America. The European and Asia-Pacific naming registries are managed by Réseaux IP Européen (RIPE) and the Asia-Pacific NIC (APNIC), respectively.

These authorities, in turn, delegate most of the country TLDs to national registries (such as RNP in Brazil and NIC-Mexico), which have ultimate authority to assign local domain names. An excellent overview of the recent history and anticipated future of the registry system can be found in "Development of the Regional Internet Registry System" (D. Karrenberg et al.) in the *IP Journal*, Vol. 4, No. 4.

Different countries may organize the country-based subdomains in any way that they want. Many countries use a subdomain similar to the TLDs, so that.*com.mx* and.*edu.mx* are the suffixes for commercial and educational institutions in Mexico, and.*co.uk* and.*ac.uk* are the suffixes for commercial and educational institutions in the United Kingdom.

The *us* domain is largely organized on the basis of geography or function. Geographical names in the *us* name space use names of the form *entity-name.city-telegraph-code.state-postal-code*.us. The domain name *cnri.reston.va.us*, for example, refers to the Corporation for National Research Initiatives in Reston, Virginia. Functional branches are also reserved within the name space for schools (K12), community colleges (CC), technical schools (TEC), state government agencies (STATE), councils of governments (COG), libraries (LIB), museums (MUS), and several other generic types of entities. Domain names in the state government name space usually take the form *department*.state.*state-postal-code*.us (*e.g.*,

The domain name *dps.state.vt.us* points to the Vermont Department of Public Safety). The K12 name space can vary widely, usually using the form *school.school-district*.k12.*state-postal-code*.us (*e.g.*, the domain *ccs.cssd.k12.vt.us* refers to the Charlotte Central School in the Chittenden South School District which happens to be in Charlotte, Vermont.) More information about the *us* domain may be found in RFC 1480.

The biggest change to the TLD process was the introduction, in 2010, of TLDs that do not use Latin characters. These Internationalized Domain Names are described in detail at ICANN's Web site. More information about TLDs, the registration process, and new TLDs can be found at the ICANN New TLD Programme Web page.

Last but not least, there is the never-ending issue of who owns domain names and IP addresses. I will make no claim to provide an authoritative answer but... domain names are owned by whoever registers them. This alone is a potential problem. Some ISPs are obtaining names on behalf of their customers *and paying the annual fee*. The issue has already arisen, "Who owns the name? The registrar or the customer?" Most ISPs have stated that they believe that the customer owns the name, even if the ISP registers the name, because there would be no reason for them to keep the name. Consider, however, that *if* an ISP insisted that it owned a name, it essentially ties a customer to an ISP forever, destroying the concept of domain name portability.

There is also an issue of violation of trademark, service mark, or copyright in the choice and ownership of domain names. The Eagles Nest in Corfu, NY. I don't know anything about The Eagles Nest of Corfu, NY but it should not be mistaken for either Eagles Nest

Enterprises of Grapevine, TX (the owner of *eaglesnest.com*) nor The Eagles Nest Internet Services of Newark, OH (owner of *theeaglesnest.com*).

In any case, suppose that Microsoft decided that someone using their service mark was not in their best interest and they pursued the issue; could they wrestle that domain name away from another registrant? Today's general rule of thumb is that if an organization believes that it's name or mark is being used in someone else's domain name in an unfair or misleading way, then they can take legal action against the name holder and the assignment of the name will be held up pending the outcome of the legal action.

More information about this issue can be found at ICANN's Uniform Domain-Name Dispute-Resolution Policy Web page. By the way, this is, of course, the question behind the new industry of cybersquatting; someone registers a domain name hoping that someone else with buy it from them later on!

And what about IP addresses? Prior to the widespread use of CIDR, individual organizations were assigned an address (usually a Class C!) and domain name at the same time. In general, the holder of the domain name owned the IP address and if they changed ISP, routing tables throughout the Internet were updated.

After 1994, domain name and IP number ownership were separated. Today, ISPs are assigned addresses in blocks called *CIDR blocks*. A customer today, whether they already own a domain name or are obtaining a new one, will be assigned an IP address from the ISP's CIDR block. If the customer changes ISP, they have to relinquish the IP address.

A good overview of the naming and addressing procedures can be found in RFC 2901, titled "Guide to Administrative Procedures of the Internet Infrastructure."

TCP/IP Protocol Architecture

TCP/IP is most commonly associated with the Unix operating system. While developed separately, they have been historically tied, as mentioned above, since 4.2BSD Unix started bundling TCP/IP protocols with the operating system. Nevertheless, TCP/IP protocols are available for all widely-used operating systems today and native TCP/IP support is provided in OS/2, OS/400, all Windows versions since Windows 9x, and all Linux and Unix variants.

Interface Layer

The TCP/IP protocols have been designed to operate over nearly any underlying local or wide area network technology. Although certain accommodations may need to be made, IP messages can be transported over all of the technologies shown in the figure, as well as numerous others. It is beyond the scope of this paper to describe most of these underlying protocols and technologies.

Two of the underlying network interface protocols, however, are particularly relevant to TCP/IP. The Serial Line Internet Protocol (SLIP, RFC 1055) and Point-to-Point Protocol (PPP, RFC 1661), respectively, may be used to provide data link layer protocol services where no other underlying data link protocol may be in use, such as in leased line or dial-up environments.

Most commercial TCP/IP software packages for PC-class systems include these two protocols. With SLIP or PPP, a remote computer can attach directly to a host server and, therefore, connect to the Internet using IP rather than being limited to an asynchronous connection.

PPP

It is worth spending a little bit of time discussing PPP because of its importance in Internet access today. As its name implies, PPP was designed to be used over point-to-point links. In fact, it is the prevalent IP encapsulation scheme for dedicated Internet access as well as dial-up access. One of the significant strengths of PPP is its ability to negotiate a number of things upon initial connection, including passwords, IP addresses, compression schemes, and encryption schemes. In addition, PPP provides support for simultaneous multiple protocols over a single connection, an important consideration in those environments where dial-up users can employ either IP or another network Layer protocol.

Internet Layer

The Internet Protocol (RFC 791), provides services that are roughly equivalent to the OSI Network Layer. IP provides a datagram (connectionless) transport service across the network. This service is sometimes referred to as *unreliable* because the network does not guarantee delivery nor notify the end host system about packets lost due to errors or network congestion. IP datagrams contain a message, or one fragment of a message, that may be up to 65,535 bytes (octets) in length. IP does not provide a mechanism for flow control.

Domain Name System

While IP addresses are 32 bits in length, most users do not memorize the numeric addresses of the hosts to which they attach; instead, people are more comfortable with host names. Most IP hosts, then, have both a numeric IP address and a name. While this is convenient for people, however, the name must be translated back to a numeric address for routing purposes. Earlier discussion in this paper described the domain naming structure of the Internet. In the early ARPANET, every host maintained a file calledhosts that contained a list of all hosts, which included the IP address, host name, and alias(es). This was an adequate measure while the ARPANET was small and had a slow rate of growth, but was not a scalable solution as the network grew.

[*Note*: A hosts file is still found on Unix systems although usually used to reconcile names of hosts on the local network to cut down on local DNS traffic; the file can usually be found in the/etc directory. On Microsoft Windows systems, the HOSTS file can typically be found in thec:\windows folder; in Windows NT, 2000, and later, it can be found in c:\winnt\system32\drivers\etc.]

To handle the fast rate of new names on the network, the Domain Name System (DNS) was created. The DNS is a distributed database containing host name and IP address information for all domains on the Internet. There is a single *authoritative name server* for every domain that contains all DNS-related information about the domain; each domain also has at least one secondary name server that also contains a copy of this information. Thirteen *root servers* around the globe maintain a list of all of these authoritative name servers. Although most of the root servers have multiple instances around the globe to improve performance and minimize vulnerability to attack, most of the primary DNS root servers are in the U.S. with the remainder in Asia and Europe).

When a host on the Internet needs to obtain a host's IP address based upon the host's name, a DNS request is made by the initial host to a local name server. The local name server may be able to respond to the request with information that is either configured or cached at the name server; if necessary information is not available, the local name server forwards the request to one of the root servers. The root server, then, will determine an appropriate name server for the target host and the DNS request will be forwarded to the domain's name server.

ARP and Address Resolution

Early IP implementations ran on hosts commonly interconnected by Ethernet local area networks (LAN). Every transmission on the LAN contains the local network, or medium access control (MAC), address of the source and destination nodes. MAC addresses are 48-bits in length and are non-hierarchical, so routing cannot be performed using the MAC address. MAC addresses are never the same as IP addresses.

When a host needs to send a datagram to another host on the same network, the sending application must know both the IP and MAC addresses of the intended receiver; this is because the destination IP address is placed in the IP packet and the destination MAC address is placed in the LAN MAC protocol frame. (If the destination host is on another network, the sender will look instead for the MAC address of the default gateway, or router.)

Unfortunately, the sender's IP process may not know the MAC address of the intended receiver on the same network. The Address Resolution Protocol (ARP), described in RFC 826, provides a mechanism so that a host can learn a receiver's MAC address when knowing only the IP address. The process is actually relatively simple: the host sends an ARP Request packet in a frame containing the MAC broadcast address; the ARP request advertises the destination IP address and asks for the associated MAC address. The station on the LAN that recognizes its own IP address will send an ARP Response with its own MAC address. As Figure 2 shows, ARP message are carried directly in the LAN frame and ARP is an independent protocol from IP. The IANA maintains a list of all ARP parameters.

IP Routing: OSPF, RIP, and BGP

As an OSI Network Layer protocol, IP has the responsibility to route packets. It performs this function by looking up a packet's destination IP NET_ID in a routing table and forwarding based on the information in the table. But it is *routing protocols*, and *not* IP, that populate the routing tables with routing information. There are three routing protocols commonly associated with IP and the Internet, namely, RIP, OSPF, and BGP.

OSPF and RIP are primarily used to provide routing within a particular domain, such as within a corporate network or within an ISP's network. Since the routing is *inside* of the domain, these protocols are generically referred to as *interior gateways protocols.*

The Routing Information Protocol version 2 (RIP-2), described in RFC 2453, describes how routers will exchange routing table information using a distance-vector algorithm. With RIP, neighboring routers periodically exchange their entire routing tables. RIP uses hop count as the metric of a path's cost, and a path is limited to 16 hops.

Unfortunately, RIP has become increasingly inefficient on the Internet as the network continues its fast rate of growth. Current routing protocols for many of today's LANs are based upon RIP, including those associated with NetWare, AppleTalk, VINES, and DECnet. The IANA maintains a list of RIP message types.

The Open Shortest Path First (OSPF) protocol is a link state routing algorithm that is more robust than RIP, converges faster, requires less network bandwidth, and is better able to scale to larger networks. With OSPF, a router broadcasts only changes in its links' status rather than entire routing tables, making it more robust and scalable than RIP. OSPF Version 2 is described in RFC 1583.

The Border Gateway Protocol version 4 (BGP-4) is an *exterior gateway protocol* because it is used to provide routing information between Internet routing domains. BGP is a distance vector protocol, like RIP, but unlike almost all other distance vector protocols, BGP tables store the actual route to the destination network.

BGP-4 also supports policy-based routing, which allows a network's administrator to create routing policies based on political, security, legal, or economic issues rather than technical ones. BGP-4 also supports CIDR. BGP-4 is described in RFC 1771, while RFC 1268describes use of BGP in the Internet. In addition, the IANA maintains a list of BGP parameters.

As an alternative to using a routing protocol, the routing table can be maintained using "static routing." One example of static routing is the configuration of a default gateway at a host system; if the host needs to send an IP packet off of the local LAN segment, it is just blindly forwarded to the default gateway (router). Edge router's, too, commonly use static routing; the single router connecting a site to an ISP, for example, will usually just have a static routing table entry indicating that all traffic leaving the local LAN be forwarded to the ISP's access router.

Since there's only a single path into the ISP, a routing protocol is hardly necessary. All IP hosts and routers maintain a table that lists the most up-to-date routing information that that device knows.

On a Windows system, you can examine the routing table by issuing a route print command; on Unix systems, use netstat -r.

IP Version 6

The official version of IP that has been in use since the early 1980s is *version 4.* Due to the tremendous growth of the Internet and new emerging applications, it was recognized that a new version of IP was becoming necessary. In late 1995, IP version 6 (IPv6) was entered into the Internet Standards Track.

The primary description of IPv6 is contained in RFC 1883 and a number of related specifications, including ICMPv6. The architecture and structure of IPv6 addresses is described in RFC 2373. In July 1999, the IANA delegated the initial IPv6 address space to the worldwide regional registries in order to begin immediate worldwide deployment of IPv6 addresses. More information can be found at APNIC, ARIN, and RIPE.

Transport Layer Protocols

The TCP/IP protocol suite comprises two protocols that correspond roughly to the OSI Transport and Session Layers; these protocols are called the Transmission Control Protocol and the User Datagram Protocol (UDP).

Ports

Higher-layer applications are referred to by a port identifier in TCP/UDP messages. The port identifier and IP address together form a *socket*, and the end-to-end communication between two hosts is uniquely identified on the Internet by the four-tuple (source port, source address, destination port, destination address).

Port numbers are specified by a 16-bit number. Port numbers in the range 0-1023 are called *Well Known Ports.* These port numbers are assigned to the server side of an application and, on most systems, can only be used by processes with a high level of privilege (such as root or administrator).

Port numbers in the range 1024-49151 are called *Registered Ports*, and these are numbers that have been publicly defined as a convenience for the Internet community to avoid vendor conflicts. Server or client applications can use the port numbers in this range. The remaining port numbers, in the range 49152-65535, are called *Dynamic and/or Private Ports* and can be used freely by any client or server.

TCP

TCP, described in RFC 793, provides a virtual circuit (connection-oriented) communication service across the network. TCP includes rules for formatting messages, establishing and terminating virtual circuits, sequencing, flow control, and error correction.

Most of the applications in the TCP/IP suite operate over the *reliable* transport service provided by TCP. The TCP data unit is called a segment; the name is due to the fact that TCP does not recognize messages, per se, but merely sends a block of bytes from the byte stream between sender and receiver.

The fields of the segment are:

- Source Port and Destination Port: Identify the source and destination ports to identify the end-to-end connection and higher-layer application.
- Sequence Number: Contains the sequence number of this segment's first data byte in the overall connection byte stream; since the sequence number refers to a byte count rather than a segment count, sequence numbers in contiguous TCP segments are not numbered sequentially.
- Acknowledgment Number: Used by the sender to acknowledge receipt of data; this field indicates the sequence number of the next byte expected from the receiver.
- Data Offset: Points to the first data byte in this segment; this field, then, indicates the segment header length.

UDP

UDP, described in RFC 768, provides an end-to-end datagram (connectionless) service. Some applications, such as those that involve a simple query and response, are better suited to the datagram service of UDP because there is no time lost to virtual circuit establishment and termination.

UDP's primary function is to add a port number to the IP address to provide a socket for the application.

ICMP

The Internet Control Message Protocol, described in RFC 792, is an adjunct to IP that notifies the sender of IP datagrams about abnormal events. This collateral protocol is particularly important in the connectionless environment of IP. ICMP is not a classic host-to-host protocols like TCP or UDP, but is host-to-host in the sense that one device (*e.g.*, a router or computer) is sending a message to another device (*e.g.*, another router or computer).

The commonly employed ICMP message types include:

- *Destination Unreachable*: Indicates that a packet cannot be delivered because the destination host cannot be reached. The reason for the non-delivery may be that the host or network is unreachable or unknown, the protocol or port is unknown or unusable, fragmentation is required but not allowed (DF-flag is set), or the network or host is unreachable for this type of service.
- *Echo and Echo Reply*: These two messages are used to check whether hosts are reachable on the network. One host sends an Echo message to the other, optionally containing some data, and the receiving host responds with an Echo Reply containing the same data. These messages are the basis for the Ping command.
- *Parameter Problem*: Indicates that a router or host encountered a problem with some aspect of the packet's Header.

TCP Logical Connections and ICMP

The server responds with a segment with the syn- and ack-bits set, a Sequence Number of 1567, and an Acknowledgement Number of 801. The syn-bit and ISN of 1567 have the same meaning as above. The ack-bit indicates the value of the Acknowledgement Number field is valid and the ACK value of 801 is the way in which the server confirms the client's ISN. The final part of the three-way handshake is when the client sends a segment with just the ack-bit set. Note that the Acknowledgement Number field (1568) is one greater than the server's ISN.

This three-way handshake is sometimes referred to as an exchange of"syn, syn/ack, and ack" segments. It is important for a number of reasons. For individuals looking at packet traces, recognition of the three-way handshake is how to find the start of a connection. For firewalls, proxy severs, intrusion detectors, and other systems, it provides a way of knowing the direction of a TCP connection setup since rules may differ for outbound and inbound connections.

The second part of the TCP connection is data exchange. The information here is more or less made up for example purposes only; it shows a POP server sending a banner message to the client system, the user sending the"quit" command, and the server signing off. (Note that the"\n" indicates an"end-of-line" indicator.) These segments show the changing of, and relationship between, the client's and server's sequence and acknowledgement numbers.

The final phase is connection termination. Although TCP connections are full-duplex (even if a given application does not allow two-way simultaneous communication), the TCP protocol views the logical connection as a pair of simplex links.

Therefore, connection termination requires four segments or, more properly, two pair of segments. In this case, the client sends the server a segment with the fin- and ack-bits set; the server responds with a segment with just the ack-bit set and the Acknowledgment Number is incremented. The server then sends a fin/ack segment to the client.

The paragraphs above describe a normal scenario setting up a TCP connection between a client and server. Two UDP hosts communicate in a similar fashion; one host sends a UDP datagram to the other which is presumably listening on the port indicated in the datagram.

TCP/IP Application Layer

The TCP/IP Application Layer protocols support the applications and utilities that are the Internet. This section will list a number of these applications and show a sample packet decode of all protocol layers.

TCP and UDP Applications

Commonly used protocols (as shown in include:

- *Archie:* A utility that allows a user to search all registered anonymous FTP sites for files on a specified topic. Obsolete by the late-1990s, obviated by the World Wide Web.
- *BGP:* The Border Gateway Protocol version 4 (BGP-4) is a distance vector exterior gateway routing protocol, commonly used between two ISPs or between a customer site and ISP if there are multiple links. defines the structure of Internet names and their association with IP addresses, as well as the association of mail and name servers with domains.
- *Finger:* Used to determine the status of other hosts and/or users (RFC 1288).
- *FTP:* The File Transfer Protocol allows a user to transfer files between local and remote host computers (RFC 959).

- *Gopher:* A tool that allows users to search through data repositories using a menu-driven, hierarchical interface, with links to other sites. Obsolete today, obviated by the World Wide Web (RFC 1436).
- *HTTP:* The Hypertext Transfer Protocol is the basis for exchange of information over the World Wide Web (WWW). Various versions of HTTP are in use over the Internet, with HTTP version 1.1 (RFC 2616) being the most current. WWW pages are written in the Hypertext Markup Language (HTML), an ASCII-based, platform-independent formatting language (RFC 1866).
- *TACACS+:* The Terminal Access Controller Access Control System plus is a remote access protocol.
- *Telnet:* Short for Telecommunication Network, a virtual terminal protocol allowing a user logged on to one TCP/IP host to access other hosts on the network (RFC 854).
- *TFTP:* The Trivial File Transfer Protocol (TFTP) is used for some specialized simple file transfer applications.
- *Time/NTP:* Time and the Network Time Protocol (NTP) are used so that Internet hosts can synchronize their system time from well-known Internet time servers.

Protocol Analysis

Today's protocol analysers are usually software running on a computer or a specialized piece of hardware. In either case, the device's network interface card (NIC) operates in promiscuous mode so that the NIC captures every packet that flies by on the wire rather than only those packets addressed to this particular NIC.

Most protocol analysers also provide a display with at least a partial interpretation of the packets.

After IP is the TCP information. Note that the destination port number is 110, the port associated with a POP3 server. Since the POP3 server port is the destination, it means that this packet contains a POP command to the server from the client (which we knew anyway by looking at the summary of frame 80 above).

Finally we see the POP3 command itself. When a POP3 client connects to the server, the first thing it does is send the username using the POP3 USERcommand. If the username is valid, the server asks for a password, which is sent from the client in a POP3 PASS command, which is shown here.

The discussion here is only meant to readers a taste of one of the coolest tools that we get to play with in data communications; it is also an important tool for network managers and security administrators.

There are a fair number of free or inexpensive software packet sniffers that one can acquire for Linux or Windows systems. One of the most popular istcpdump, which comes with many Linux distributions (*e.g.*, Red Hat 7.1).

WinDump is a tcpdump implementation for Windows, and the same group distributes Analyser, a GUI packet sniffer. Ethereal is another GUI analyser, with version for both Windows and Linux. More information on these packages can be found at the author's Packet Sniffing and Protocol Analysis Software page.

communication protocol

TCP/IP is not merely a pair of communication protocols but is a suite of protocols, applications, and utilities. Increasingly, these protocols are referred to as the Internet Protocol Suite, but the older name will not disappear anytime soon. Applications and utilities reside in host, or end-communicating, systems. TCP provides a reliable, virtual circuit connection between the two hosts. (UDP, not shown, provides an end-to-end datagram connection at this layer.) IP provides a datagram (DG) transport service over any intervening subnetworks, including local and wide area networks. The underlying subnetwork may employ nearly any common local or wide area network technology.

Note that the term gateway is used for the device interconnecting the two subnets, a device usually called a router in LAN environments orintermediate system in OSI environments. In OSI terminology, a gateway is used to provide protocol conversion between two networks and/or applications. Internet specifications, standards, reports, humour, and tutorials are distributed as Request for Comments (RFC) documents. RFCs are all freely available on-line, and most are available in ASCII text format. Internet standards are documented in a subset of the RFCs, identified with an"STD" designation. RFC 2026 describes the Internet standards process and STD 1 always contains the official list of Internet standards.

Practical Extraction and Report Language

Language historians will also note some vestiges of csh, Pascal, and even BASIC-PLUS. Expression syntax corresponds quite closely to C expression syntax. Unlike most Unix utilities, perl does not arbitrarily limit the size of your data -- if you've got the memory, perl can slurp in your whole file as a single string. Recursion is of unlimited depth. And the hash tables used by associative arrays grow as necessary to prevent degraded performance.

Perl uses sophisticated pattern matching techniques to scan large amounts of data very quickly. Although optimized for scanning text, perl can also deal with binary data, and can make dbm files look like associative arrays (where dbm is available). Setuid perl scripts are safer than C programmes through a dataflow tracing mechanism which prevents many stupid security holes.

If you have a problem that would ordinarily use sed or awk or sh, but it exceeds their capabilities or must run a little faster, and you don't want to write the silly thing in C, then perl may be for you. There are also translators to turn your sed and awk scripts into perl scripts. OK, enough hype.

Starting Perl

Upon startup, perl looks for your script in one of the following places:

- Specified line by line via -e switches on the command line.
- Contained in the file specified by the first filename on the command line. (Note that systems supporting the #! notation invoke interpreters this way.)
- Passed in implicitly via standard input. This only works if there are no filename arguments -- to pass arguments to a stdin script you must explicitly specify a - for the script name.

Data Types and Objects

Perl has three data types: scalars, arrays of scalars, and associative arrays of scalars. Normal arrays are indexed by number, and associative arrays by string. The interpretation of operations and values in perl sometimes depends on the requirements of the context around the operation or value. There are three major contexts: string, numeric and array. Certain operations return array values in contexts wanting an array, and scalar values otherwise.

(If this is true of an operation it will be mentioned in the documentation for that operation.)

Operations which return scalars don't care whether the context is looking for a string or a number, but scalar variables and values are interpreted as strings or numbers as appropriate to the context.

A scalar is interpreted as TRUE in the boolean sense if it is not the null string or 0. Booleans returned by operators are 1 for true and 0 or'' (the null string) for false.

There are actually two varieties of null string: defined and undefined. Undefined null strings are returned when there is no real value for something, such as when there was an error, or at end of file, or when you refer to an uninitialized variable or element of an array. An undefined null string may become defined the first time you access it, but prior to that you can use the defined() operator to determine whether the value is defined or not.

References to scalar variables always begin with'$', even when referring to a scalar that is part of an array. Thus:

```
$days          # a simple scalar variable
$days[28]      # 29th element of array @days
$days{'Feb'}   # one value from an associative array
$#days         #. last index of array @days
but entire arrays or array slices are denoted by'@':
@days          # ($days[0], $days[1],\|... $days[n])
@days[3,4,5]   # same as @days[3.\|.5]
@days{'a','c'}# same as ($days {'a'}, $days {'c'})
and entire associative arrays are denoted by'%':
%days          # (key1, val1, key2, val2...)
```

Any of these eight constructs may serve as an lvalue, that is, may be assigned to (It also turns out that an assignment is itself an lvalue in certain contexts). Assignment to a scalar evaluates the righthand side in a scalar context, while assignment to an array or array slice evaluates the righthand side in an array context.

You may find the length of array @days by evaluating"$#days", as in csh. (Actually, it's not the length of the array, it's the subscript of the last element, since there is (ordinarily) a 0th element.) Assigning to $#days changes the length of the array. Shortening an array by this method does not actually destroy any values. Lengthening an array that was previously shortened recovers the values that were in those elements.

You can also gain some measure of efficiency by preextending an array that is going to get big. (You can also extend an array by assigning to an element that is off the end of the array. This differs from assigning to $#whatever in that intervening values are set to null rather than recovered.) You can truncate an array down to nothing by assigning the null list () to it. The following are exactly equivalent

```
@whatever = ();
$#whatever = $[- 1;
```

If you evaluate an array in a scalar context, it returns the length of the array. The following is always true:

```
scalar(@whatever) == $#whatever - $[+ 1;
```

If you evaluate an associative array in a scalar context, it returns a value which is true if and only if the array contains any elements. (If there are any elements, the value returned is a string consisting of the number of used buckets and the number of allocated buckets, separated by a slash.)

Multi-dimensional arrays are not directly supported, but see the discussion of the $; variable later for a means of emulating multiple subscripts with an associative array. You could also write a subroutine to turn multiple subscripts into a single subscript.

Every data type has its own namespace. You can, without fear of conflict, use the same name for a scalar variable, an array, an associative array, a filehandle, a subroutine name, and/or a label. Since variable and array references always start with'$','@', or'%', the"reserved" words aren't in fact reserved with respect to variable names. (They ARE reserved with respect to labels and filehandles, however, which don't have an initial special character.

Hint: you could sayopen(LOG,'logfile') rather than open(log,'logfile'). Using uppercase filehandles also improves readability and protects you from conflict with future reserved words.) Case IS significant--"FOO","Foo" and"foo" are all different names. Names which start with a letter may also contain digits and underscores. Names which do not start with a letter are limited to one character, *e.g.*"$%" or"$$". (Most of the one character names have a predefined significance to perl. More later.)

Numeric literals are specified in any of the usual floating point or integer formats:

```
12345
12345.67
.23E-10
0xffff        # hex
0377        # octal
4_294_967_296
```

String literals are delimited by either single or double quotes. They work much like shell quotes: double-quoted string literals are subject to backslash and variable substitution; single-quoted strings are not (except for \' and \e). The usual backslash rules apply for making characters such as newline, tab, etc., as well as some more exotic forms:

```
\t   tab
\n   newline
\r   return
\f   form feed
\b   backspace
\a   alarm (bell)
\e   escape
\033 octal char
\x1b hex char
\c[  control char
\l   lowercase next char
\u   uppercase next char
\L   lowercase till \E
\U   uppercase till \E
\E   end case modification
```

You can also embed newlines directly in your strings, *i.e.* they can end on a different line than they begin. This is nice, but if you forget your trailing quote, the error will not be reported until perl finds another line containing the quote character, which may be much further on in the script.

Variable substitution inside strings is limited to scalar variables, normal array values, and array slices. (In other words, identifiers beginning with $ or @, followed by an optional bracketed expression as a subscript.) The following code segment prints out"The price is $100."

```
$Price ='$100';  # not
interpreted
print"The price is $Price.\n"; # interpreted
```

Note that you can put curly brackets around the identifier to delimit it from following alphanumerics. Also note that a single quoted string must be separated from a preceding word by a space, since single quote is a valid character in an identifier.

Two special literals are __LINE__ and __FILE__, which represent the current line number and filename at that point in your programme. They may only be used as separate tokens; they will not be interpolated into strings. In addition, the token __END__ may be used to indicate the logical end of the script before the actual end of file.

Any following text is ignored, but may be read via the DATA filehandle. (The DATA filehandle may read data only from the main script, but not from any required file or evaluated string.) The two control characters ^D and ^Z are synonyms for __END__.

A word that doesn't have any other interpretation in the grammar will be treated as if it had single quotes around it. For this purpose, a word consists only of alphanumeric characters and underline, and must start with an alphabetic character. As with filehandles and labels, a bare word that consists entirely of lowercase letters risks conflict with future reserved words, and if you use the –w switch, Perl will warn you about any such words.

Bibliography

Agrawal, Meenu : *Consumer Behaviour and Consumer Protection in India*, New Century Pub, Delhi, 2006.

Armstrong, G. & Kotler, P., : *Marketing: An Introduction*. New Jersey: Pearson Education Inc., 2005.

Baily, M.N., and A.K. Chakrabarti: *Innovation and the Productivity Crisis,* Brookings Institution Press, Washington, DC, 1988.

Bateson, J.E.G. : *Managing Services Marketing : Text and Readings*, The Dryden Press, USA, 1991.

Center, Allen & Jackson, Patrick: *Public Relations Practices : Managerial Case Studies and Problems*, Prentice-Hall, UK, 1990.

Churchill, G. A. and Iacobucci, D. : *Marketing Research: Methodological Foundations,* South-Western/Thomson Learning, Mason, Ohio, 2002.

Danton, J. Periam: *The Dimensions of Comparative Librarianship*, American Library Association, Chicago, 1973.

De Pelsmacker, P., Gevens, M., Van De Berg, J., :*Marketing communications*. Harlow, England: Prentice Hall, 2001.

Feigenbaum, Edward A.: *Computers and Thought*, New York: McGraw-Hill, 1963.

Fernie John and Sparks Leigh : *Logistics and Retail Management*, Viva Books, Delhi, 2010.

Fill, C., :. *Marketing Communications. Contexts, Contents and Strategies*. London, UK: Prentice Hall Europe, 1995.

Gabriel, Richard P.: *Patterns of Software: Tales from the Software Community*, New York: Oxford University Press, 1996.

Gentle, James E.: *Random Number Generation and Monte Carlo Methods*, Springer-Verlag, New York, 1998.

Harrison, S., : *Public Relation: An Introduction*. London, UK: Business Press Thomson Learning, 2000.

Hockey, Susan: *A Guide to Computer Applications in the Humanities*, Baltimore: John Hopkins Univerisity Press, 1980.

Iversen, G.R.: *Bayesian Statistical Inference (Quantitative Applications in the Social Sciences)*, Newbury Park, CA: Sage Publications, 1984.

Jagadish Chakravarthy: *Net, Media and Mass Communication*, Authorspress, Mumabi, 2004.

Jhully, Sut : *The Codes of Advertising: Fetishism and the Political Economy of Meaning*, Routledge, 1990.

Keller, Kevin Lane : *Conceptualizing, Measuring, and Managing Customer-Based Brand Equity*, Journal of Marketing, 1993.

Lasch, Christopher : *The Culture of Narcissism: American Life in an Age of Diminishing Expectations*, New York, 1995.

Lears, Jackson : *Fables of Abundance: A Cultural History of Advertising in America*, Basic Books, 1995.

Malhotra, N. K. : *Marketing Research: An Applied Orientation*, Prentice-Hall International, London, 2004.

Nicosia, F.M. : *Advertising Management, Consumer Behaviour and Simulation*, Journal of Advertising Research, 1968.

Nundo Lal Dey: *The Geographical Dictionary of Ancient and Mediaeval India*, Orient, Delhi, 1984.

Parama Sen: *Media Sensitivity to Conflicts : A Comparative Study of India and the United States 1999-2004*, Progressive Pub, Delhi, 2009.

Ronald M. Atlas: *Handbook of Media for Environmental Microbiology*, CRS Press, Taylor and Francis Group, Delhi, 2010.

Sarita Kumari and D. S. Srivastava: *Education: Assessment, Evaluation and Remedial*, Isha Books, Delhi, 2005.

Saunders, M., Lewis, P. : *Research Methods for Retail Business Students*, Financial Times Prentice Hall, Harlow, 2003.

Thompson, Hugh A.: *Internet Resources: A Subject Guide*, Chicago: Association of College and Research Libraries, 1995.

Vaske, H., : Radical Advertising. *Nico Interviews & Fashion*, Summer 2008, p. 143- 145, 2008.

Vicari, S., :. *Brand Equity. Il potenziale generativo della fiducia*. Milan, Italy: EGEA, 1995.

Webster, Frank, and Robins, Kevin: *Information Technology—A Luddite Analysis*, Ablex, Norwood, NJ, 1986.

Wernick, Andrew : *Promotional Culture: Advertising, Ideology and Symbolic Expression*, London: Sage Publications Ltd, 1991.

Yaffee, R.A. and McGee, M.: *An Introduction to Time-Series Analysis and Forecasting: With Applications*, Burlington, MA: Academic Press, 2000.

Zachary, G. Pascal: *Showstopper! The Breakneck Race to Creat Windows NT and the Next Generation at Microsoft*, New York: The Free Press, 1994.

Index

M

N

O

P

R

S

T

U

V

W

❑❑❑